Lecture Notes in Computer Science 4433

Commenced Publication in 1973
Founding and Former Series Editors:
Gerhard Goos, Juris Hartmanis, and Jan van Leeuwen

Erol Şahin William M. Spears
Alan F. T. Winfield (Eds.)

Swarm
Robotics

Second SAB 2006 International Workshop
Rome, Italy, September 30-October 1, 2006
Revised Selected Papers

 Springer

Volume Editors

Erol Şahin
KOVAN Research Lab - Dept. of Computer Engineering
Middle East Technical University
06531, Ankara, Turkey
E-mail: erol@ceng.metu.edu.tr

William M. Spears
University of Wyoming
Computer Science Department
Laramie, WY, 82071, USA
E-mail: wspears@cs.uwyo.edu

Alan F. T. Winfield
University of the West of England
Computing, Engineering and Mathematical Sciences
Bristol, UK
E-mail: Alan.Winfield@uwe.ac.uk

Library of Congress Control Number: 2007925713

CR Subject Classification (1998): F.1, I.2.9, I.2.11, C.2.4, E.1, F.2.2

LNCS Sublibrary: SL 1 – Theoretical Computer Science and General Issues

ISSN   0302-9743
ISBN-10   3-540-71540-1 Springer Berlin Heidelberg New York
ISBN-13   978-3-540-71540-5 Springer Berlin Heidelberg New York

Springer is a part of Springer Science+Business Media

springer.com

© Springer-Verlag Berlin Heidelberg 2007
Printed in Germany

Typesetting: Camera-ready by author, data conversion by Scientific Publishing Services, Chennai, India
Printed on acid-free paper   SPIN: 12038909   06/3180   5 4 3 2 1 0

Preface

Swarm robotics is the study of how large numbers of relatively simple physically embodied agents can be designed such that a desired collective behavior emerges from the local interactions among agents and between the agents and the environment. Swarm robotics has emerged as a novel approach to the coordination of large numbers of robots and is inspired from observation of social insects – ants, termites, wasps and bees – which stand as fascinating examples of how a large number of simple individuals can interact to create collectively intelligent systems. Social insects are known to coordinate their actions to accomplish tasks that are far beyond the capabilities of a single individual: termites build large and complex mounds, army ants organize impressive foraging raids, ants can collectively carry large prey. Such coordination capabilities are still well beyond the reach of current multi-robot systems.

Research on swarm robotics has seen a significant increase in the last 5 years. A number of successful swarm robotic systems have now been demonstrated in the laboratory and the study of the design, modelling, implementation and analysis of swarm robotic systems has become a hot topic of research. This workshop was organized within SAB 2006, as a sequel to the successful first swarm robotics workshop in 2004, with the aim of reviewing and updating recent advances on the topic.

We received 21 full papers (20 research + 1 review) and accepted 14 (13 research + 1 review). Overall, we, as organizers, were pleased with the number of submissions, and a number of our reviewers explicitly commented on the generally high quality of the papers.

The workshop was held in Rome, Italy, as a two-day event at the SAB 2006 conference (From Animals to Animats) on October 31 and November 1. The workshop opened with an invited talk given by Marco Dorigo. In his talk Dorigo reviewed the results obtained from the successful Swarm-bots project and briefly introduced the research visions for the new EU FP6 Swarmanoids project. The workshop took place in a warm atmosphere with high-quality presentations[1] on recent research on swarm robotics, interspersed with lively and thought-provoking discussions.

The papers included in this volume can be split into four groups: (1) Algorithms, (2) Modelling and Analysis, (3) Hardware, and (4) Evolutionary Approaches.

Algorithms: In their paper, Schmickl and Crailsheim present a novel navigation principle for swarm robotics based on slime mold signal propagation. Using this principle, simulated robots successfully performed a collective cleaning task

---

[1] The presentations are available at http://www.swarm-robotics.org/SAB06/.

and showed the ability to find the shortest path between two targets. Liu et. al. propose a simple adaptation mechanism for a swarm foraging task, enabling the swarm to be more energy efficient by dynamically changing the number of foragers. Their results demonstrate successful adaptive emergent dynamic task allocation (division of labor) between foragers and resters and show that robots need to cooperate more when energy is scarce. Schmickl et. al. investigate the issue of "collective perception," i.e., how a robot swarm is able to join multiple instances of individual perceptions to obtain a global picture. First they examine the "hop-count" strategy, which is often used in swarm robotics. Then they propose a novel trophallaxis-inspired strategy. They conclude that the latter strategy was successful at measuring sizes of target areas, while the former strategy was not. Miller et. al. examine the important issue of "task selection" in multi-agent swarms. The goal is to allocate the desired number of swarm robots to each task while reducing inter-task latencies and communication overhead. The authors propose a polynomial-time heuristic-based algorithm for the NP-Complete distributed task selection problem. Their results indicate that those heuristics in which each swarm robot considers both the effects of other robots on tasks and its own relative position to other robots achieve better efficiency.

Modelling and analysis: Soysal and Şahin study the self-organized aggregation of a swarm of robots in a closed arena. They then propose a macroscopic model for predicting the final distribution of the aggregates. Their results indicate that the simulated final aggregate distributions match those of their model, despite the fact that the simulations do not explicitly enforce all the assumptions of the model. Hamann and Woern also examine swarm foraging and present a macroscopic model based on partial differential equations, using virtual pheromones as the medium for communication. Robot density, food flow, and a qualitative description of the stability of the system can be extracted from the model. Berman et. al. propose a three-level macroscopic/microscopic methodology that can be used to characterize, analyze and synthesize swarm behaviors. The methodology is applied to a dynamical model of ant house hunting. Their multi-level simulations demonstrate that they produced a rigorously correct microscopic model from the macroscopic descriptions. Gazi and Fidan give a review of the field of multi-agent dynamic systems, from the system dynamic and control perspective. They present a number of classic problems with respect to the coordination and control of multi-agent systems, and summarize some of the recent results on stability, robustness and performance. They conclude with a number of open problems, such as asynchronism, and sensor and communication delays. These problems are also inherent in swarm robotics.

Hardware: Cianci et. al. present swarm robotics from an educational perspective. They first discuss the "e-puck," a low-cost small-scale mobile robotic platform designed for educational use. Then they present a custom module for local radio communication, enabling communication between robots and any other IEEE 802.15.4-compatible device. Finally, they conclude with a demonstration of this module facilitating a collective decision among a group of ten robots.

As De Nardi and Holland state, achieving flocking or swarming of real vehicles with complex dynamics is still an unsolved problem. To address this issue, the authors present their work on the development of autonomous miniature helicopters. Since no detailed dynamic model of the helicopter is available, a controller is designed using artificial evolution. Preliminary results of tackling the problem of flocking are presented. Spears et. al. present a novel platform-independent swarm robotics localization technique, based on the use of ultrasonic and RF transceivers. The technique is fully distributed, inexpensive, scalable, robust and provides a unified framework for merging localization with information exchange between robots. Furthermore, it does not rely on global information provided by GPS, beacons, landmarks or maps. This localization technique is tested on three robots in a number of applications, including a quite difficult chemical plume tracing task.

Evolutionary approaches: Ampatzis et. al. also consider the issue of communication in swarms of robots. Artificial evolution is used as a means to engineer robot neuro-controllers capable of guiding groups of robots in a categorization task. Communication behavior emerges, despite the absence of explicit selective pressure to favor signaling over non-signaling groups. Finally, one evolved controller is ported to real robots. Eiben et. al. examine the role of specialization in a collective search and find task. The authors propose a novel collective neuro-evolution method and compare it with a heuristic method. Results indicate that the best performing group converged to a specialized group composition that resembled the group composition of the highest performing specialized group tested with the heuristic method. The authors conclude that conventional neuro-evolution techniques fail due to their lack of specialization. Vicentini and Tuci investigate the important issue of scalability in swarm robotics. The authors also evolve neural network controllers using evolutionary algorithms. The results indicate that the controllers are potentially scalable. However, an analysis of a single controller identified elements that can significantly hinder scalability. This analysis helps in understanding the principles underlying the concepts of scalability and in designing more scalable solutions.

We are completely satisfied with the quality of the event, and are confident that the workshop is now recognized as one of the premier venues for swarm robotics research. We would like to thank all contributors for this success: SAB 2006 organizers Stefano Nolfi, Gianluca Baldassarre, Raffaele Calabretta, John C.T. Hallam, Davide Marocco, Jean-Arcady Meyer, Orazio Miglino and Domenico Parisi, for giving us the opportunity to organize this workshop within the SAB conference; all the authors for submitting their papers; and the Program Committee members for making the review process smooth through their high-quality and on-time reviews that provided detailed and thorough feedback to the authors. The Program Committee consisted of: Marco Dorigo, John Feddema, Paolo Gaudiano, Veysel Gazi, Kristina Lerman, Alcherio Martinoli, Francesco Mondada, Lynne E. Parker, David Payton, Joerg Seyfried, Kasper Støy, Guy Théraulaz, Cem Unsal, and Richard Vaughan.

Erol Şahin thanks Levent Bayındır for his help during the organization of the workshop. Erol Şahin also acknowledges the support of the Department of Computer Engineering, Middle East Technical University. Alan Winfield is grateful for the support of the Bristol Robotics Laboratory and the Faculty of Computing, Engineering and Mathematics at the University of the West of England, Bristol.

February 2007

Erol Şahin
William M. Spears
Alan F.T. Winfield

Organization

The Second International Workshop on Swarm Robotics was organized by the Middle East Technical University (Turkey), the University of Wyoming (USA), and the University of the West of England (UK), in cooperation with SAB 2006.

Organization Committee

Erol Şahin (Middle East Technical University, Ankara, Turkey)
William M. Spears (University of Wyoming, Laramie, Wyoming, USA)
Alan F. T. Winfield (University of the West of England, Bristol, UK)

Program Committee

Marco Dorigo (Université Libre de Bruxelles, Brussels, Belgium)
John Feddema (Sandia National Laboratory, Albuquerque, New Mexico, USA)
Paolo Gaudiano (Icosystem Corporation, Cambridge, Massachusetts, USA)
Veysel Gazi (TOBB University of Economics and Technology, Ankara, Turkey)
Kristina Lerman (USC Information Sciences Institute, Marina del Rey, California, USA)
Alcherio Martinoli (École Polytechnique Fédérale de Lausanne, Lausanne, Switzerland)
Francesco Mondada (Laboratoire de Systèmes Robotiques, Lausanne, Switzerland)
Lynne E. Parker (University of Tennessee, Knoxville, Tennessee, USA)
David Payton (HRL Laboratories, Malibu, California, USA)
Joerg Seyfried (Universitaet Karlsruhe, Karlsruhe, Germany)
Kasper Støy (University of Southern Denmark, Odense, Denmark)
Guy Théraulaz (Université Paul Sabatier, Toulouse, France)
Cem Unsal (Yoriwa Inc., San Jose, CA, USA)
Richard Vaughan (Simon Fraser University, Burnaby, British Columbia, Canada)

Table of Contents

A Navigation Algorithm for Swarm Robotics Inspired by Slime Mold Aggregation

Thomas Schmickl and Karl Crailsheim

Department for Zoology, Karl-Franzens-University Graz,
Universitaetsplatz 2, A-8010 Graz, Austria
schmickl@nextra.at,
karl.crailsheim@uni-graz.at
http://zool33.uni-graz.at/schmickl/

Abstract. This article presents a novel bio-inspired navigation principle for swarm robotics that is based on a technique of signal propagation that was inspired by slime mold. We evaluated this strategy in a variety of simulation experiments that simulates a collective cleaning scenario. This scenario includes several sub-tasks like exploration, information propagation and path finding. Using the slime mold-inspired strategy, the simulated robots successfully performed a collective cleaning scenario and showed the ability of finding the shortest path between two target places. Finally, the parameters of the strategy were optimized by artificial evolution and the discovered optima are discussed.

1 Motivation

In swarm robotics a high number of robots is used to perform tasks collectively. The high number of robots usually results in a miniaturization of the single robot unit. The abilities of these miniaturized robots are usually rather limited, so that a single robot cannot reach the collective goal; but the whole swarm of robots can succeed by cooperation. These limitations of the robots ask for simple navigation strategies and for simple communication protocols.

During our research for the I-SWARM project [1], we browsed the biological world for possible coordination algorithms that can be transformed into robot control algorithms for the I-SWARM robots. The final swarm size of the I-SWARM project will be 1000 robots, one single robot will be very small (approx. 8mm³) and it will be significantly limited in motion (speed, d.o.f.) and in communication (LED-light pulses). To allow testing of suggested control algorithms, a special robot platform (JASMINE) was designed that is bigger in size (approx. 16 cm³) but offers similar communication principles [2] [3]. Based on simulation of both platforms (I-SWARM, JASMINE), we recently published two swarm control strategies: the 'trophallaxis-inspired' strategy [4] and the 'vector-based' strategy [5]. Both strategies were analyzed in our multi-agent simulation platform 'LaRoSim' (Large Robot-Swarm Simulator), which implements the basic architecture of both robot types in a cleaning scenario [4][5]. Figure 1 shows the basic morphology of the JASMINE robot and the

E. Şahin et al. (Eds.): Swarm Robotics Ws, LNCS 4433, pp. 1–13, 2007.
© Springer-Verlag Berlin Heidelberg 2007

communication principle it uses. In contrast to the situation depicted in figure 1, the strategy that we present in this article does not rely on bi-directional communication, and in contrast to the strategies that we published in [4] and [5], our new strategy uses much more narrow communication channels, thus we assume it is better suitable for hardware platforms with limited abilities in communication.

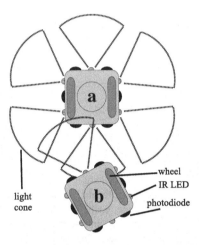

Fig. 1. Morphology of the robots in the used simulation environment with special emphasis on the communication system (infrared LEDs, photo-diodes) and on the movement systems. In the picture, the two robots can establish a bidirectional communication, because one receptor of each robot is within the light cone of the other robot.

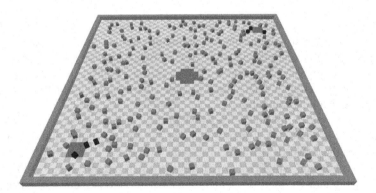

Fig. 2. A screenshot of our simulation platform LaRoSim. In the upper right corner and in the lower left corner, two 'dust' areas are located (gray floor patches, square). The 'dump' area is located in the center of the arena (gray floor patches, circular). The arena is occupied by empty robots (small gray cubes) that explore the arena. A good swarm strategy will guide loaded robots (black cubes) directly towards the 'dump' area.

2   The Simulation Platform and the Swarm Scenario

LaRoSim basically implements a scenario of collective 'floor cleaning'. Within this scenario, the robot swarm has to explore the arena collectively for areas that contain a number of dust particles and propagate information about found dust sites within the whole swarm. With the final I-SWARM robot, these particles can be small dust particles. For the JASMINE robot, a magnetic gripper for metal objects is currently under development. The propagation of information about the location of the dust sites is then used to aggregate empty (unloaded) robots at these dust sites. Loaded robots, that are robots that have picked up one particle, then have to move to a designated 'dump' area to drop the item there. The empty robots also have to explore the location of the dump area first. The information about the location of the dump has then to be propagated throughout the swarm. Figure 2 shows a screenshot of LaRoSim.

3   The 'Slime Mold' Strategy

An impressive biological aggregation scenario inspired the control strategy we suggest in this article: the aggregation of tens of thousands of slime mold amoebas. Similar collective behaviors are also found in bacteria [6]. In nature, the amoebas of the slime mold *Dictyostelium discoideum* feed on bacteria and move almost randomly. If their food gets scarce, they starve and dramatically change their behavior: They produce cAMP (a chemical substance called 'cyclic adenosine 3',5'-monophosphate') and release it to their outside (extracellular) environment. This releasing was found to happen in an oscillatory way with a frequency of 5 to 10 minutes. It was found that higher cAMP concentrations lead to higher cAMP production and that the amoebas use the cAMP gradient in the environment to navigate. So far, this process represents a positive feedback loop, which can already serve as inspiration for an algorithm of swarm aggregation. Many other cases are found in nature where the releasing of pheromones is used for aggregation (e.g., ants, bark beetles) and several approaches in swarm robotics have been performed to establish similar gradients within a robot swarm [4] [7] [8] [9] [10]. But in *D. discoideum*, a second process is working simultaneously that makes the aggregation principle unique: If the extracellular cAMP concentration exceeds a certain threshold, the amoebas release their intercellular reserve of cAMP in a very large pulse. A high concentration of extracellular cAMP desensitizes the receptors for cAMP, so that amoebas fall into a 'refractory' state for some time after such a large pulse. During this refractory state, the amoebas do not release an additional pulse of cAMP secretion. This process leads to travelling waves of cAMP pulses that head through the 'swarm' of amoebas from an initial triggering cell, at least if the packing of amoebas is already dense enough. The emergence of these waves (which can be circular or spiral shaped) leads to the impressive aggregation patterns that are found in nature: The cells move along nested, self-organized trails towards the aggregation center ('cell streaming', see photographs in [6]).

To imitate these processes in a control algorithm for swarm robotics, we had to omit several aspects of the biological source of inspiration. For our swarm robots, it is impossible to deposit something that represents cAMP in the environment. Thus we decided to implement only the cAMP pulses in our swarm strategy. The chemical cAMP pulses are represented by light signals (boolean) that are emitted by robots in all directions (broadcast). This sort of communication does not require bi-directional communication channels. Because we did not implement the chemical cAMP gradient, we call this version of the slime mold strategy also the 'binary slime mold strategy'. In section 4.5, we show results of another version of this strategy, which is called the 'gradient slime mold strategy'.

A robot that finds a target emits a light pulse. Each of the neighboring robots that receive this light pulse starts in turn to emit one light pulse for a given time (*fire_time*). Afterwards, each robot switches to the refractory state for a given time (*refractory_time*). In this state, a robot is insensitive for further light pulses. The global pattern that emerges in the swarm of robots is a wave of light pulses that travels away from the place where it was initially triggered. In our cleaning scenario, the robot swarm exploits 2 different kinds of light pulses, e.g., distinguishable by color. One type of wave emerges from the discovered dust areas and one emerges from the discovered dump areas. The empty robots mostly head against the direction of the first type of wave, the loaded robots move mostly against the direction of the latter one. See figure 3 for a scheme of the finite state automatons that we implemented into our robots and that collectively generate these waves.

If the robots aggregate too densely at the target places, the space between the targets may become sparsely filled with robots what might prevent the signal waves from reaching all parts of the arena. To overcome this problem, we implemented two additional features: The parameter '*fraction_random_walkers*' designates a certain fraction of the robots to the role 'random-walker'. These robots do not aggregate; they perform a pure random walk and therefore continue to explore the arena throughout the runtime of the cleaning experiment. They also act as communicational bridges that connect the areas of aggregation and allow the waves to reach the whole arena. Additionally, the robots that are not 'random-walkers' do not always move against the travelling wave. The parameters *weight_dust* and *weight_dump* adjust the strength of this directed navigation. A weight of **0.0** represents pure random walk and a weight of **1.0** represents only directed navigation. In addition to that, we implemented collision avoidance by a method that uses virtual potential fields. To allow preferential avoidance of loaded robots and of random-walkers, we implemented two additional boolean (on/off) signals that are emitted (see table 1). The parameter *priority_collision_dist* determines the strength of the repellence of random-walkers and of loaded robots. The parameters *loaded_coll_avoid_dist* and *empty_coll_avoid_dist* determine how far these two robot cohorts try to move away from other robots.

4   Detailed Description of the Strategy and of the Simulator

In the following section, we describe the 'slime mold' strategy in the cleaning scenario according to 6 sub-domains of the global problem. We suggest using this scheme of describing swarm strategies, because it allows addressing similarities and differences between strategies and between scenarios in a well-structured way.

Table 1. Swarm scenario classification. Description of the „slime mold'-inspired control strategy for robot swarms.

Sub-domain	Description
Collective goal	The swarm should clean up all 72 dust particles in the arena as fast as possible.
Individual goal	Empty robot: find dust particle as soon as possible. Loaded robot: find dump as soon as possible. Random-walker: minimize collisions with other robots.
Individual states	'I': Inactive (ready to perceive a light pulse) 'A': Activated (emitting a light pulse) 'R': Refractory (insensitive for light pulses).
Collective states	Our swarm never changes its collective global state.
Individual behavior	Empty robot: Head against the direction of wave 1 (dust). Loaded robot: Head against the direction of wave 2 (dump). Random-walker: Random walk with collision avoidance
Collective behavior	The empty robots aggregate at the dust, the loaded robots aggregate at the dump. Random-walkers fill the empty space in between and work as bridges for the travelling waves.
Internal implementation of robots	Finite state automatons as depicted in figure 3.
Communication domain	Signal 1 (1 bit) for the wave emerging at the dust. Signal 2 (1 bit) for the wave emerging at the dump. Signal 3 (1 bit) Emitted by loaded robots for preferential collision avoidance. Signal 4 (1 bit) Emitted by random-walkers (for coll. avoid).

Table 2. Robot constraints. Our simulator works scale-free, so the unit 'rd' ('robot diameter') is used for modeling distance measurements.

Constraint	Parameter	Units	Value
Max. communication radius	Com_radius	rd	3.5
Error distance-measurement	Err_distance	%	10%
False communication	P(comm_break)	%	5%
Robot speed	Robot_speed	rd	0.5/step

In addition to the detailed implementation of the robot, our simulation platform deals also with several important constraints. These are given in table 2. Our simulator assumes that robots have no long-distance perception for dump or for dust areas, so that the robots can detect these areas only when they are located directly above them. We furthermore assumed that robots could measure robot-to-robot distances only within 3 range classes 'near', 'medium', and 'far'. These measurements are only used in the potential-fields based collision avoidance functions. The robots cannot detect the exact angle to another robot but they can determine which photodiode received the message and therefore assume the 'side' the other robot is located. If several robots are located within one LED-emitted light cone, only the nearest robot can perceive the signal (shadow).

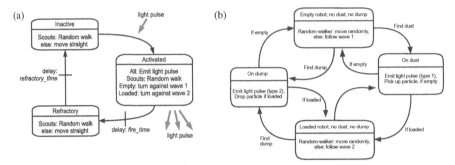

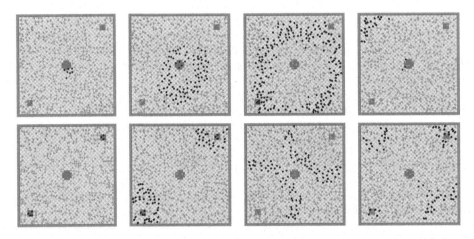

Fig. 3. State diagram of the internal finite state automatons. (a) The state automaton that is responsible for the wave. (b) The state automaton that is responsible for navigation. Please note that we implemented the left state automaton twice into each robot (one per wave type). The right state automaton is implemented only once per robot.

Fig. 4. The propagation of the light pulses throughout the robots swarm. The upper row shows the dynamics of the wave emerging from the dump; the lower row shows the dynamics of the waves emerging form the dust areas. Colliding waves extinguish each other. The very left column shows time step 3, the very right column shows step 15. The waves travel much faster than the robots move, as it is also in the biological counterpart (*D. discoideum*). Parameters: 500 robots, *fire_dump* = *fire_dust* = 2 steps, *refractory_dump* = *refractory_dust* = 7 steps.

5   Results

Our experiments successfully generated wave propagation within the robot swarm. These waves emerge, as expected, from the target areas (dump, dust) and the robots can exploit these waves for navigation. Figure 4 shows how the waves move through the robot swarm and figure 5 shows how loaded robots were directed towards the dump area in the center of the arena.

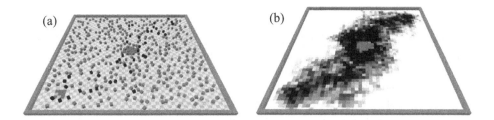

Fig. 5. Resulting collective behavior. (a) The loaded robots (dark cubes) form trails heading towards the dump area. The empty robots (gray) are spread throughout the arena. (b) The cumulative paths of loaded robots reveal that the navigation of the loaded robots is directed from the dust towards the central dump area. The darker a floor-patch is, the more often a loaded robot was located on this floor patch. Parameter settings: *fire_dump* = *fire_dust* = 2 time steps, *refractory_dump* = *refractory_dust* = 7 time steps, *weight_dust* = 0.3, *weight_dump* = 1.0, *density_of_robots* = 0.18, *fraction_random_walkers* = 5%, simulated period = 800 time steps.

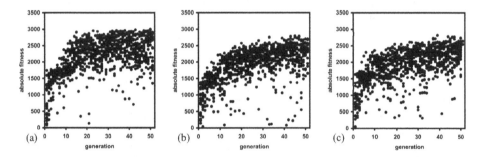

Fig. 6. Results of 3 runs of artificial evolution that shaped the parameters of the slime mold strategy. The fitness function accounts for the number of picked up dust items and for the number of dust items that were successfully delivered to the dump. N=3000 simulations / run.

5.1 Evolving Optimal Parameters

We performed three runs of an 'Evolutionary Strategy' (ES) to shape the parameters of the slime mold strategy. In each ES, we used a population size of 20 swarms. The fitness function accounts for the number of picked up dust items (+20 points each), for delivered dust items (+40 points each), and for the number of collisions (-40 points each divided by the number of robots). As soon as a swarm delivers its first dust particle at the dump, it earns a bonus of 200 points. For results, see figure 6 and table 3. In the ES, we used a mutation rate of 0.5, a crossover rate of 0.2. The best 3 swarms were transferred to the next generation unchanged (elitism). Each evolution was performed for 50 generations. In total, 3000 simulation runs were performed.

5.2 Evaluation of Critical Parameters

In a swarm of robots that depends on information propagation, the density of the robots is a critical factor. A swarm that has a low density has problems with the spread of information due to the limited communication radius of the single robot. In contrast to that, swarms with high density of robots have problems with 'traffic jams' that lead to unwanted clustering of robots. So we assumed that a swarm with a medium density represents an optimal solution. The three evolutionary runs led to swarms with densities between 0.12 and 0.16 which means that 12% to 16% of the arena floor was covered with robots. We performed an additional analysis run to investigate the role of robot densities. We chose the fittest swarm of the three evolutionary runs, which achieved an absolute fitness of 3001 fitness points and varied the swarm density between 5% and 40%. In total, 2401 robots fill the arena, so a density of 15% represents 360 robots. A run lasted for a maximum of 1800 time steps, but was terminated earlier as soon as the robots picked up all dust particles and delivered 66 particles at the dump. Figure 7 shows that a swarm density of 15% represents an optimal solution. Robot collisions are still in a moderate range and the work can be performed on a straight and quick way.

Table 3. Evolved parameters in the top 250 swarms of each evolutionary run (means ± st.d.)

Parameter name	Run 1	Run 2	Run 3
Density_of_robots	0.16 ± 0.02	0.12 ± 0.01	0.17 ± 0.02
Fraction_random_walkers	0.04 ± 0.02	0.05 ± 0.03	0.07 ± 0.03
Robot_speed	0.46 ± 0.03	0.49 ± 0.01	0.45 ± 0.04
Weight_dust	0.63 ± 0.07	0.45 ± 0.06	0.40 ± 0.07
Weight_dump	0.97 ± 0.03	0.85 ± 0.05	0.94 ± 0.04
Priority_collision_dist	0.37 ± 0.08	0.41 ± 0.13	0.41 ± 0.14
Loaded_coll_avoid_dist	0.31 ± 0.05	0.32 ± 0.03	0.34 ± 0.04
Empty_coll_avoid_dist	0.86 ± 0.05	0.91 ± 0.07	0.78 ± 0.20
Fire_dust (f_{dust})	4.05 ± 0.74	5.85 ± 1.96	3.55 ± 1.75
Refractory_dust (r_{dust})	16.32 ± 2.17	9.49 ± 2.37	10.89 ± 4.29
Fire_dump (f_{dump})	2.07 ± 0.26	3 ± 0.42	1.78 ± 0.83
Refractory_dump (r_{dump})	6.68 ± 0.73	8.6 ± 1.54	7.18 ± 1.09
r_{dust}/f_{dust}	4.26 ± 1.53	2.25 ± 2.12	4.11 ± 2.74
r_{dump}/f_{dump}	3.26 ± 0.48	2.92 ± 0.74	4.92 ± 2.02

5.3 Alternative 'Good' Parameter Settings

The trails formed by the loaded robots that lead to the fastest cleaning of the arena are rather loose (see figure 5), which is efficient, because it minimizes the problem of traffic jams. We were interested if we could generate more solid (and thus more slime-mold-like trails) by changing parameters of our strategy. We did this by reducing the robot speed from 0.5 to 0.1 and by increasing the density of robots to 25% to ensure good wave propagation. As figure 8 shows, the slower robots form now more dense trails towards the dump.

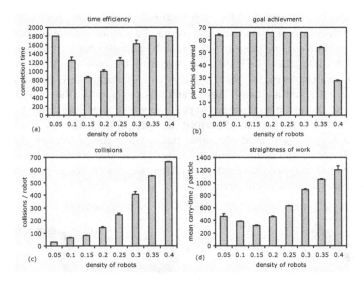

Fig. 7. Simulation runs with varying densities of robot swarms (medians and third quartiles, N=6). *fire_dump* = 2, *fire_dust* = 4, *refractory_dump* = 7, *refractory_dust* = 15, *weight_dust* = 0.66, *weight_dump* = 1.0, *fraction_random_walkers* = 4%, simulated period = 1800 time steps.

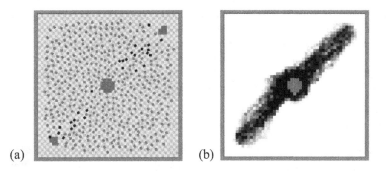

Fig. 8. Resulting collective behavior with reduced robot speed. (a) The loaded robots (dark cubes) form now better directed trails heading towards the dump. (b) The cumulative paths of loaded robots. The darker a floor-patch is, the more often a loaded robot was located on this floor patch. Parameter settings: *fire_dump* = *fire_dust* = 2, *refractory_dump* = *refractory_dust* = 7, *weight_dust* = 0.75, *weight_dump* = 1.0, *density_of_robots* = 0.20, *fraction_random_walkers* = 5%, *priority_collision_dist* = 0.50, *loaded_coll_avoid_dist* = 0.1, *empty_coll_avoid_dist* = 0.81, simulated period = 3000 time steps.

5.4 Way Finding and Trail Formation

After we found parameter settings that produced slime-mold-like trails of robots, we were interested which further collective abilities the swarm possesses. Recent studies have shown, that another slime mold species (*Physarum polycephalum*) is able to find the shortest path in a labyrinth [11]. It is assumed that waves like those that exist in excitable media can be exploited for such 'optimal route finding' problems [12]. Our robot swarm represents such an excitable media. To test the abilities of our swarm in a route finding problem, we modified the arena by adding a barrier that contains three gates. Through these gates, the trails can move from the dust area (lower left corner) to the dump area (upper right corner). The waves of excitation (pulses) are passing through these gates and are annihilating each other as soon as they collide. So only the wave on the shortest path manages to pass the whole way from dump to dust. This fact suffices to allow the swarm to perform an optimal path finding. The three ways had different lengths. We used the same parameter settings that we used in sub-section 4.3. Figure 9 shows the resulting trails. The loaded robots in the swarm followed always the available shortest path. After we closed some gates, the swarm made a different (optimal!) collective decision.

Fig. 9. Resulting collective behavior in a setup with barriers. For this experiment we used one dust area in the lower left corner of the arena and one dump area in the upper right corner. (a) Cumulative paths of loaded robots that take the shortest way. (b) After we closed the gate for the shortest path, the robots took the second shortest one. (c) After we also closed the second shortest path, the loaded robots took the last remaining possible path from the dust area to the dump area. This path was neglected in the prior runs. All figures: The darker the color of a floor patch is, the more often a loaded was located on this patch. Parameter settings were the same that for the run in figure 7. Run time = 2000 time steps.

5.5 The 'Gradient Version' of the Slime Mold Algorithm

In section 3 we mentioned that we did not implement the cAMP gradient in our 'binary' slime mold algorithm. But we were interested if we can generate slime-mold-like aggregation behavior if we also mimic such a chemical gradient. For mimicking the cAMP gradient we used another method of robot-to-robot communication: Floating-point numbers that are passed among robots. We already used such numbers in the 'trophallaxis-inspired' strategy described in [4]. A robot that finds a target increases an internal memory place by a value of 300 units. Neighboring robots adjust their memory values by bi-directional communication and share always half of the experienced difference. This process mimics 'diffusion' and allows a gradient to spread. Each time step, each robot decreases its memory value by 25%, a process that leads to exponential decay. If a robot which is not in 'refractory' state (see figure 3), experiences a neighbor with a memory value above a threshold (70 units), it in turn releases again 300 units, switches to the state 'activated' and switches then to the internal state 'refractory'. The robots navigate always uphill in the gradient: Each robot turns into the direction of the neighbor that broadcasts the highest memory value. We set the simulation to the following parameters: *robots_speed* = 0.2rd/step, *fraction_random_walkers* = 0%. We introduced four aggregation targets in the arena. As figure 10 shows, the robots aggregate in a 'dentritic' way: nested streams of robots aggregate to each target. The pulses of high memory vales (represents cAMP) are running down these nested streams, emerging at the target areas. This result resembles the picture of aggregating slime mold amoebas very much.

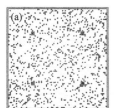 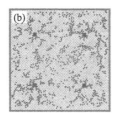 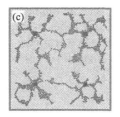 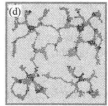

Fig. 10. Resulting collective behavior in the 'gradient version' of the slime mold strategy. The robots aggregate in nested streams at the aggregation targets. Pulses of high memory values in robots (representing local cAMP peaks) move down the nested streams, emerging from the aggregation targets. (a) Initial conditions, (b) 25 time steps, (c) 250 steps, (d) the traveling waves in the streams. Parameters: 1000 robots, *fire* =4, *refractory* = 20, *weight* = 1.0, *density_of_robots* = 0.2, *fraction_random_walkers* = 0%, all *collision_dist's* = 0.1, simulated period = 2000 time steps.

6 Discussion

Swarm robotics has been a growing field in the science of robotics in the last decade. Huge swarms of robots, like the I-SWARM, require miniaturized robots with very limited abilities. Such robots need intelligent communication principles and robust navigation to show self-organization [6] and swarm intelligence [13] in collective behavior. Several strategies have been suggested and evaluated for the hardware of the I-SWARM robot (and for the JASMINE robot). Compared to the strategy presented here, the 'trophallaxis-inspired' strategy [4] and the 'vector based' strategy [5] use a more complex internal implementation and more complex communication. Some approaches have been made to mimic the spread of 'virtual pheromones' within a robot swarm, some use hop-count techniques [7][8][10], other extend the arena with external equipment [9]. A cricket-inspired oscillator-based strategy described in [14] uses also a binary signal and a travelling wave to navigate the robots. In contrast to the oscillator-based strategy, our internal implementation of the robots is very much different. No intrinsic oscillator is used; instead a state automaton is implemented. The difference is that in times with no dust sites found, there is no excitation, and no waves are produced. This is more efficient; it increases the exploration in these times. We present here a novel decentralized control strategy for robot swarms. The strategy uses broadcast communication in a very narrow communication channel (one bit per target). The details of the strategy were inspired from a biological example, the aggregation behavior of *D. discoideum*. By using artificial evolution, the algorithm could be tailored to perform our cleaning task as fast as possible. Reduced robot speed led to a slower task completion but also led to better trails that resemble the biological counterpart. Like the biological example [11], the swarm was able to collectively find the shortest path between two points of the arena. By adding a second strategy that mimics the spread of cAMP within the swarm ('gradient version' of slime mold strategy), we could also re-generate slime-mold aggregation behavior in a swarm of 1000 simulated micro-robots. In conclusion, we can say that our strategy is robust and flexible, it uses only broadcast communication, and it uses a narrow communication channel. It allows generating robot swarms that show 'intelligent' collective behavior. In future, we will continue to investigate this strategy with hardware experiments and will further develop the gradient version of the slime-mold strategy.

Acknowledgement

This work is partially supported by: EU IST-FET-project 'I-Swarm', no. 507006.

References

1. Seyfried, J., Szymanski, M., Bender, N., Estana, R., Thiel, M., Wörn, H.: The I-SWARM Project: Intelligent Small World Autonomous Robots for Micro-Manipulation. In: Sahin, E., Spears, W.M. (eds.) Swarm Robotics. Springer LNCS 3342, (2005) 70 – 83
2. Kornienko, S., Kornienko, O., Levi, P.: Minimalistic approach towards communication and perception in microrobotic swarms. In: Proceedings of IEEE/RSJ International Conference on Intelligent Robots and Systems, Edmonton, Alberta, Canada (2005) 4005 – 4011
3. Kornienko, S., Kornienko, O., Levi, P.: Collective AI: Context awareness via communication. In: Proceedings of the Nineteenth International Joint Conference on Artificial Intelligence (IJCAI 2005), 1464-1470, Edinburg, Scotland, (2005) 1464 – 1470
4. Schmickl, T., Crailsheim, K.: Trophallaxis among swarm-robots: A biological inspired strategy for swarm robotics. In: Proceedings of BioRob 2006, Biomedical Robotics and Biomechatronics, Pisa, Italy. (2006) ISBN 1-4244-0040-6
5. Valdastri, P., Corradi, P., Menciassi, A., Schmickl, T., Crailsheim, K., Seyfried, J., Dario, P.: Micromanipulation, communication and swarm intelligence issues in a microrobotic platform. Robotics and Automation Systems (in press).
6. Camazine, S., Deneubourg, J.L., Franks, N., Sneyd, J., Theraulaz, G., Bonabeau, E.: Self-Organization in Biological Systems. Princeton University Press, NJ, USA (2001)
7. Payton, D., Daily, M., Estowski, R., Howard, M., Lee, C.: Pheromone Robotics. Autonomous Robots 11 (2001) 319 – 324
8. Payton, D., Estkowski, R., Howard, M.: Compound behaviors in pheromone robotics. Robotics and Autonomous Systems 44 (2003) 229 – 240
9. Sugawara, K., Kazama, T., Watanabe, T.: Foraging behavior of interacting robots with virtual pheromone. In: Proceedings of IEEE/RSJ International Conference on Intelligent Robots and Systems, Sendai, Japan (2004) 3074 – 3079
10. Stoy, K., How do construct dense objects with self-reconfigurable robots. In: Christensen, H.I. (eds.) European Robotics Symposium 2006, STAR 22 (2006) 27 – 37
11. Nakagaki, T.: Smart behavior of true slime mold in a labyrinth. Res. Microbiol. 152 (2001) 767 – 770

12. Steinbock, O., Toth, A., Showalter, K.: Navigating complex labyrinths: Optimal paths from chemical waves. Science 267 (1995) 868 – 871
13. Bonabeau, E., Dorigo, M., Theraulaz, G.: Swarm intelligence: From natural to artificial systems. Oxford University Press, New York, NY, USA (1999)
14. Hartbauer, M., Römer, H.: Decentralized microrobot swarm communication via coupled oscillators. In: Proceedings of BioRob 2006, Biomedical Robotics and Biomechatronics, Pisa, Italy. (2006) ISBN 1-4244-0040-6

Strategies for Energy Optimisation in a Swarm of Foraging Robots

Wenguo Liu[1,2], Alan Winfield[1], Jin Sa[1], Jie Chen[2], and Lihua Dou[2]

[1] Bristol Robotics Lab, UWE, Bristol BS16 1QY, UK
[2] Intellectual Information Technology Lab, BIT, Beijing 100081, China

Abstract. This paper presents a simple adaptation mechanism to auto-matically adjust the ratio of foragers to resters (division of labour) in a swarm of foraging robots and hence maximise the net energy income to the swarm. Three adaptation rules are introduced based on local sensing and communications. Individual robots use internal cues (successful food retrieval), environmental cues (collisions with teammates while searching for food) and social cues (teammate success in food retrieval) to dynam-ically vary the time spent foraging or resting. The paper investigates the effectiveness of a number of strategies based upon different combina-tions of cues, and demonstrates successful adaptive emergent division of labour. Strategies which employ the social cues are shown to lead to the fastest adaptation to changes in food density and we see that social cues have most impact when food density is low: robots need to cooperate more when energy is scarce.

1   Introduction

Foraging is a widely used metaphor for cooperative behaviour in swarm robotics research due to its strong biological basis. Some researchers point out that a major factor that impacts the efficiency of a group is the interference caused by competition for space. Lerman analyses the effect the size of a swarm has on the group performance based on a probabilistic model and points out that there should be an optimal number of robots to perform the foraging task in order to get the best group performance [1]. Krieger and Billeter take a threshold-based approach [2], first introduced by Théraulaz et al. in investigating the division of labour in social insects [3], to allocate their robots to each task: resting (loaf-ing) or foraging. In their experiment each robot has to be characterized with a different randomly chosen threshold in order to regulate the activity of the team. Labella et al. introduce a simple adaptive mechanism to change the ratio of foragers to resters to improve the performance of the system by adjusting the probability of leaving home based on successful retrieval of food [4]. They reward successful food retrieval and punish failure in order to adjust the probability of leaving home. A disadvantage of this approach is the absence of knowledge about the other robots. Jones and Matarić describe an adaptive labour division ap-proach in which robots observe each other but do not communicate directly [5]. Guerrero and Oliver present an auction-like task allocation model [6], partially

E. Şahin et al. (Eds.): Swarm Robotics Ws, LNCS 4433, pp. 14–26, 2007.
© Springer-Verlag Berlin Heidelberg 2007

inspired by auction and threshold-based methods, to try to determine the optimal number of robots needed for foraging, however, the demands of communication between robots during the auction process constrains the scalability of their method for large numbers of robots.

This paper builds upon previous work in task allocation or division of labour in a number of ways. Firstly, our overall goal is that the swarm maximises its net energy income. Secondly, we investigate a richer set of adaptation rules, or cues, for individual robots: internal cues (successful food retrieval), environmental cues (collisions with teammates while searching for food) and social cues (teammate success in food retrieval). Social cues are triggered by pheromone-like local communication between robots. Thirdly, we evaluate a number of control strategies based upon different combinations of these internal, environmental and social cues, in order to discover the relative merit of the cues in optimising the net energy income to the swarm. Our foraging swarm makes use of local sensing and communication only, but the overall swarm exhibits properties of emergence and adaptive self-organisation; that is adaptation to environmental changes (in food density). The approach presented in this paper thus meets the criteria for swarm robotics articulated by Şahin [7] and Beni [8].

This paper proceeds as follows. In section 2 we introduce the basic adaptation mechanism for the individual robots in the swarm. In section 3, a description of the foraging task and the experimental environment are given. Section 4 presents the experimental results, in which we compare the performance of the system with different adaptation rules. We conclude the paper in section 5.

2   Adaptation Mechanism

Our inspiration comes from the widely observed phenomena in nature, such as in schools of fish, flocks of birds etc. The group behaviour emerges from the interactions of individuals by essentially following the rule *"I do what you do"*, *"I go where you go"* [9]. Consider swarm foraging: the goal of the swarm is to forage as much food as possible over time. Assume that:

- each robot will consume energy at A units per second while searching or retrieving and at B units per second while resting, where $A > B$.
- each food item collected by a robot will provide C units of energy to the swarm.
- average retrieval time (the time spent on one successful search and retrieval cycle), denoted by t, is a function of the number of forager robots, denoted by x, and the density of the food, denoted by ρ, in the environment, say:

$$t = f(x, \rho) \tag{1}$$

According to [1], because of interference between robots, the average retrieval time increases with number of foragers increasing and decreases with density of food increasing when there are more robots than the food available allows. So we have

$$E_{consumed} = Ax + B(N - x) \quad (/sec)$$

$$E_{retrieval} = Cx/t = \frac{Cx}{f(x, \rho)} \quad (/sec) \tag{2}$$

Thus the average energy income for the swarm is:

$$E_{average} = E_{retrieval} - E_{consumed} = \left(\frac{C}{f(x, \rho)} - (A - B) \right) x - BN \tag{3}$$

where N is the size of the swarm.

Equation (3) shows that in order to maximize energy income for the swarm we need to either increase the number of foragers x or decrease the average retrieval time $f(x, \rho)$. Since $f(x, \rho)$ increases with x increasing when ρ stays the same[1], there should be an optimal value X^* for x, that is, number of foragers in the swarm, for a given food density. Moreover, X^* changes with ρ changing. However, the function $f(x, \rho)$ is quite complex and hard to model because of the complexity of the interactions between robots. Although it may ultimately be possible to develop a detailed mathematical model in order to find an optimal value of X^*, using for example the approach of [10], we first need a controller design. Thus, in this paper we adopt a bottom-up design process (a typical characteristic of the swarm robotics methodology), resulting in a swarm that is able to dynamically adapt the ratio of foragers to resters through the interaction between robots and between robots and the environment.

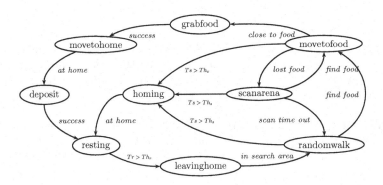

Fig. 1. State transition diagram of foraging task

---

[1] In order to investigate how the adaptation mechanism can improve the performance of the system, we only consider the situation of over-crowded robots in the searching area in which interference has a negative impact on system performance. Thus increasing the number of foragers results in more interference between robots and robots take longer to find and retrieve a food-item.

Figure 1 represents the control program for each robot in our system. The transition between states *randomwalk, scanarena, movetofood* and state *homing* is triggered by parameter *searching time* (T_s); such a transition will reduce the number of foragers which in turn minimizes the interference due to overcrowding, thus reducing the average retrieval time. The transition between state *rest* and state *leavinghome*, which is triggered by parameter *resting time* (T_r), will drive the robot back to work to collect more food for the colony, which means increasing the number of foragers in the swarm. The efficiency of the swarm might be improved if robots are able to autonomously adjust their searching time Th_s and resting time Th_r thresholds. In order to achieve this, we introduce three rules to change these two parameters based on (i) environmental cues, (ii) internal cues and (iii) social cues, explained as follows:

– Environmental cues. For a robot that is foraging (searching for food), if it collides with other robots it will reduce Th_s and increase Th_r because *"there are already enough foragers in the arena, I'd better go back to the nest sooner so I don't get in the others' way"*.
– Internal cues. After a successful food retrieval cycle, a robot will reduce Th_r because *"there may be more food, I'd better go back to work as soon as possible"*. Alternatively, if a robot fails to find food, indicated by searching time is up, the robot will increase Th_r since *"there seems to be little food available, I'd better rest for longer"*

As a social cue, we introduce a pheromone-like mechanism into the swarm. A robot will broadcast a message indicating its success or failure to find food after it has returned to the nest. All the robots resting at home will receive these messages and adjust their Th_s and Th_r based on the following rules:

– Social cues. If the robot returning home broadcasts a *successful retrieval* message, then the robots resting at home will reduce Th_r and increase Th_s because *"somebody else has found food, there may be more so I'd better get back to work sooner"*. On receiving a *failed retrieval* message, the resting robots will increase T_r and reduce T_s because *"somebody else failed to find food, there may be a food shortage so I'd better stay in the nest for longer"*

Table 1 shows all of the cues for adjusting the time thresholds in summary. The pseudocode of Algorithm 1 shows the adaptation procedure in each robot's

Table 1. Cues to adjust time threshold

	increase	decrease
Th_s	⑤	③④
Th_r	①③④	②⑤

internal cues: { ① failure retrieval
                  ② success retrieval

environmental cues: ③ collision with other robots while searching

social cues: { ④ failure retrieval by teammates
               ⑤ success retrieval by teammates

Algorithm 1. Adaptation mechanism

---

initialization:
 $robotid = id$
 $Th_r \leftarrow 0; Th_s \leftarrow Th_{s\_max}$
 $teammate\_success[id] \leftarrow 0; teammate\_failure[id] \leftarrow 0$
loop:
 $teammate\_success[id] \leftarrow teammate\_success[id] - \delta_s * (T_t - T_{t-1})$
 $teammate\_failure[id] \leftarrow teammate\_failure[id] - \delta_f * (T_t - T_{t-1})$
 if $teammate\_success[id] < 0$ **then**
  $teammate\_success[id] \leftarrow 0$
 end if
 if $teammate\_failure[id] < 0$ **then**
  $teammate\_failure[id] \leftarrow 0$
 end if
 if collision with other robots while foraging **then**
  $Th_r \leftarrow Th_r + \Delta t_{ari}$
  $Th_s \leftarrow Th_s - \Delta t_{asd}$
 else if food retrieved **then**
  $Th_r \leftarrow Th_r - \Delta t_{srd}$
  $teammate\_sucess[k] \leftarrow teammate\_sucess[k] + 1, \ (k = 0, 1, \ldots, N - 1; k \neq id)$
 else if searching time times-out **then**
  $Th_r \leftarrow Th_r + \Delta t_{fri}$
  $teammate\_failure[k] \leftarrow teammate\_failure[k] + 1, \ (k = 0, 1, \ldots, N - 1; k \neq id)$
 else if resting at home **then**
  $Th_r \leftarrow Th_r - \Delta t_{tsrd} * teammate\_success[id] + \Delta t_{tfri} * teammate\_failure[id]$
  $Th_s \leftarrow Th_s + \Delta t_{tssi} * teammate\_success[id] - \Delta t_{tfsd} * teammate\_failure[id]$
  $teammate\_success[id] \leftarrow 0; teammate\_failure[id] \leftarrow 0$
 end if
loop again

Table 2. Adjustment factor and corresponding cues

adjustment factor	comments	corresponding cues*
Δt_{ari}	increase Th_r	③
Δt_{asd}	decrease Th_s	③
Δt_{fri}	increase Th_r	①
Δt_{srd}	decrease Th_r	②
Δt_{tsrd}	decrease Th_r	⑤
Δt_{tfri}	increase Th_r	④
Δt_{tssi}	increase Th_s	⑤
Δt_{tfsd}	decrease Th_s	④

* See Table 1 for details of cues

control system. *teammate_success* and *teammate_failure* store the retrieval information of teammates. Attenuation factors δ_s and δ_f are introduced here to simulate gradually decaying rather than instantly disappearing social cues, somewhat akin to ants leaving a decaying pheromone trail while foraging. Such a mechanism should be readily implemented in a real robot implementation. As shown in Table 2, adjustment factors Δt_{ari}, Δt_{asd}, Δt_{fri}, Δt_{srd}, Δt_{tsrd}, Δt_{tfri}, Δt_{tssi} and Δt_{tfsd} indicate how the Th_s and Th_r will be changed based on the above three different cues.

3   Experimental Set-Up

We have tested our swarm foraging adaptation scheme using the sensor-based simulation tools Player/Stage [11]. Figure 2 is a snapshot of the simulation. Eight robots work in a $8m \times 8m$ octagonally shaped arena. The nest area is indicated with a green (grey) colour, with one homing spot light source located at point A to indicate the direction of the nest. Each robot is size $0.26m \times 0.26m$, the same as the real robots (Linuxbots) in our laboratory, and is equipped with 3 light intensity sensors, 3 Infra-Red proximity sensors, 1 camera, 1 colour sensor and 1 gripper. Thus the robot can sense food at a distance using the camera then grab the food using its gripper; the robot also has the ability to find its way back to the nest using the three front mounted light intensity sensors and to know whether it is at home or not with the bottom mounted colour sensor. The control programs for each robot are identical, as shown in Fig.1. Note that to keep the diagram clear, with the exception of state *resting*, each state will transition to state *avoidance*, not shown in Fig.1, whenever the proximity sensors are triggered. The behaviours for the foraging task are:

leavinghome: robot exits the nest region and resumes its search.
randomwalk: robot moves forward and at random intervals turns left or right through a random arc.

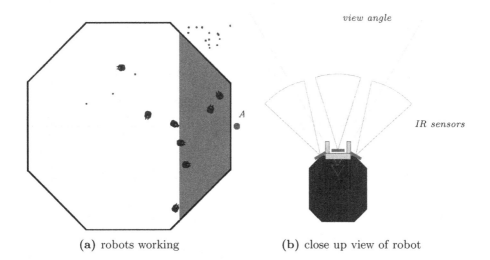

(a) robots working   (b) close up view of robot

Fig. 2. Snapshot of simulation

movetofood: if food is sensed, move towards the food.

grabfood: if the food is close enough, close the gripper and grab the food.

scanarena: because of interference between robots, sometimes a robot will lose sight of its target food item when moving towards it, the robot will then scan the area by turning a random angle to find the lost food. If successful, it will move to the food again, if not, then randomwalk.

movetohome: move towards the home location with the food.

deposit: food.

resting: rest at home.

homing: if searching time is up and no food has been grabbed, return home.

avoidance: robot avoids obstacles, walls and other robots whenever its proximity sensors are triggered; after completing a successful avoidance behaviour, the robot returns to the state it was in before the collision.

At the start of the simulation, all robots are in state *resting* with the same time threshold $Th_s(= Th_{s\_max})$ and $Th_r(= 0)$. In order to maintain the food density ρ at a reasonably constant level over time, a new food item is placed randomly in the searching arena with probability P_{new} each second. Collected food deposited in the home area will be removed to prevent robots from retrieving the food that has already been collected. In each time step of the simulation, a robot will consume an amount of energy varying with its state since the robot uses different sensors and actuators in different states. For example, a robot will consume more energy when carrying food back to the nest than when wandering in the search area because the grippers are used in the former state. Table 3 shows the energy consumed per second for each state. Note that the energy consumed in state *avoidance* also varies depending on whether the robot is carrying a food item. Moreover, the robot will consume a small amount of energy even when resting at home, currently *1 unit/sec*. A successful food retrieval will deliver *2000 units* of energy to the swarm.

Table 3. Energy consumed

state	energy consumed(units/sec)
leavinghome	6
randomwalk	8
movetofood	8
grabfood	12
scanarena	8
movetohome	12
deposit	12
resting	1
homing	6
avoidance	6 or 9

4   Experimental Results and Analysis

In order to investigate whether and how our foraging adaptation mechanism can improve the energy efficiency of the swarm, we run four types of experiments (strategies) in simulation (10 times each), each with a different combination of cues. Table 4 shows the cue configuration of each experiment. Each simulation lasts for 10000 seconds and P_{new} is set to 0.03 during the whole experiment, Th_{s_max} is set to 100 seconds, the value of parameters for adjusting Th_s and Th_r are given in Table 5.

Table 4. The four strategies: cue combinations

	with internal cues	with environment cues	with social cues
S_1	×	×	×
S_2	✓	×	×
S_3	✓	×	✓
S_4	✓	✓	✓

Table 5. Value of time adjustment factors

Δt_{ari}	Δt_{asd}	Δt_{fri}	Δt_{srd}	Δt_{tsrd}	Δt_{tfri}	Δt_{tssi}	Δt_{tfsd}	δ_s	δ_f
5	5	20	20	20	40	10	10	0.1	0.1

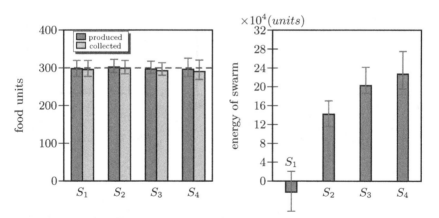

Fig. 3. Food produced and collected   **Fig. 4.** Energy of swarm after 10000 sec

With equal P_{new}, the total amount of food appearing in the search area over time is almost the same in all four experiments, and as we would expect almost all of the food is collected by the robots, as shown in Fig.3. However, from Fig.4, it is clear that the swarm which makes use of all cues S_4 can gain much more net energy than the one which does not use any cues S_1. Swarm S_1 uses up all of the energy collected while swarm S_4 saves 37.8% of the energy collected

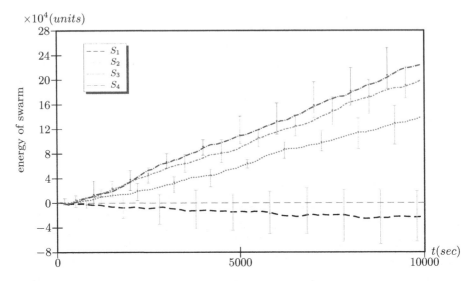

Fig. 5. Instantaneous net energy of swarm

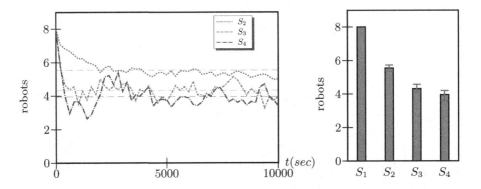

Fig. 6. Number of foraging robots   **Fig. 7.** Average foragers

(300 food items donate 60×10^4 energy units to the swarm while the average energy for S_4 after 10000 sec is 22.7×10^4). Figure 4 also shows that the social cues have a greater impact than the environmental cues, comparing the final energy in experiments S_2, S_3 and S_4. The instantaneous energies of the four swarms are plotted in Fig. 5, and we are surprised to see the rates of increase of swarm energy for experiments S_2, S_3 and S_4 are almost linear, and the swarm using all cues has the fastest rate of energy increase of all experiments.

Measuring the number of foragers in the swarm in the four experiments, which is 8.0, 5.55, 4.32, 3.95 on average for S_1, S_2, S_3 and S_4 respectively, the swarm with all cues used has the lowest average number of foragers over time, as shown in Fig.7, i.e. more energy is saved using fewer foragers for a given food source density. A more interesting result is seen in Fig.6: the number of foragers in experiments S_3 and S_4 keep oscillating with time, while staying near an average value. That means that a dynamic equilibrium between the number of foragers and the number of resters is reached when we introduce the adaptation mechanism into the swarm system. Thus, the overall swarm task allocation (division of labour) emerges from the low-level interactions between robots, and the environment.

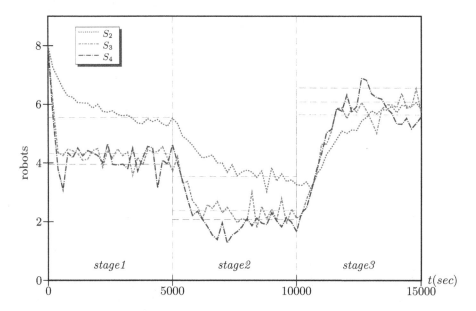

Fig. 8. Number of foraging robots: food density changes at $t = 5000$ and $t = 10000$

We now introduce a step change of probability P_{new} from 0.03 to 0.015 at $t = 5000$ and then from 0.015 to 0.045 at $t = 10000$ and run the four types of experiments 10 times each, see Fig.8. The simulation lasts 15000 seconds and other parameters remain as above. As expected, a new dynamic equilibrium for the number of foragers in the swarm is observed each time the food source density is changed. The swarms using social cues, experiments S_3 and S_4, adapt more rapidly to the change of environment than the swarm without social cues, experiment S_2. The reason for this is that social cues provide more information about the environment (food density) for the individuals. Figure 8 also shows the steady-state average number of foragers in the different stages. The relative change in average foragers between experiments S_3 and S_4 is bigger when P_{new} is smaller, 0.37/4.32, 0.30/2.37, 0.44/6.08 for stages 1, 2 and 3 respectively, so the environmental cues have a bigger impact on the performance of the swarm when the food source is poor ($P_{new} = 0.015$) than when the food source is rich

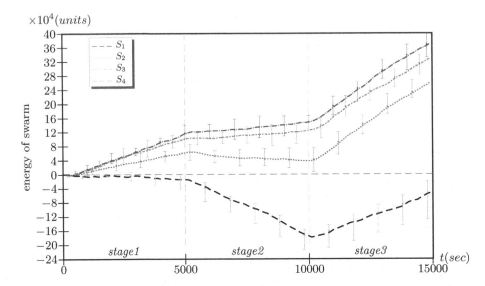

Fig. 9. Instantaneous net energy of swarm: food density changes at $t = 5000$ and $t = 10000$

($P_{new} = 0.03\,or\,0.045$); this is because the robots not carrying food collide with each other more often in a low density food source environment. Figure 9 plots the energy of the swarm for each experiment, as we might now expect the gradient changes when food density changes for a specific experiment. However, surprisingly the energy gradient seems to be very close for the high food density $P_{new} = 0.045$ in experiments S_2, S_3 and S_4. This is because in this situation the average number of foragers in each experiment is high and close, 5.06, 5.26, 5.14 for experiments S_2, S_3 and S_4 respectively. The relative change in average foragers between experiments S_2 and S_3 is 0.47/6.56 in stage 3 but 1.22/5.55 and 0.98/3.35 for stage 1 and stage 2. Thus we can deduce that the social cues have less impact on the performance of the swarm when the food source is rich, but more impact when the food source is poor; robots need to cooperate more when energy is scarce.

5   Conclusion

In this paper, we have proposed a simple adaptation mechanism for a swarm foraging task which is able to dynamically change the number of foragers and thus make the swarm more energy efficient. The individuals in the swarm use only internal cues (successful or unsuccessful food retrieval), environmental cues (collision with other robots while searching) and social cues (teammate food retrieval success or failure) to determine whether they will rest in the nest for longer to either save energy or minimize interference, or be actively engaged in foraging, which costs more energy for the individual but potentially gains more energy for the swarm. With the adaptation mechanism, the swarm system demonstrates:

- Significantly improved performance compared with the swarm with no adaptation mechanism
- Emergent dynamic task allocation (division of labour) between foraging and resting
- Robustness to environmental change (in food density)

The most interesting conclusions are, firstly, that the swarms utilising social cues (communication between teammates) achieve the highest net energy income to the swarm and the fastest adaptation in ratio of foragers to resters when the food density changes; and, secondly, that the same social cues have the greatest impact when the food density is low.

This is a work in progress and so we have not tested the scalability or robustness of the approach, however given the minimal local communication between robots we have good reason to suppose the approach is scalable. We also believe that the approach will exhibit a high level of robustness to failure of individual robots, in keeping with the level of robustness commonly seen in swarm robotic systems.

Currently, in Algorithm 1, all values of time adjustment factors are chosen on a trial and error basis and all experiments in this paper use the same time adjustment values (see Table 5). Future work will include: (i) introducing a learning mechanism so that the swarm can find its own time adjustment values, and (ii) analysing both how these values affect the performance of the swarm and to what extent the system will be able to remain robust over a range of time adjustment values. Future work will also (iii) seek to develop a probabilistic model for our foraging swarm.

References

1. Lerman, K.: Mathematical model of foraging in a group of robots: Effect of interference. Autonomous Robots **13**(2) (2002) 127–141
2. Krieger, M.J.B., Billeter, J.B.: The call of duty: Self-organised task allocation in a population of up to twelve mobile robots. Robotics and Autonomous Systems **30**(1-2) (January 2000) 65–84
3. Théraulaz, G., Bonabeau, E., Deneubourg, J.L.: Response threshold reinforcement and division of labour in insect societies. In: the Royal Society B: Biological Sciences. Volume 265. (1998) 327–332
4. Labella, T.H., Dorigo, M., Deneubourg, J.L.: Efficiency and task allocation in prey retrieval. In: Proceedings of the First International Workshop on Biologically Inspired Approaches to Advanced Information Technology. Volume 3141. (2004) 32–47
5. Jones, C., Matarić, M.J.: Adaptive division of labor in large-scale multi-robot systems. In: IEEE/RSJ International Conference on Intelligent Robots and Systems (IROS). (2003) 1969–1974

6. Guerrero, J., Oliver, G.: Multi-robot task allocation strategies using auction-like mechanisms. In: Artificial Research and Development in Frontiers in Artificial Intelligence and Applications. (2003)
7. Şahin, E.: Swarm robotics: From sources of inspiration to domains of appliction. In Şabin, E., Spears, W., eds.: Swarm Robotics Workshop: State-of-the-art Survey. Volume 3342 of Lecture Notes in Computer Science., Springer (2005) 10–20
8. Beni, G.: From swarm intelligence to swarm robotics. In Şahin, E., Spears, W., eds.: Swarm Robotics Workshop: State-of-the-art Survey. Volume 3342 of Lecture Notes in Computer Science., Springer (2005) 1–9
9. Camazine, S., Franks, N.R., Sneyd, J., Bonabeau, E., Deneubourg, J.L., Théraulaz, G.: Self-Organization in Biological Systems. Princeton University Press (2001)
10. Martinoli, A., Easton, K.: Modeling swarm robotic systems. International Journal of Robotics Research **23**(4) (2004) 415–436
11. Gerkey, B.P., Vaughan, R.T., Howard, A.: The player/stage project: Tools for multi-robot and distributed sensor systems. In: Proceedings of the International Conference on Advanced Robotics. (2003) 317–323

A Macroscopic Model for Self-organized Aggregation in Swarm Robotic Systems

Onur Soysal and Erol Şahin

KOVAN Research Lab.
Department of Computer Engineering
Middle East Technical University,
06531, Ankara, Turkey
{soysal,erol}@ceng.metu.edu.tr
http://kovan.ceng.metu.edu.tr/{~soysal,~erol}

Abstract. We study the self-organized aggregation of a swarm of robots in a closed arena. We assume that the perceptual range of the robots are smaller than the size of the arena and the robots do not have information on the size of the swarm or the arena. Using a probabilistic aggregation behavior model inspired from studies of social insects, we propose a macroscopic model for predicting the final distribution of aggregates in terms of the parameters of the aggregation behavior, the arena size and the sensing characteristics of the robots. Specifically, we use the partition concept, developed in number theory, and its related results to build a discrete-time, non-spatial model of aggregation in swarm robotic systems under a number of simplifying assumptions. We provide simplistic simulations of self-organized aggregation using the aggregation behavior with different parameters and arena sizes. The results show that, despite the fact that the simulations did not explicitly enforce to satisfy the assumptions put forward by the macroscopic model, the final aggregate distributions predicted by the macroscopic model and obtained from simulations match.

1 Introduction

Aggregation, defined as "the collecting of units or parts into a mass or whole"[1], can be considered as one of the fundamental behaviors of swarms. In nature, aggregation behaviors, observed in organisms ranging from bacteria to social insects and mammals[2], increase the survival chance of the swarm in hostile environments. Although some of these aggregations can be traced back to environmental cues, others are self-organized.

We believe that self-organized aggregation, that do not require a cue from the environment or centralized control, is an essential competence for swarm robotic systems[3,4]. In these systems, aggregation behaviors can act as precursors for more complex behaviors such as flocking, pattern formation or self-assembly[5]. However, like other behaviors that produce self-organization, engineering aggregation behaviors is a major challenge. Although the general structure of aggregation behaviors can be inspired from studies of social insects, the relationship

E. Şahin et al. (Eds.): Swarm Robotics Ws, LNCS 4433, pp. 27–42, 2007.
© Springer-Verlag Berlin Heidelberg 2007

of behavioral parameters, and environmental factors to the performance of self-organized aggregation remains an open problem.

In this paper, we propose a probabilistic aggregation behavior for swarm robotic systems and develop a macroscopic model to predict the performance of the aggregation behavior under different parameters of the swarm system.

2   Related Studies

2.1   Aggregation

Studies of aggregation can be grouped in three different but related fields; namely, social insect studies, control theory, and swarm robotics. In social insect studies, aggregation, a rather common phenomenon in ants, cockroaches, etc., is a rather well-studied phenomenon. In [6], Deneubourg et al. studied the aggregation behavior of cockroaches, that aggregate in hiding sites. They studied the modulation of the resting time, defined as the time a cockroach spends in an aggregation. They observed that the resting time of cockroaches is proportional to the number of individuals in the aggregate. Hence, individuals tend to spend more time in large aggregations, and that this provides a positive feedback for growth of aggregations. In another study[7], Jeanson et al. presented a model of aggregation in cockroach larvae in homogeneous conditions. It was observed that the behavior of individuals depend on the number of larvae in their close vicinity. The authors computed the parameters of their model through systematic experiments on the larvae, and showed that similar aggregations can be obtained in simulations using these parameters.

In control theory, aggregation is often referred as the gathering, the agreement or the rendezvous problem. In most of these studies[8,9], however, the robots are modeled as points without orientation neglecting even the physical embodiment of the robots. Also, it is usually assumed that all robots can perceive the location of all the other robots in the swarm. In these studies, the major axis of research focus on the convergence characteristics of aggregation methods. For instance, in [10], it was shown that explicit bounds on the swarm size and bounds on the time of convergence can be obtained for aggregation.

When perception range is limited, however, aggregation of robots into a single aggregate becomes a more difficult problem. Deterministic algorithms work only when there are no isolated robots in the swarm [11]. Even without isolated robots, it was noted that, convergence may take an infinitely long time [8] in some scenarios. In the same study, Flocchini et. al proposed an aggregation algorithm which can provide guaranteed aggregation in finite time that required limited visibility with distinguishable robots and a common orientation decided by the robots. In a similar approach proposed in [12], Lin et al. utilized the geometric constraints on the behavior of robots to develop an aggregation behavior.

In swarm robotic systems, the problem of engineering and evaluation of aggregation behaviors have been tackled by a number of studies. We would like to first note that, aggregation refers to the forming of aggregates by the robots themselves, and is fundamentally different from the aggregation of passive items (like pucks) by a swarm of robots. We consider the latter problem as the clustering problem, and distinguish it from the aggregation problem.

In [13], one of the early studies on the problem, robots were required to form aggregates of pre-determined size around infrared beacons. Inspired by birds and frogs, the proposed method used a chorus consisting of individuals who can approximate the size of the aggregates using variations in sound. This method was also tested on systems without infrared beacons that trigger aggregation. The results indicated that, self-organized aggregation can be obtained with this method only in virtually noiseless environments.

In [14], Trianni et. al used genetic algorithms to study the evolution of neural networks to generate aggregation behaviors for a swarm of robots. Aggregation behaviors that were evolved in simulation, were partially tested on physical robots. It was shown that evolution was able to generate two different aggregation strategies: (1) static aggregation behaviors where robots remain still in aggregates, and (2) dynamic aggregation behaviors where robots continue moving in aggregates. It was shown that the evolved behaviors demonstrated a certain degree of scalability to generating aggregates in larger swarm sizes and larger arenas than the ones that the behaviors were evolved in.

Bahçeci et. al [15] investigated the use of evolutionary methods for developing aggregation behaviors. They systematically investigated the performance of behaviors evolved with different evolution parameters for the aggregation task. Based on the results of the systematic experiments, they proposed a number of rule of thumbs that can be used for evolving behaviors for swarm robot systems.

In a former study[16], we used a probabilistic aggregation behavior for studying aggregation in simulated swarm robotic systems. We investigated the effect of probabilistic parameters on aggregation performance through systematic experiments on a physics-based robot simulator, and identified different control parameters that lead to dynamic and static aggregation strategies.

2.2   Modeling

The engineering and evaluation of behaviors that generate self-organization in swarm robotic systems, such as self-organized aggregation, is a challenging problem. Although it is easy to propose generic behaviors for self-organization, it is hard to set their parameters and predict their performances for different swarm sizes and environments. Conducting systematic experiments is a difficult task, even with simulated swarm robotic systems, requiring a large amount of computation time. Despite this, however, the results obtained from such experiments provide little insight to the relationships between the performance of the behaviors and the parameters of the swarm system.

Constructing macroscopic models to describe the behavior of swarms can provide a viable approach to guide the design of swarm behaviors [17]. Macroscopic models, once developed, can provide explicit relationships between the parameters of the swarm system and its performance. Through such relationships, one can derive or evaluate the performances of a behavior under different parameters settings, and choose the optimum parameter values for a desired task. Despite these advantages, however, building macroscopic models for swarm robotic systems is a challenging task and there are few studies in the literature.

Most of the existing macroscopic models[17,18,19] used rate equations and Markovian processes to model the behavior of swarm robotic systems. These models generally represent the environment and behavioral states with probabilistic variables and define the change of these variables. In [20], Martinoli et. al proposed a probabilistic model for puck clustering task. In this problem, a number of pucks that are initially dispersed within a bounded arena, are clustered by a swarm of robots. The robots grip pucks in the arena and transporting them closer to other puck clusters. The model developed in this study was validated against the simulated and physical robots through experiments. In [19], Agassounon et. al. extend the object aggregation model described in [20] to a macroscopic level.

In [21], Kazadi defined the global goals as mathematical constraints an synthesize behaviors as to satisfy them. The behavior of the system can be investigated using the goal constraints. Lee et. al applied this concept to robot aggregation in their recent work [22] and showed that a controller for aggregation can be constructed using results form the clustering algorithm.

3   Aggregation Problem

We define aggregation as the gathering of a swarm of robots, that are initially dispersed into a closed arena, into preferably a single aggregate. We assume that; (1) The arena is bounded. (2) The perceptual range of robots is smaller than the size of the arena and that the initial positioning of the individuals may not necessarily form a connected graph. (3) The individuals in the swarm do not have any knowledge regarding the size of the arena or the swarm.

The first assumption removes the possibility that some robots may get lost during the aggregation process and is very common in the aggregation studies with social insects[7] and swarm robotic systems[13,14]. The second assumption makes the aggregation problem more realistic and difficult. It also rules out any centralized coordination mechanisms that may be proposed for the problem. The third assumption rules out any solutions to the aggregation problem that may be specific for a particular swarm and/or arena size.

4   Aggregation Behavior

In this study, we use an aggregation behavior that is implemented as a finite state machine as shown in Figure 1(a). The behavior consists of three basic behaviors, namely *random walk*, *wait* and *approach*. The *random walk* behavior, once activated, controls the robot for a certain pre-specified duration, moving the robot in the arena randomly while avoiding other robots and the walls of the arena. After the expiration of the *random walk* behavior, if the robot has an aggregate in its perceptual view, the robot switches to the *approach* behavior, else, the robot switches into the *wait* behavior, creating a one-robot aggregate.

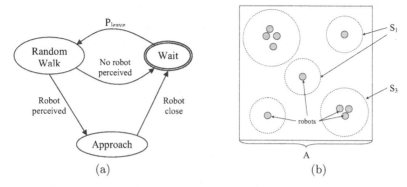

Fig. 1. (a) Aggregation behavior. Ovals display the simple behaviors and arrows represent the behavior transitions. **(b)** A sketch of the environment. The square frame represents the arena. The gray circles represent the robots and dashed circles represent the part of environment where the robot aggregate can be perceived by another robot, i.e S_m's. See text for more details.

In the *wait* behavior, the robot remains still with a certain probability to switch to the *random walk* behavior. The probability of leaving the *wait* behavior is denoted as P_{leave}. In the *approach* behavior, the robot moves toward the closest aggregate perceived. When the robot gets into the close proximity of the aggregate, the robot switches into the *wait* behavior.

We believe that the proposed aggregation behavior is consistent with the ones observed in natural swarms and is generic enough to represent different aggregation strategies through changes in transition probabilities. However, the performance comparison of different aggregation strategies that can be generated from this generic behavior, remains a challenge, and will be our motivation for constructing a macroscopic model.

5   A Macroscopic Model for Aggregation

We assume that there are n robots randomly placed in a closed arena of size A. We define an *aggregate* of robots as the group of robots who are in local proximity of each other, i.e. a connected group of robots who can sense each other through their proximity sensors. An aggregate which consists of m robots is called as an *m-aggregate*. The area within which an *m-aggregate* can be perceived by another robot is called as S_m, representing the area of the *attraction region* for the aggregate. Although, S_m would depend on the grouping of the *m-aggregate*, we will assume that all *m-aggregate*s have a rather compact grouping and that the area of their attraction regions can be approximated with a single S_m value. Figure 1(b) shows an exemplary sketch of the environment.

In the macroscopic model, the state of the swarm aggregation is denoted as a configuration $C_{a_1,a_2,..,a_k}$, where each a_k represent the existence of an a_k-*aggregate* in the arena and that $\sum_{i=1..k} a_k = n$. The configuration of a sample aggregation state shown in Figure 1(b) is denoted as $C_{4,3,1,1,1}$ indicating that there exist five aggregates in the arena with sizes 4, 3, 1, 1 and 1. Such a representation corresponds to the notion of *partition* in mathematics which is formally defined as an unordered set of positive integers whose sum is n [23]. Finally, we would like to note that, in this representation the spatial positioning of the aggregates are ignored, and two distributions are considered equivalent if they have equal number of aggregates, all with the same size.

In order to analyze the evolution of the configuration of the robots, we need to consider possible changes in the size of aggregates. These changes occur when robots leave their current aggregates to form a new one-robot aggregate or to join an existing aggregate. Such changes can be modeled as transitions in the configuration of the swarm. Our ultimate goal is to construct a macroscopic model that can model these transitions to make predictions about the time evolution and performance of a certain aggregation strategy. However, within this paper, we will construct a constrained macroscopic model which will make two simplifying constraints; (**1**) Only single robot transitions happen among the aggregates. (**2**) The probability of robot transitions between two aggregates is independent of the distance in between.

The first constraint assumes that the probability of multi-robot transitions among aggregates is small and can be neglected to simplify the temporal analysis of the aggregation process. In swarm robotic systems, such an assumption can be approximately made to hold by choosing a small P_{leave} value for the aggregation behavior. The second constraint assumes that the probability for a robot, which left its current aggregate, to join another aggregate is independent of the distance between the two aggregates. This assumption is made to simplify the spatial analysis and can be considered to approximately hold when the duration of the *random walk* behavior is chosen long enough with respect to the size of the arena.

The changes in configurations can be modeled as probabilistic transitions and that a graph can be constructed to visualize them, as shown in Figure 2. In this graph, each node corresponds to a configuration and directed weighted edges represent the probabilistic transitions from one configuration to another. The central view of our macroscopic model is that, if one can compute the probability of transitions between these configurations from the parameters of the swarm system, it is possible to deduce the evolution of the aggregation in time. Here, the parameters of a swarm system consists of the parameters of the aggregation behavior, P_{leave}, the sensing characteristics of the robots through S_m values, the size of the swarm n, and the area of the arena A.

Note that the limitation of transitions to single-robot transitions simplifies the connectivity of the graph greatly reducing the complexity of the model. However, despite this, the number of possible configurations and the probabilistic transitions among them grows exponentially making it difficult, if not impossible, to compute the transition probabilities of the model.

Here, we would like to point out that, the ultimate goal of aggregation is to form a single aggregate that contains all the individuals in the arena. Hence, we propose to use the size of the largest aggregate in a configuration, as its performance

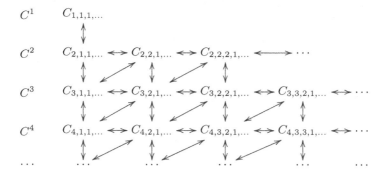

Fig. 2. Configuration graph re-ordered according to equivalence classes

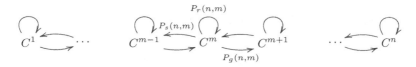

Fig. 3. Equivalence classes and the transitions between them

metric. With this metric, we can group all the different configurations with the same metric value, into equivalence classes. All the configurations that contain one or more *m-aggregate*s as their largest aggregate(s) can be lumped into a single equivalence class denoted by C^m. Hence, the transition graph of different configurations can be arranged according to their equivalence classes.

As a result of this grouping , in a swarm of size n, there can be only n equivalence classes. Also, using the single-robot transition assumption, we can limit the probabilistic transitions among these classes to transitions among consecutive equivalence classes in Figure 3.

Figure 4 shows all possible configurations of $n = 7$ robots as grouped into 7 equivalence classes. Note that, the spatial location of the aggregates is left out by our representation, and that the locations of the aggregates drawn on the figure is only exemplary.

With this representation, the system can only stay in one equivalence class or change into a neighboring equivalence class in one transition. The transitions between the equivalence classes will be denoted with three probabilities:

$P_s(n, m)$: the probability that the largest aggregate shrinks.
$P_g(n, m)$: the probability that the largest aggregate grows.
$P_r(n, m)$: the probability that the largest aggregate remains the same.

5.1   Probabilities for Shrinking

Shrinking is defined as a change in the configuration such that the largest aggregate is reduced by one as the result of a single-robot transition. Effectively,

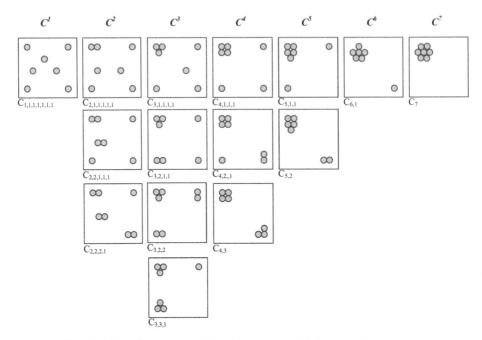

Fig. 4. All configurations of 7 robots grouped into equivalence classes

it means a transition from a configuration in equivalence class C^m to another configuration in equivalence class C^{m-1}.

First, note that the number of m-aggregates must be 1 such that shrinking can occur. Let's call the number of m-1-aggregates as k. If $k = 0$, meaning there is no aggregate with size $m - 1$ then there is a single aggregate the robot should not join for shrinking to occur, that is the aggregate it left. If $k > 0$ then the robot should not join any of these k aggregates and the aggregate it left. Therefore, the probability of shrinking when there are k m-1-aggregates is

$$\frac{A - (k + 1) \cdot S_{m-1}}{A},$$

which denotes the probability that the robot would not end up in the attraction regions of the m-1-aggregates in the arena.

The transition probabilities between configurations in consecutive classes needs to be integrated over all the configurations in the initial class. Hence, the probability of being in a configuration that included only one m-aggregate and a certain number of m-1-aggregates over all possible configurations need to be calculated. In order to calculate these probabilities, we will depend heavily on number theory concepts. A *partition function* $q(n, m)$, gives the number of ways to write n in terms of positive integers where the largest one is less than or equal to m [24] . If we fix the first aggregate to size m, the number of ways to write the rest with the largest being m gives us the number of configurations in C^m. This is equivalent to $q(n - m, m)$.

In C^m, the number of configurations that contain k *m-1-aggregates* and a single *m-aggregate* can be calculated using the partition function

$$q(n - m - k(m - 1), m - 2).$$

This formulation guarantees that the rest of the aggregates are neither of size m nor of size $m - 1$ by limiting the required largest aggregate size to $m - 2$.

Combining these, we can derive the shrinking probability for C^m as:

$$\boldsymbol{P}_s(n,m) = \frac{m \cdot P_{leave}}{n} \cdot \sum_{k=0}^{\left\lfloor \frac{n-m}{m-1} \right\rfloor} \frac{q(n - m - k \cdot (m - 1), m - 2)}{q(n - m, m)} \cdot \frac{A - (k + 1) \cdot S_{m-1}}{A},$$

where k ranges from 0 to the maximum number of aggregates of size $m - 1$ in C^m, which can be computed as $\left\lfloor \frac{n-m}{m-1} \right\rfloor$.

Note that for $n = m$, corresponding to the case that there is a single cluster that contains all robots, $q(0, m) = 1$ as zero is considered to have a single partition which is the empty partition. Therefore, $P_s(n, n)$ is reduced to

$$P_{leave} \cdot \frac{A - S_{n-1}}{A},$$

which reflects the case that the single large cluster will shrink if any of the robots leaves the cluster and does not come back.

5.2   Probabilities for Growth

Growth is defined as a change in the configuration such that the largest aggregate is increased by one as the result of a single-robot transition. Effectively, it means a transition from a configuration in equivalence class C^m to another configuration in equivalence class C^{m+1}.

First, note that the growth probabilities depend on two factors: the size of the aggregate that the robot is and the number of *m-aggregates*, denoted by t and k respectively. For given t and k, the probability of growth can be computed as:

$$\frac{\alpha}{q(n - m, m)} \cdot \frac{t \cdot P_{leave}}{n} \cdot \frac{k \cdot S_m}{A},$$

where α is the number of *t-aggregates* in all configurations of C^m that also contain k *m-aggregates*.

Here, the value of α can be computed using $\hat{p}(n, t)$ and $\hat{q}(n, m, t)$ functions. $\hat{p}(n, t)$ corresponds to the number of occurrences of t in all partitions of n and $\hat{q}(n, m, t)$ corresponds to the number of occurrences of t in all partitions of n where largest term is less than or equal to m. $\hat{p}(n, t)$ can be calculated with the following recurrence relation:

$$\hat{p}(n, t) = \begin{cases} 0 & t > n \\ 1 & t = n \\ q(n - t, n - t) + \hat{p}(n - t, t) & t < n. \end{cases}$$

In the recursion step, we can add t to all possible partitions of $n - t$, that will each have one more t. Since partitions of $n - t$ may contain more t's we add $\hat{p}(n - t, t)$. We now define $\hat{q}(n, m, t)$ as:

$$\hat{q}(n, m, t) = \begin{cases} 0 & t > m \\ q(n - t, m) + \hat{q}(n - t, m, t) & t = m, t < n \\ \hat{q}(n, m - 1, t) + \hat{q}(n - m, m, t) & t < m < n, t < n \\ \hat{p}(n, t) & \text{otherwise.} \end{cases}$$

In the first recursion case, we follow a similar construction with $\hat{p}(n, t)$. This time, $q(n - t, m)$ is used instead of $q(n - t, n - t)$ since we want to limit largest aggregate size to m. The second recursion case splits the partitions into two disjoint sets; the first one containing no terms equal to m, and the second one containing at least one term equal to m. The number of occurrences of t is sum of occurrences in these two sets. Note that, $t < m$ in this case, hence the number of occurrences in the second set discounts this mandatory term m.

If there are k m-aggregates, the number of occurrences of t in all such configurations is:

$$\hat{q}(n - k \cdot m, m - 1, t).$$

Using $\hat{q}$ and the previous result, we can calculate the total probability of growth for all aggregates of size t. We call this function γ:

$$\gamma(n, m, t, k) = \frac{\hat{q}(n - k \cdot m, m - 1, t)}{q(n - m, m)} \cdot \frac{t \cdot P_{leave}}{n} \cdot \frac{k \cdot S_m}{A}; t < m.$$

Note that this definition of γ is only valid for $t < m$ since the transitions between m-aggregate do not fit the rule explained above. Handling this special case is not very difficult since we know that there are exactly k aggregates of size m. The number of configurations with exactly k aggregates of size m can be computed with $q(n - k \cdot m, m - 1)$. In each of these configurations, a robot from k different aggregates can join one of the $k - 1$ aggregates to increase the size of largest aggregate. So we extend the definition of γ as follows:

$$\gamma(n, m, k, t) = \begin{cases} \frac{\hat{q}(n - k \cdot m, m - 1, t)}{q(n - m, m)} \cdot \frac{t \cdot P_{leave}}{n} \cdot \frac{k \cdot S_m}{A} & ; t < m \\ \frac{k \cdot q(n - k \cdot m, m - 1)}{q(n - m, m)} \cdot \frac{t \cdot P_{leave}}{n} \cdot \frac{(k - 1) \cdot S_m}{A} & ; t = m \end{cases}$$

The total probability of growth is the sum of these probabilities for all possible k and t values. For each different number of aggregates of size m, we need to consider all aggregate sizes that can lose a robot that could increase the size of the largest aggregate. These separate cases add up to the total growth probability.

$$P_g(n, m) = \sum_{k=1}^{\lfloor \frac{n}{m} \rfloor} \sum_{t=1}^{m} \gamma(n, m, k, t).$$

5.3   Probabilities to Remain Same

Once the shrinking and the growth probabilities are derived, the probability of remaining in the same equivalence class can be derived as:

$$P_r(n,m) = 1 - P_s(n,m) - P_g(n,m).$$

5.4   Macroscopic Model

The probability distribution of being at different equivalence classes C^m at time t is represented with $F(t)$ which is a probability vector (i.e. have positive real-valued entries summing up to 1) with n entries. Using M we can calculate the value of $F(t+1)$ with:

$$F(t+1) = M \cdot F(t).$$

Here, M is called the system matrix which consist of the probability values derived above as:

$$M_{m,i} = \begin{cases} P_g(n,m) & m = i - 1 \\ P_s(n,m) & m = i + 1 \\ P_r(n,m) & m = i \\ 0 & \text{otherwise.} \end{cases}$$

The steady state behavior of the system can then be obtained by iterating the system for infinite number of steps:

$$F(\infty) = M^\infty \cdot F(0).$$

Notice that M is a *left-stochastic* matrix since its rows are probability vectors. Stochastic matrices can be considered as representations of the transition probabilities of a first-order finite Markov chain. Furthermore, the M matrix is *regular* since the matrix power M^k will contain only strictly positive entries for some k [25]. According to the Perron-Frobenius theorem, such a system has a unique convergence point [26] meaning that it will converge to a steady-state vector representing the distribution of configurations as time goes to infinity. The final steady-state of the system would be the eigenvector of the matrix corresponding to the eigenvalue of unity.

6   Experimental Results

The predictions of the macroscopic model beg to be compared against results obtained from simulated or real robots. We have developed a simple 2D robot simulator for this purpose. The simulator supported simplified physical interactions between the robots, and the robot and the environment based on collision detection and recovery. The simulated robots have a radius of 3 units. They have infrared proximity sensors around them, to detect the existence of other robots and also avoid the walls of the arena. The characteristics of the proximity sensors control the *Robot close* condition which ends the *approach behavior*. The robots are also equipped with a omnidirectional long-range sensor through which they can sense each other within 30 units. This sensor, gives the center of mass for the robots in the perceptual view of the robot and determine the attraction regions (S_m) of the aggregates. The S_1 is computed as 2826 $unit^2$ (computed as $\pi \cdot 30 \cdot 30$) using the range of the long-range sensor. Through empirical experiments, S_{20} was measured to be approximately 5800 $unit^2$. The S_m values for the aggregate sizes in between was obtained using a linear interpolation between these two values. The random walk behavior duration is determined experimentally to be 20,000 simulation steps where robots can move around 1 units per simulation step. Finally, we would like to note that, the simulator does not restrict the movement of the robots and that more than one robot can be on the move at a given time.

We have conducted two sets of experiments and compared the final aggregate distributions obtained in simulation against those predicted by the macroscopic model. In the first set of experiments, we have studied the effect of the P_{leave} on the performance of the self-organized aggregation. In natural swarm systems, individuals are known to perceive the aggregates that they are in, and to modulate their leaving probability with respect to the size of the aggregate[7]. Specifically, we simulated three different strategies for setting the leave probability: **(1)** Constant: $P_{leave}(i) = G$, **(2)** Inversely proportional to aggregate size: $P_{leave}(i) = G/i$ and **(3)** Inversely proportional to the square of aggregate size: $P_{leave}(i) = G/i^2$. G is chosen to be 0.00002 in all the experiments.

Each strategy was tested with three different swarm and arena sizes: **(1)** 5 robots in a 150×150 arena, **(2)** 10 robots in a 212×212 arena and, **(3)** 20 robots in a 300×300 arena. These setups keep the robot density approximately same while increasing the number of robots. Each simulation run lasted for 50,000,000 simulation steps, which was observed to be sufficient for stabilization.

For each of the nine cases, 50 simulation runs were made, and the largest aggregate formed at the end of the simulations are recorded. Similarly, we used the macroscopic model to predict the final distribution of the aggregates for the same given parameters. The predictions of the model and the histogram of the largest aggregates obtained from simulations are plotted in Figure 5. The results indicate good match between model and the results of the simulation experiments. The model correctly predicts that constant leave probabilities, that is $P_{leave} = G$, should lead to small aggregates, whose mean size is determined by the size of the swarm as shown in the top row of the figure. The plots shown in the middle row indicates a phase transition from the top row to the bottom row. The plots in the bottom row of the figure clearly show that for leave probabilities set to be inversely proportional to the square of the aggregate size, that is $P_{leave}(i) = G/i^2$), the aggregation performance of the swarm is high. For three different arena sizes, it can be seen that the aggregation behavior was able to generate aggregates that contain all of the robots in the swarm for most runs.

These results are in aggreement with the results in [7]. In that study, Jeanson et. al reported poor aggregation performance when the agents ignored the number of agents in their close proximity, which corresponds to constant probabilities

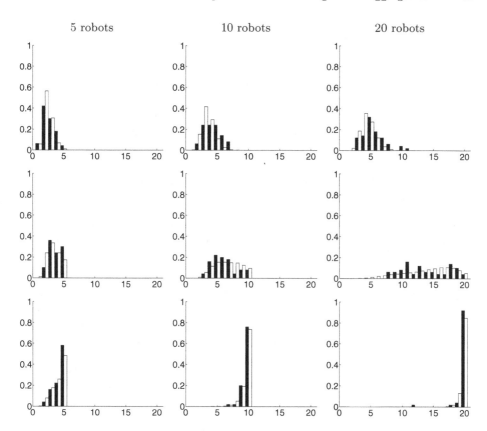

Fig. 5. The comparison of macroscopic model predictions against results obtained from simulations. Each plot shows the histogram of largest aggregates at the end of each run. White boxes show the prediction of the macroscopic model and black boxes show the results of experiments. Top row: $P_{leave}(i) = G$. Middle row: $P_{leave}(i) = \frac{G}{i}$. Bottom row: $P_{leave}(i) = \frac{G}{i^2}$. Note that, the black boxes do not have any error bars, since they represent the normalized histograms obtained from 50 runs.

in our model. They also reported successful aggregation when rest durations are increased more than linearly with respect to aggregate size which is similar to the quadratic case in our experiments. The results with quadratic probabilities are also comparable to results by Lee et. al, in which the controller is defined to use decreasing leave probabilities for aggregates [22].

In a second set of experiments, we investigate the effect of swarm density, which can be defined as the number of robots in the swarm divided by the arena size, on the performance of the aggregation. We studied the aggregation behavior of 5 robots in three different arenas: 150×150, 212×212 and 300×300.

When we used the leave probability setting, $P_{leave}(i) = G/i^2$, which was shown to be the best performer in the first set of experiments. The results of the simulations and the predictions of the model are plotted in Figure 6. It can be

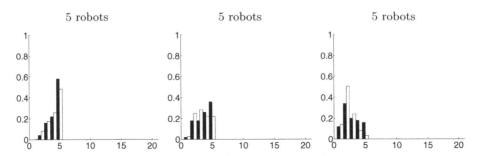

Fig. 6. Comparison of model predictions with experimental results with respect to arena size. Each diagram shows the histogram of largest aggregates at the end of each run. White boxes show the prediction of macroscopic model and black boxes show the results of experiments. $P_{leave}(i) = \frac{G}{i^2}$ where i is the number of robots in the aggregate. Note that, the black boxes do not have any error bars, since they represent the normalized histograms obtained from 50 runs.

seen that there is an approximate match between the model's predictions and the results of the simulations. The results show that the aggregation performance degrades with decreasing robot density, indicating that the constant used in the leave probability is related to the density of the robots in the area for a desired performance.

7   Conclusion

In this study we proposed a macroscopic model for self-organized aggregation behavior in swarm robotic systems and compared its aggregation performance predictions against results obtained from simulations. The macroscopic model, resulting in a simple mathematical form allows detailed analysis, such as the optimization of behavioral parameters for desired aggregation performance if given the number of robots, their perception range and the size of the environment.

However, we would like to explicitly state that the work presented in this paper is not complete yet and the model presented here relies on a number of restricting assumptions. As a possible result of these, there are a number of small discrepancies between the model predictions and the simulation results, such as the middle plot in Figure 6. There are many potential sources for these discrepancies. As stated, the macroscopic model relies on a number of assumptions, which are not fully satisfied in the simulations: **(1)** Single-robot transitions were not explicitly enforced in the simulations, **(2)** spatial information regarding the positions of the aggregates were excluded from the model, and **(3)** attraction regions of the aggregates were based on rough estimations. Other than these, cases like two aggregates joining into a single aggregate through a interconnecting robot were completely neglected. A detailed analysis of these unsatisfied assumptions on the performance of the aggregation remains a future challenge for our studies.

Acknowledgements

This work was partially funded by the "KARİYER: Kontrol Edilebilir Robot Oğulları" Career Project (Project no: 104E066) awarded to Erol Şahin by TÜBİ-TAK (Turkish Scientific and Technical Council).

The authors would like to thank Maya Çakmak for her help on both the discussions that led to the development of this model as well as her help on writing the manuscript.

References

1. "aggregation": (Merriam-webster online dictionary, 2006.) http://www.merriam-webster.com.
2. Camazine, S., Franks, N.R., Sneyd, J., Bonabeau, E., Deneubourg, J.L., Theraulaz, G.: Self-Organization in Biological Systems. Princeton University Press, Princeton, NJ, USA (2001) ISBN: 0691012113.
3. Dorigo, M., Şahin, E.: Swarm robotics - special issue editorial. Autonomous Robots **17**(2) (2004)
4. Şahin, E.: Swarm robotics: From sources of inspiration to domains of application. In Şahin, E., Spears, W., eds.: Swarm Robotics Workshop: State-of-the-art Survey. Number 3342 in Lecture Notes in Computer Science, Berlin Heidelberg, Springer-Verlag (2005) 10–20
5. Dorigo, M., Tuci, E., Groß, R., Trianni, V., Labella, T.H., Nouyan, S., Ampatzis, C.: The swarm-bots project. In Şahin, E., Spears, W., eds.: Swarm Robotics Workshop: State-of-the-art Survey. Number 3342 in Lecture Notes in Computer Science, Berlin Heidelberg, Springer-Verlag (2005) 31–44
6. Deneubourg, J.L., Lioni, A., Detrain, C.: Dynamics of aggregation and emergence of cooperation. Biological Bulletin **202** (2002) 262–267
7. Jeanson, R., Rivault, C., Deneubourg, J., Blanco, S., Fournier, R., Jost, C., Theraulaz, G.: Self-organised aggregation in cockroaches. Animal Behaviour **69** (2005) 169–180
8. Flocchini, P., Prencipe, G., Santoro, N., Widmayer, P.: Gathering of asynchronous robots with limited visibility. Theoretical Computer Science **337**(1-3) (2005) 147–168
9. Gordon, N., Wagner, I.A., Bruckstein, A.M.: Gathering multiple robotic a(ge)nts with limited sensing capabilities. In: Lecture Notes in Computer Science. Volume 3172. (2004) 142–153
10. Gazi, V., Passino, K.M.: A class of attractions/repulsion functions for stable swarm aggregations. International Journal of Control **77**(18) (2004) 1567–1579
11. Lin, Z., Francis, B., Ma, M.: Necessary and sufficient graphical conditions for formation control of unicycles. IEEE Transactions on Automatic Control **50**(1) (2005) 121–127
12. Lin, J., Morse, A.S., Anderson, B.D.O.: The multi-agent rendezvous problem. In: 42nd IEEE Conference on Decision and Control. Volume 2. (2003) 1508–1513
13. Melhuish, C., Holland, O., Hoddell, S.: Convoying: using chorusing to form travelling groups of minimal agents. Journal of Robotics and Autonomous Systems **28** (1999) 206–217

14. Trianni, V., Groß, R., Labella, T., Şahin, E., Dorigo, M.: Evolving aggregation behaviors in a swarm of robots. In Banzhaf, W., Christaller, T., Dittrich, P., Kim, J.T., Ziegler, J., eds.: Advances in Artificial Life - Proceedings of the 7th European Conference on Artificial Life (ECAL). Volume 2801 of Lecture Notes in Artificial Intelligence., Springer Verlag, Heidelberg, Germany (2003) 865–874

15. Bahçeci, E., Şahin, E.: Evolving aggregation behaviors for swarm robotic systems: A systematic case study. In: Proc. of the IEEE Swarm Intelligence Symposium, Pasadena, California (2005) 333–340

16. Soysal, O., Şahin, E.: Probabilistic aggregation strategies in swarm robotic systems. In: Proc. of the IEEE Swarm Intelligence Symposium, Pasadena, California (2005) 325–332

17. Lerman, K., Martinoli, A., Galstyan, A.: A review of probabilistic macroscopic models for swarm robotic systems. In Şahin, E., Spears, W., eds.: Swarm Robotics Workshop: State-of-the-art Survey. Number 3342, Berlin Heidelberg, Springer-Verlag (2005) 143–152

18. Kazadi, S., Chung, M., Lee, B., Cho, R.: On the dynamics of clustering systems. Robotics and Autonomous Systems **46** (2004) 1–27

19. Agassounon, W., Martinoli, A., Easton, K.: Macroscopic modeling of aggregation experiments using embodied agents in teams of constant and time-varying sizes. Autonomous Robots **17** (2004) 163–192

20. Martinoli, A., Ijspeert, A., Mondada, F.: Understanding collective aggregation mechanisms: From probabilistic modelling to experiments with real robots. Robotics and Autonomous Systems **29** (1999) 51–63

21. Kazadi, S.T.: Swarm Engineering. PhD thesis, Caltech (2000)

22. Lee, C., Kim, M., Kazadi, S.: Robot clustering. In: IEEE International Conference on Systems, Man and Cybernetics. Volume 2. (2005) 1449–1454

23. Weisstein, E.W.: Partition from mathworld–a wolfram web resource (2005) `http://mathworld.wolfram.com/Partition.html`.

24. Weisstein, E.W.: Partition function q from mathworld–a wolfram web resource (2002) `http://mathworld.wolfram.com/PartitionFunctionq.html`.

25. Wikipedia: Stocastic matrix from wikipedia, the free encyclopedia (2006) `http://en.wikipedia.org/wiki/Stochastic_matrix`.

26. Wikipedia: Perron - frobenius theorem from wikipedia, the free encyclopedia (2006) `http://en.wikipedia.org/w/index.php?title=Perron-Frobenius_theorem`.

An Analytical and Spatial Model of Foraging in a Swarm of Robots

Heiko Hamann and Heinz Wörn

Institute for Process Control and Robotics,
Universität Karlsruhe (TH)
76128 Karlsruhe, Germany
{hamann,woern}@ira.uka.de

Abstract. The foraging scenario is important in robotics, because it has many different applications and demands several fundamental skills from a group of robots, such as collective exploration, shortest path finding, and efficient task allocation. Particularly for large groups of robots emergent behaviors are desired that are decentralized and based on local information only. But the design of such behaviors proved to be difficult because of the absence of a theoretical basis. In this paper, we present a macroscopic model based on partial differential equations for the foraging scenario with virtual pheromones as the medium for communication. From the model, the robot density, the food flow and a quantity describing qualitatively the stability of the behavior can be extracted. The mathematical model is validated in a simulation with a large number of robots. The predictions of the model correspond well to the simulation.

Keywords: macroscopic model, foraging, swarm robotics, mathematical analysis.

1 Introduction

The ongoing advances in electronics and robotics have made it possible to build small robots of sizes below $3 \times 3 \times 3$ cm^3 at low cost. See website [6] for example which is part of the European project I-SWARM [18] and also gives an overview over other existing platforms. This evolution made it feasible to implement large groups of 50 or more robots. While the hardware is available, the development of the control software is still a problem. To minimize the complexity of the entire system, the development targets simple rules and, in an allusion to nature, one hopes for emergent behavior of the robot group that leads to the solution of the predefined task. However, both the design of the general strategy and the configuration of many influential parameters are in general not supported by any guideline based on theoretical results. Therefore, the software is just implemented using simple heuristics based on experience and a trial-and-error process. To fill this gap, a scientific basis that describes the behavior of robot swarms would be desirable.

A first step could be the development of analytical models, that support us in understanding the results obtained by simulations and experiments in a better

E. Şahin et al. (Eds.): Swarm Robotics Ws, LNCS 4433, pp. 43–55, 2007.
© Springer-Verlag Berlin Heidelberg 2007

way. Additionally, such models help to save resources, because they are usually faster than simulations and they give some insights before a single robot is implemented. The use of such models for finding optimal parameters is limited but possible, if a mapping from the abstract level to reality exists [13].

Although research in this field has just begun, a lot of results have been published recently: A probabilistic, analytic, and macroscopic model based on rate equations has been introduced and applied to several different scenarios by Lerman, Martinoli, Matarić, and others and performs very well in predicting the ratios of robots being in a certain state at a certain time [9,12,11]. It is based on the assumption that the space is uniform, so that for example scenarios involving pheromones cannot be represented using this model. However, there exist many models that approximate spatial characteristics: For example the dimensionality of space is reduced by modeling the movement of agents as a graph or a line of decision points [5,4], space is discretized using cellular automata [3], or space is fully but only microscopically modeled using Monte Carlo simulations [21,2]. An analytical microscopic model with respect to space based on Brownian motion has been presented by Schweitzer [15,16]. In some cases the derivation of a macroscopic model from the microscopic descriptions has been performed and presented.

The foraging scenario is an old problem in robotics and hence it has been investigated intensively. There are many variants of this scenario: A single robot or a group of robots has to find and collect or basically only transport (food) items to some random locations or to one defined place. A brief overview of the work in robotics on this scenario is given in [10]. Here we focus on the situation having one place where food can be found (we will refer to this as *food*) and another place where the food should be delivered (*nest*). Our approach will make use of pheromones as the tool for communication and will utilize a large number of robots. In [14] an overview of simulations connected to this special scenario is given and an approach is presented using two dynamic pheromones, i.e. their distributions change over time.

An analytical macroscopic model for a variant of foraging is presented in [10]. The given rate equations are based on the assumption of homogeneous space and no pheromones are used in the investigated scenario. In [17,15], a spatial model for trail formation by ants using two pheromones is given. The model is based on differential equations that describe the agents microscopically.

2   Simulation

The analytical model will be validated with results of a simulation. As the framework for our simulation we use the Breve simulator by J. Klein [8]. Here, we simulate a homogeneous swarm in continuous space combined with a discrete implementation of the pheromones. Since we want to simulate big numbers of robots over many runs, we depend on a rather simple model of the robot, that is computationally easy to handle. In our model, the robot has circumferential visibility, can measure distances to objects within the coverage of its sensors, and can distinguish between other robots, the nest, food, and the wall, that circumscribes the arena. It is also able to perceive a pheromone gradient in two mutually orthogonal directions and to drop a certain amount of pheromone. The robots' locomotion is assumed to be ideal, i.e. an acceleration towards an arbitrary direction is possible at all times (holonomic drive mechanism). The control of the robot is totally reactive and based on the principle of virtual physics (potential field techniques), i.e. other objects have a repelling effect on it depending on their distance and visibility [19,7,1]. This defines the avoidance behavior to be similar to the collision of two particles in our real physical world.

A robot is in one of two possible states: looking for food (s_f) or returning home to the nest (s_n). Initially, all robots are randomly positioned close to the nest with a random velocity heading to a random direction and all start in state s_f. If a robot in state s_f perceives the food, it transitions to state s_n. Robots in state s_n perform a transition to state s_f, if they perceive the nest. We are using two pheromones: one that should be established to increase in intensity towards the food (p_f) and another one that increases towards the nest (p_n). To avoid immense instabilities and to simplify the scenario, pheromone p_n is chosen to be present and constant at all times. It is always guaranteed to have a smooth gradient leading to the nest at any position. However, at least in a grid world based on a concept of dying agents it has been shown, as mentioned above, that a stable behavior can be reached with two dynamic pheromones with the advantage of finding shortest paths around obstacles [14]. As a second consequence, the robots will only be able to deposit the pheromone p_f, which they will do in state s_n. The amount that is dropped by the robot at each simulation step is set to an initial value (drop size, see Table 1) at the state transition and decreases exponentially over time thereafter (drop decrease rate).

The pheromones are implemented by a grid of so-called patches that is laid over the whole arena. The patches are quadratic and we have chosen a size of $s = 6$ cm (for comparison: a patch fits into the area covered by the robot's sensors). The performance of the swarm is independent of this size as long as it is reasonably small and both the evaporation and the diffusion rate are adapted to it. But choosing the patch size is computationally critical because the evaporation and diffusion process of pheromone p_f is executed at every time step, which has to handle every single patch (complexity is $O(\frac{1}{s^2})$), another option could be to update the grid only every m time steps for $m > 1$). Every patch has an associated pheromone intensity i that is updated per step by

$$i_{t+1} = (1 - e - d)i_t + \sum_{n \in \mathcal{N}} n(1 - e)\frac{d}{4}, \tag{1}$$

where e denotes the evaporation rate, d the diffusion rate and $\mathcal{N}$ the set of intensities of the patches in the von Neumann neighborhood of range one except the current patch itself. If a robot deposits some pheromone p_f, the dropped amount will be added to the intensity associated with the patch where the robot is located at that moment. Pheromone p_n is time-invariant as discussed above (see Section 4 for the definition).

To implement the gradient ascending, the two components of the gradient are computed from the intensities of the neighboring patches independent of the robot's orientation: $g_x = n_{x+} - n_{x-}$, where n_{x+} denotes the intensity of the neighboring patch in positive x-direction and n_{x-} in negative x-direction; g_y is computed analogously. The overall acceleration vector of the robot is a weighted sum of $\frac{(g_x,g_y)^T}{|(g_x,g_y)^T|}$ (if $|(g_x,g_y)^T| = 0$ the term is set to 0) and another vector depending on sensed objects that implements the avoidance behavior.

Table 1. Simulation parameters

Parameter	Value
arena size	258 cm × 258 cm
nest position	(129 cm, 195 cm)
food position	(129 cm, 63 cm)
patch size	6 cm
agent diameter	2 cm
proximity sensor range	5 cm
iteration step	0.05 s
max. speed	7 cm/s
evaporation rate	0.0392 1/s
diffusion rate	0.1568 1/s
drop decrease rate	0.095 1/s
initial drop size	0.5

3   Analytical Model

In [16] macroscopic equations are presented, that are derived from microscopic equations to describe the behavior of so-called "heatbugs". The "heatbug" simulation bears resemblance to the scenario addressed here: Corresponding to the pheromone, it is also a spatial property – the heat, that influences the movements of the bugs and which is also manipulated by them. We use the equation of the agent density from [16] as a starting point:

$$\frac{\partial}{\partial t}S(\mathbf{r},t) = D\frac{\partial^2 S(\mathbf{r},t)}{\partial \mathbf{r}^2} - \alpha\frac{\partial}{\partial \mathbf{r}}\left[\frac{\partial P(\mathbf{r},t)}{\partial \mathbf{r}}S(\mathbf{r},t)\right] \tag{2}$$

$$= D\nabla^2 S(\mathbf{r},t) - \alpha\nabla\left[\nabla P(\mathbf{r},t)S(\mathbf{r},t)\right], \tag{3}$$

where $S(\mathbf{r},t)$ denotes the density of robots at position $\mathbf{r}$ at time t, $P(\mathbf{r},t)$ the intensity of the pheromone, D the diffusion constant, α the greediness of following the gradient, and ∇ the gradient.

The first term describes a standard diffusion process according to Fick's Second Law that models the exploring robots as well as robots avoiding collisions. The underlying assumption to motivate the application of this equation to the scenario investigated here is: If the density of robots in the arena is inhomogeneous then the robots tend to move away from spots of higher density into areas with less density. Please note that our approach of using virtual physics in our simulation meets this assumption. Thus, the diffusion term is a suitable mathematical description of robots performing some kind of random walk.

Because the rate of diffusion usually depends on the local density, the choice of using a constant diffusion coefficient is a simplification justified by two considerations: First, in the steady state the regions of highest density are most relevant and these densities reside within a small interval. Second, typically the diffusion constant has to be measured in an experiment or simulation. Having to measure the diffusion as a function of the density means higher overhead and demands longer running times to reach a reasonable accuracy.

The second term describes for $\alpha > 0$ a gradient ascent of the robots proportional to the pheromone gradient. Although applications of the pheromone scenario could exist in which such a behavior of the robots might be desired, we drop the proportionality to the pheromone intensity of the gradient ascent, because this corresponds to a more efficient control software of robots and results in better stability in both the simulation and the used numerical solver of the analytical model. This is achieved by normalizing the gradient of P to one:

$$\frac{\partial}{\partial t} S(\mathbf{r}, t) = D\nabla^2 S(\mathbf{r}, t) - \alpha\nabla \left[\frac{\nabla P(\mathbf{r}, t)}{|\nabla P(\mathbf{r}, t)|} S(\mathbf{r}, t) \right]. \tag{4}$$

In the case of $|\nabla P(\mathbf{r}, t)| = 0$ the second term is set to 0. However, this model does not support several states, several pheromones, or state transitions and an extention is necessary (note that in [15] another way of incorporating internal states and several potential fields is given). First, we introduce the densities S_f and S_n that describe the densities of robots in state s_f and s_n respectively. Accordingly, we introduce the pheromone intensities P_f and P_n that correspond to the pheromones introduced in the previous section. This leads to two partial differential equations (PDE) in the same form as equation 4:

$$\frac{\partial}{\partial t} S_f(\mathbf{r}, t) = D_f\nabla^2 S_f(\mathbf{r}, t) - \alpha_f\nabla \left[\frac{\nabla P_f(\mathbf{r}, t)}{|\nabla P_f(\mathbf{r}, t)|} S_f(\mathbf{r}, t) \right], \tag{5}$$

$$\frac{\partial}{\partial t} S_n(\mathbf{r}, t) = D_n\nabla^2 S_n(\mathbf{r}, t) - \alpha_n\nabla \left[\frac{\nabla P_n(\mathbf{r}, t)}{|\nabla P_n(\mathbf{r}, t)|} S_n(\mathbf{r}, t) \right]. \tag{6}$$

Now we are investigating a system with multicomponent diffusion but we are still using Fick's law that does not model the coupling of the two diffusion coefficients and is only exact for two components. However, this is a common approximation in physics and is the more accurate the higher the concentration of the supporting medium (here: space) is, which is a suitable assumption here. Thus these two PDE are coupled only indirectly by the state transitions and the pheromones, which will be defined in the following.

The nest and the food are modeled as areas with special boundary conditions that implement the state transitions. Say $\partial\Omega_n$ is the boundary of the arena around the nest. Then we define the boundary conditions at the nest as the following:

$$\forall \mathbf{r} \in \partial \Omega_n : \frac{\partial S_f}{\partial t}(\mathbf{r}, t) = D_f \nabla^2 S_f(\mathbf{r}, t) - \alpha_f \nabla \left[\frac{\nabla P_f(\mathbf{r}, t)}{|\nabla P_f(\mathbf{r}, t)|} S_f(\mathbf{r}, t) \right]$$
$$+ D_n \nabla^2 S_n(\mathbf{r} - \epsilon \mathbf{n}, t) - \alpha_n \nabla \left[\frac{\nabla P_n(\mathbf{r} - \epsilon \mathbf{n}, t)}{|\nabla P_n(\mathbf{r} - \epsilon \mathbf{n}, t)|} S_n(\mathbf{r} - \epsilon \mathbf{n}, t) \right] \tag{7}$$

$$\forall \mathbf{r} \in \partial \Omega_n : S_n(\mathbf{r}, t) = 0, \tag{8}$$

where $\mathbf{n}$ denotes the exterior normal to the boundary (pointing towards the nest center). The intuitive interpretation of these equations is simple: The robots in state s_n, that are close to the nest, perform a transition to s_f, because they have finished their mission to find the nest. In a trivial grid discretization of these PDE, the boundary conditions are implemented by adding the amount of S_n to S_f and setting $S_n = 0$ within the area of the nest after each iteration. The boundary conditions at the food are defined in an analog way. The boundaries of the arena are modeled as total isolation.

The pheromone P_n leading to the nest is assumed to be constant over time and is just defined as it is implemented in the simulation:

$$P_n(\mathbf{r}) = c_1 (\sqrt{d_{max}} - \sqrt{d(\mathbf{r}, \mathbf{r}_n)}), \tag{9}$$

where $d(\mathbf{r}, \mathbf{r}_n)$ is the distance to the center of the nest, d_{max} the maximal possible distance, and some constant c_1 that is used to adapt P_n to the absolute intensities of P_f (see Table 2). However, every function that provides a gradient pointing towards the nest at all positions could be used, since our model as well as the simulation are both independent of the absolute values.

Pheromone P_f is modeled to depend on S_n directly:

$$P_f(\mathbf{r}, t) = S_n(\mathbf{r}, t) c_2^{c_3 d(\mathbf{r}, \mathbf{r}_f)}, \tag{10}$$

where $d(\mathbf{r}, \mathbf{r}_f)$ is the distance to the center of the food, and some constants $c_2 < 1$ and c_3 depending on the pheromone dropping procedure. The underlying consideration is that the amount of pheromone dropped per step by a robot decreases exponentially with time. Thus the amount of pheromone that can be dropped by a robot at a certain spot is limited by the time a robot needs to travel from the food to this spot. Assuming a constant velocity this time is proportional to the distance to the food.

Note that no dependency on the history of S_n is incorporated. Intuitively, one might argue, that this direct coupling corresponds to a high evaporation rate of the pheromone and thus could cause instabilities in the modeled overall behavior, that would not emerge for appropriate parameter settings. However, for reasonable values of diffusion D, the history is intrinsically modeled. For the steady state this is quantitatively true and can be shown under the assumption that at each patch the pheromone diffusion net flux is zero. Since the robots depend on the normalized gradient only, a qualitatively correct representation of the gradient is sufficient. For visualization, imagine a large group of robots in state s_n starting at the food and moving towards the nest following the gradient greedily and leaving behind only few other robots that moved to different directions due to diffusion. On the line between food and nest they would create a pheromone trail starting high at the food and decreasing exponentially towards the nest because of the dropping method. Since the density of the robots left behind would not exponentially increase towards the nest, this situation is represented qualitatively correct in our model. Similar considerations imply that equation 10 is a good approximation.

Table 2. Pheromone parameters

Parameter	Value
c_1	$1.4 \cdot 10^{-4}$
c_2	0.998
c_3	10

4   Results

To simplify the following investigations, we restrict ourselves to a special case and set $\alpha_f = \alpha_n := \alpha$ and $D_f = D_n := 1 - \alpha = D$. This class of parameter settings is of special interest, because for example one would expect that the configuration with the maximal flow of food belongs to this class of symmetric diffusion settings, which is also supported by the results of our simulations. Now only a single variable that connects the model to the simulation is left – the diffusion D.

This diffusion parameter might be directly extracted from the robot control, if the control method enforces a certain amount of diffusion. However, the diffusion will typically depend on the local density also and here the diffusion is not explicitly implemented in our control software. Thus it has to be determined from the overall behavior in the simulation. This was done by measuring the amount of robots that follow the pheromone gradient approximately in comparison to those that move to any other direction at many different positions in the arena. The average diffusion was computed by weighting these values by their local density averaged over time.

The solution of the PDE provides us basically with the stationary density distributions of robots in states s_f and s_n, if they exist. Fig. 1(a) shows a typical solution and Fig. 1(b) the corresponding averaged density of 30 simulation runs. The accuracy of the model is good at positions between nest and food. However, close to the nest and the food it suffers from the unmodeled acceleration processes of the robots and the impossibility to represent the infinite slope of the densities in the simulation.

Furthermore, we are interested in the resulting flow of food that is the same as the rate of robots that perform a transition from s_n to s_f per time. The amount

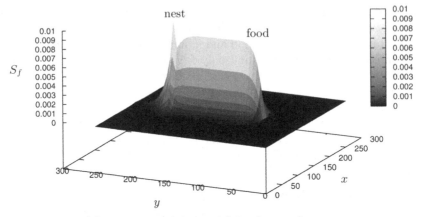

(a) Prediction of the model for the steady-state

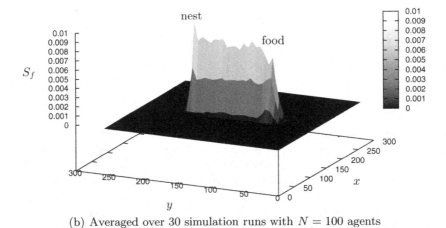

(b) Averaged over 30 simulation runs with $N = 100$ agents

Fig. 1. Distribution of S_f for $D \approx 0.55$

of robots that perform a transition at the boundaries of the nest and the food per time in our model gives a good prediction of the flow. Another estimate of the converged flow, that turned out to be less sensitive to correctly measuring the diffusion, is obtained by integrating the densities of the steady-state over a line in the mid between nest and food, that is orthogonal to the shortest path between nest and food. Say the result of this integration is I then the prediction of the flow for the given diffusion constant D would be $I(1 - D) = I\alpha$. This is a good approximation because the component of the pheromone gradient in the direction orthogonal to this plane is typically small. Thus the diffusion in this direction will also be small following Fick's First Law that gives the diffusion flux in the steady state: $J(\mathbf{r}) = -D\frac{\partial P(\mathbf{r})}{\partial \mathbf{r}}$. This is the method we used to predict the flow.

In every simulation run, we drew 36 samples equidistant in time after a transient. The results are averaged over the samples of 30 runs. More runs would be

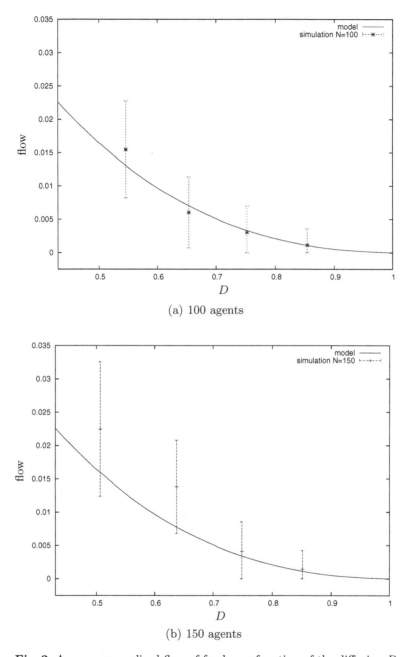

(a) 100 agents

(b) 150 agents

Fig. 2. Average normalized flow of food as a function of the diffusion D

desirable for a better statistical significance, however, due to limited resources and the high computational demand of the simulation, that could not be achieved. Two sets of simulation runs with two different swarm sizes $N \in \{100, 150\}$ were

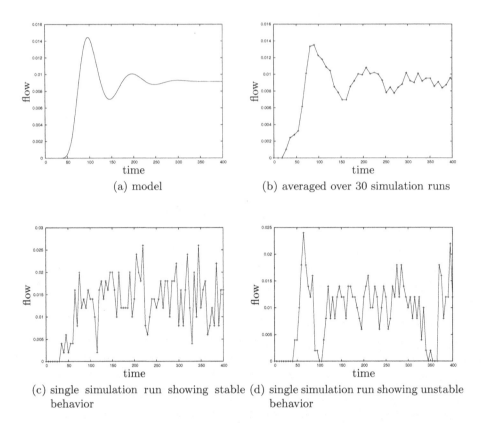

(a) model

(b) averaged over 30 simulation runs

(c) single simulation run showing stable behavior

(d) single simulation run showing unstable behavior

Fig. 3. Food flow over time

performed and we could only reach diffusion rates in the interval $0.5 < D < 0.9$. The flow decreases with the diffusion, as expected (see Fig. 2, the error bars show the 95% confidence interval based on the t-distribution).

In order to maximize the flow and following these results one would like to set the diffusion as low as possible. However, our observations of the simulation indicate that the lower the diffusion rate is the more unstable the system becomes. Please note that the situation described here will only occur in simulations that implement interference effects between agents and an unbiased gradient ascent. If the robots follow the pheromone gradient $\frac{\partial P_f}{\partial r}$ very greedily, it becomes highly probable that they accumulate at certain spots. This might be caused by and lead itself to local maxima in the pheromone intensities P_f, where robots of state s_f are attracted. These groups of robots block others in state s_n traveling in the opposite direction. Hence, the local intensities P_f are reinforced and more and more robots accumulate at this spot. As a consequence, the flow of food might even break down temporarily (compare to Fig. 3). This fact is not directly represented by the flow prediction of our model as it only gives the average flow of a functioning swarm without modeling effects of interference. While in the flow diagram of the model the intensity and number of oscillations only increases

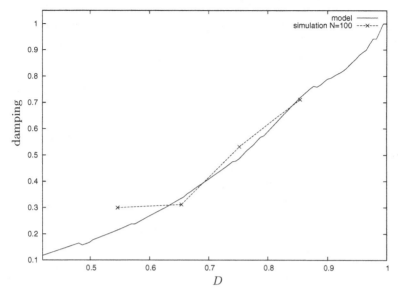

Fig. 4. Damping as a function of the diffusion D

with decreasing diffusion, the batch-wise flow caused by robots moving in large groups and the temporary stop of the flow appears as an overshooting in the flow diagram of the simulation. These observations give rise to another measure introduced in the following.

As a qualitative measure for the instability of the system we use a damping constant d as it is used in control theory. The run of the flow over time can be interpreted as a step response and modeled by a 2nd-order lag element (P-T2). Such an element is stable for $0 < d < 1$ (underdamped) as well as for $d \geq 1$ (overdamped) and shows oscillating behavior in the former region. Our observations showed that as well in the model as in the simulation the number and amplitude of these oscillations decrease with the diffusion.

To get reasonable results, we had to average over all available simulation results and thus cannot give any statistical measure. For too high numbers of robots leading to high densities the effects by interference induce a higher damping for low diffusion rates than predicted. However, a trend can be noticed in Fig. 4 and shows that the damping of the P-T2 element can serve as a qualitative model for the stability of the swarm behavior.

5   Conclusion and Outlook

The application of this analytical model to the foraging scenario has shown that the overall behavior of large groups of robots can be predicted well and described by the use of mathematical methods. Compared to the simulation the average behavior is computed faster by three or more orders of magnitude. The diffusion constant can be measured by the simulation within minutes. However, this constant models abstractly a variety of basic behaviors like exploration and collision avoidance. A direct connection to the control software does usually not exist. Thus a found optimal diffusion constant can only serve as a broad guideline for the development of the software.

There are a variety of possible extensions to this model: At first, it would be desirable to model also the interferences between robots that accumulate densely at one place, to investigate the characteristics of scalability in this scenario. This might be achieved by combining this model and the one presented in [10] or by better approximations of the diffusion process (Wilke or Maxwell-Stefan diffusion). Furthermore, a scenario with two dynamic pheromones and obstacles as well as the adaptability to food sources that change in position or quality over time could be investigated.

We plan to implement the presented scenario on real robots following the approach of Sugawara et al., that implemented it for a number of up to three robots [20]. At our institute, a swarm of 40 Jasmine robots is available (see [6]), that will be extended soon. We also have a combination of a video projector and a video camera installed above the arena. Additionally, light sensors on the top of the robots are under development and will be used by the robots to perceive the virtual pheromone gradient, i.e. a light gradient. The robots are able to drop pheromones by lighting an LED on their top, which will be detected by a computer connected to the camera and it will adapt the image projected onto the arena accordingly. With this setting it is easily possible to simulate scenarios physically that would actually need more technical overhead, e.g. following a gradient of temperature or gas concentrations. Even the combination of the two paradigms of self-organization and central control (on demand) might lead to synergies for example in microassembly. Self-organizing techniques provide robustness and scalability while central control techniques provide highest accuracy if needed.

Acknowledgments. The authors want to thank the anonymous referees for their excellent report, which has largely improved the clarity and content of the paper. This work was partially supported by the German Research Foundation (DFG) within the Research Training Group GRK 1194 Self-organizing Sensor-Actuator Networks.

References

1. Arkin, R. C.: Motor schema based mobile robot navigation. International Journal of Robotics Research **8** (1989) 92–112
2. Bonabeau, E., Thraulaz, G., Fourcassi, V. and Deneubourg, J.: The phase-ordering kinetics of cemetery organization in ants. Technical Report 98-01008, Santa Fe Institute, 1998.
3. Cole, B.J. and Cheshire, D.: Mobile Cellular Automata Models of Ant Behavior: Movement Activity of Leptothorax allardycei. American Naturalist, Vol. **148** (1996), pp. 1–15

4. Deneubourg, J.L., Aron, S., Goss, S. and Pasteels, J.M.: The self-organizing exploratory pattern of the Argentine ant. Journal of Insect Behavior **3** (1990) 159–168
5. Goss, S., Aron, S. , Deneubourg, J.L. and Pasteels, J.M.: Self-organized shortcuts in the Argentine ant. Naturwissenschaften **76** (1989) 579–581
6. Jasmine Robot - Project Website. `http://www.swarmrobot.org/`. (2006)
7. Khatib, O.: Real-time obstacle avoidance for manipulators and mobile robots. International Journal of Robotics Research **5** (1986) 90–98
8. Klein, J.: Continuous 3D Agent-Based Simulations in the breve Simulation Environment. In: Proceedings of NAACSOS Conference (North American Association for Computational, Social, and Organizational Sciences). (2003)
9. Lerman, K.: A model of adaptation in collaborative multi-agent systems. Adaptive Behavior **12** (2004) 187–198
10. Lerman, K., Galstyan, A. Mathematical Model of Foraging in a Group of Robots: Effect of Interference. Autonomous Robots **13** (2002) 127–141
11. Lerman, K., Jones, C., Galstyan, A. and Mataric, M.: Analysis of Dynamic Task Allocation in Multi-Robot Systems. Int. J. of Robotics Research (2006)
12. Lerman, K., Martinoli, A. and Galstyan, A.: A Review of Probabilistic Macroscopic Models for Swarm Robotic Systems In: Sahin, E., Spears, W. (eds.): Swarm Robotics Workshop: State-of-the-art Survey. Springer-Verlag, Berlin Heidelberg New York (2005)
13. Martinoli, A., Easton, K. and Agassounon, W.: Modeling Swarm Robotic Systems: A Case Study in Collaborative Distributed Manipulation. In: Siciliano, B. (editor): Special Issue on Experimental Robotics, Int. Journal of Robotics Research **23** (2004) 415–436.
14. Panait, L. and Luke, S.: Ant Foraging Revisited. In: Pollack, J., Bedau, M., Husbands, P. and Ikegami, T. (eds.): ALife IX Proceedings. MIT Press, Cambridge (2004)
15. Schweitzer, F.: Brownian Agents and Active Particles. On the Emergence of Complex Behavior in the Natural and Social Sciences. Springer-Verlag, Berlin Heidelberg New York (2003)
16. Schweitzer, F.: Brownian Agent Models for Swarm and Chemotactic Interaction. In: Polani, D., Kim, J., Martinetz, T. (eds.): Fifth German Workshop on Artificial Life. Abstracting and Synthesizing the Principles of Living Systems. Akademische Verlagsgesellschaft Aka (2002)
17. Schweitzer, F., Lao, K., Family, F.: Active Random Walker Simulate Trunk Trail Formation by Ants. BioSystems **41** (1997) 153–166
18. Seyfried, J., Szymanski, M., Bender, N., Estana, R., Thiel, M. and Wörn, H.: The I-SWARM project: Intelligent Small World Autonomous Robots for Micromanipulation. In: Sahin, E. and Spears, W. (eds.): Swarm Robotics Workshop: State-of-the-art Survey. Springer-Verlag, Berlin Heidelberg New York (2005)
19. Spears, W.M. and Gordon, D.F.: Using Artificial Physics to control agents. In: IEEE International Conference on Information, Intelligence, and Systems. (1999)
20. Sugawara, K., Kazama, T. and Watanabe, T.: Foraging Behavior of Interacting Robots with Virtual Pheromone. In: Proceedings of 2004 IEEE/RSJ International Conference on Intelligent Robots and Systems. (2004)
21. Theraulaz, G., Gautrais, J., Camazine S. and Deneubourg, J.L.: The formation of spatial patterns in social insects: from simple behaviours to complex structures. Phil. Trans. R. Soc. Lond. A **361** (2003), 1263–1282

Algorithms for the Analysis and Synthesis of a Bio-inspired Swarm Robotic System

Spring Berman[1], Ádám Halász[1], Vijay Kumar[1], and Stephen Pratt[2]

[1] University of Pennsylvania, Philadelphia PA 19104, USA
{spring,halasz,kumar}@grasp.upenn.edu
[2] Arizona State University, Tempe AZ 85287, USA
Stephen.Pratt@asu.edu

Abstract. We present a methodology for characterizing, analyzing, and synthesizing swarm behaviors using both a macroscopic continuous model that represents a swarm as a continuum and a macroscopic discrete model that enumerates individual agents. Our methodology is applied to a dynamical model of ant house hunting, a decentralized process in which a colony attempts to emigrate to the best site among several alternatives. The model is hybrid because the colony switches between different sets of behaviors, or modes, during this process. Using the model in [1], we investigate the relation of site population growth to initial system state with an algorithm called Multi-Affine Reachability analysis using Conical Overapproximations (MARCO) [2]. We then derive a microscopic hybrid dynamical model of an agent that respects the specifications of the global behavior at the continuous level. Our multi-level simulations demonstrate that we have produced a rigorously correct microscopic model from the macroscopic descriptions.

Keywords: multiscale modeling, synthesis, abstractions of swarms, reachability analysis, stochastic simulation, insect house hunting.

1 Introduction

Coordinated multi-agent systems have yielded robust, efficient, and cost-effective solutions to diverse objectives, such as the establishment of a mobile sensor network for environmental monitoring, surveillance, or reconnaissance; object manipulation and transportation; and search-and-rescue tasks. One multi-agent paradigm is a swarm robotic system, which consists of many anonymous agents that operate autonomously under decentralized control laws. Although each agent follows relatively simple rules, the group can collectively achieve complex tasks at the macroscopic level. In this sense, robot swarm systems can draw inspiration from the self-organized processes of natural aggregations such as social insect colonies [3], which accomplish global objectives such as nest construction, foraging, brood sorting, and colony relocation through local interactions, both among individuals and between individuals and their environment. In a robotics

E. Şahin et al. (Eds.): Swarm Robotics Ws, LNCS 4433, pp. 56–70, 2007.

context, the simplicity and identical nature of swarm agents offer the advantages of system robustness and control scalability with population size.

Our goal in this paper is to establish a general methodology to solve the so-called *inverse problem*: the design of individual behaviors to achieve a desired macroscopic behavior for the group. This work is related in spirit to the work of [4], which presents a systematic approach to translate group behaviors, modeled as vector fields on a low-dimensional abstract manifold, into agent behaviors in a high-dimensional manifold derived from copies of an agent's state space. As in recent work on modeling and analyzing swarm robotic systems [5] [6] [7], we employ a multi-level representation of swarm activity. At the highest level, we consider a *macro-continuous* model, also called the Rate Equation model [8], characterized by differential equations in which the state variables represent population fractions engaged in different tasks or roles. We distinguish the *macro-discrete* level, which models a discrete number of agents in each task according to the Stochastic Master Equation [9], as an intermediate level. This level permits behaviors synthesized at the highest level to be translated into difference equations involving integers, in effect representing the system as a finite automaton. At the bottom of the hierarchy, the *microscopic* level [8] models agents in a physical setting, incorporating the geometry and dynamics of individual agents and possibly modeling heterogeneity.

Several types of distributed robot systems have been modeled by translating an individual robot controller into a description of collective behavior. Collaborative stick-pulling [5] and object clustering [6] have been modeled with Probabilistic Finite State Machines, whose states represent both (a) the possible behaviors of a single agent at the microscopic level, and (b) the average number of agents in each task at a certain time step at the macro-continuous level. The robots obey the semi-Markovian property: their state transitions depend only on their present state and the amount of time they have occupied the state. Adaptive robots that change their task based on a history of local observations have been modeled in a multi-foraging scenario [7]. In this work, the macro-continuous and macro-discrete levels are derived from a microscopic model that abstracts away physical robot behaviors. In all of the systems, it is assumed that robots and their stimuli are uniformly spatially distributed. The state transition rates in the macro-continuous model are computed from physical robot parameters, sensor measurements, and geometrical considerations. The macro-continuous models are validated by comparing steady-state variables and other quantities of interest to the results of embodied simulations and experiments.

In addition to the bottom-up design methodology just described, a top-down approach has been used to synthesize agent controllers [10]. An algorithm is first designed assuming that agents have global information, which is then replaced with local information that is exchanged among agents. In an application to the multi-foraging scenario [7], the probability of a state transition is generated through the gradient descent of an objective function with a minimum at the robot state distribution that matches the task type distribution.

In the methods just discussed, the main challenge is to derive an appropriate mathematical form for the task state transition rates [8]. In contrast, the top-down design approach that we present assumes that these rates are known beforehand. To investigate the effect of changing them, we do not need to simulate the system under many different conditions; instead, our macroscopic analysis technique allows us to determine the global influence of ranges of such parameters. In addition, we provide a framework for synthesizing a desired system outcome and then translating the macroscopic behaviors into individual agent behaviors. This technique does not require progressive model decentralization and calibration of the fully distributed system, as does the top-down approach in [10]. Finally, our macro-discrete level can capture phenomena that occur at the microscopic level but are lost at the macro-continuous level. This is because the stochastic formulation of a system has a more legitimate physical basis than the deterministic formulation [9]. Examples of such phenomena include state fluctuations in relatively small populations, potentially leading to stochastic transitions between equilibria of multi-stable systems [11].

We apply our methodology to a model inspired by the work of [1], which studies the process by which a colony of *Temnothorax albipennis* ants chooses a new home from several sites and emigrates through quorum-dependent recruitment mechanisms. The quorum dependency creates a hybrid system in which the ants switch tasks, which can be thought of as sets of controllers, based on their surroundings. The quorum sensing mechanism is key to the collective decision-making process of nest site selection. The authors present models at the two macroscopic levels. However, because they were not interested in models of individual ants and their dynamics, the microscopic-level modeling is absent.

From a robotics perspective, an analogy can be drawn between the ants and robotic agents with limited communication that must distribute themselves or transport objects optimally among several locations. We are concerned with three interesting questions on the biological phenomena and their implications for robotics. (1) Why do the ants behave as they do and is their behavior optimal in any sense? (2) Can we prove that this behavior leads to successful migration to the best nest? (3) Can this behavior be realized on robotic systems? Our paper addresses the second and third questions. We answer (2) using a reachability analysis technique that permits us to explore all possible states reached by a macro-continuous level model. We answer (3) by deriving a methodology that allows macro-continuous level abstract behaviors (as in [4]) to be realized at the macro-discrete level and then at the microscopic level.

2   Methodology

We consider a population of N agents moving in the continuous state space $X_a \subset \mathbb{R}^2$. At any given time, an agent's actions are determined by one of a set L_a of l_a controllers or behaviors. We can describe the agent as a hybrid automaton, $H_a = \{X_a, L_a\}$, to indicate that its activity is governed by both continuous and discrete dynamics. Figure 1a shows how this high-dimensional microscopic level can be mapped to lower-dimensional representations, the macro-discrete and macro-continuous levels, through the abstractions $\mathcal{F}_d$ and $\mathcal{F}_c$, respectively.

Representing the swarm as a continuous quantity, the macro-continuous level models its dynamics with a set of differential equations whose variables, x_i $(i = 1, ..., b)$, are the population fractions associated with different tasks or roles. Each agent mode $l \in L_a$ corresponds to one of these tasks, and possibly to a subdivision of activity within a task. It is assumed that the population is conserved, so one variable may be removed through the conservation constraint. The variables therefore comprise a continuous state space $X_p \subset \mathbb{R}^{b-1}$. If the model is a hybrid system, then the state space is divided into a set L_p of l_p regions, called population modes, each of which is associated with different continuous dynamics. The system may then be described by a hybrid automaton $H_p = \{X_p, L_p\}$. The macro-discrete level, which considers a swarm as a collection of discrete agents rather than a continuum, maintains a count of the number of agents in each of the b tasks or roles.

As Figure 1b shows, our methodology for designing a swarm system and analyzing its behavior relies on all three of these levels of abstraction. We shall illustrate our methodology with the concept of an emigrating ant colony whose rules of behavior, either known (as in biological systems) or designable (as in artificial swarms), are within our control.

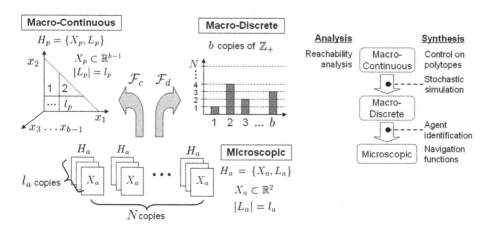

Fig. 1. (a) Levels of abstraction of a swarm; (b) Analysis and synthesis methodologies

The macro-continuous level is used to define and plan the execution of the general task that the system should achieve. In nature, a signature of self-organizing systems is multi-stability, with the most adequate stable states selected according to their fitness [12]. This trait lends robustness to the system under perturbations. In our engineered house-hunting scenario, however, we may want to control the system so that there is always one outcome: the emigration of the entire colony to the optimal nest among several available sites. In addition, let us suppose that we want the emigration to allow at most a fraction of the colony, say 25%, to be separated from the rest for no more than T time units.

The macro-continuous level analysis checks whether or not the continuous model satisfies the requirements. The first condition can be verified by using steady-state analysis to ensure that the model has a single stable equilibrium that corresponds to the entire colony's settlement in the best site. The traditional approach to checking the second condition, or to identifying a range of parameter values that produces a desired result, is to solve the continuous model for many different initial states and parameter sets. This verification can be done more efficiently with *reachability analysis*, which determines the set of states that are attainable from an initial set A. If set B consists of the states in which over 25% of the colony is separated from the rest, then the analysis can show whether (1) A ever reaches B and, if so, whether (2) the system remains there for longer than time T. Problem (1) is a standard reachability question that can be investigated by overapproximating the reachable set on a discrete abstraction of the system or on the state space directly. Problem (2) can be converted into (1) by adding a clock s for which $\dot{s} = 1$ if the system is in B and $\dot{s} = 0$ otherwise, and seeing whether the augmented system reaches the set $s > T$. Similarly, the system behavior over a parameter range can be analyzed by adding the parameter p as a state with $\dot{p} = 0$ and including an interval over p in set A. The macro-continuous model may be solved with the parameters that are chosen from this analysis to ensure that they produce the desired system evolution.

If reachability analysis reveals that the system exhibits undesirable behavior, then control terms can be added to the macro-continuous model to meet the requirements. [13] presents a method of defining feedback control laws on a piecewise-linear hybrid system. Control inputs are defined at the vertices of a polytope state-space region that corresponds to a mode, and a convex combination of these inputs is used to drive states inside the polytope to the next desired mode.

The macro-discrete level connects the macro-continuous level to the microscopic level, which is needed for the ultimate implementation. This level is still a macroscopic model that abstracts away agent identities; however, now we consider an integer number of agents. We simulate transitions between tasks by incrementing and decrementing the number of agents in each task. To synthesize this level, we apply a simulation algorithm from [9], which has been used in the mathematically similar problem of replacing a differential equation description of chemical kinetics with individual molecular reactions. The algorithm generates a sequence of transitions and their times according to a probability density function that is rigorously derived from the known physical principles that govern the underlying chemical processes. In our case, the rules producing the transitions may be stochastic, intrinsically and/or by design, or deterministic. Transition times in the house-hunting model are governed by a Poisson distribution. As $N \to \infty$, the Poisson transition probabilities per unit time become transition rates, and the macro-discrete level simulation approaches the macro-continuous level solution. Transitions have a deterministic component if they are delayed by the time an agent takes to perform an action necessary to change its state, such as navigation.

If we wish to construct a robot swarm that behaves similarly to the ant colony, we need to prescribe the behavior of each agent in all situations it may encounter. This occurs at the microscopic level, where agent identities and spatial considerations become important. At this level, travel between two sites is implemented using navigation functions [14], which can be defined on environments of a certain topological class to guide an agent to a goal while steering it away from obstacles. The resulting mean travel times are used as time delays in the macro-discrete level. For the microscopic level to be abstracted to the macro-discrete level, state transitions should not depend on the previous history of the agent (the Markov property), and spatial information must be either discarded or converted into substates associated with regions in the physical space.

We note that aside from its specification of navigation controllers, our microscopic model is still a coarse-grained representation [8] since it abstracts away ant behaviors such as quorum estimation, recruiter-recruitee communication, and avoidance of collisions with other ants. Thus, the model still requires more detail in order to constitute an executable robot controller. We point out that the quorum dependency does not pose a theoretical impediment to synthesizing such a controller. In our model, only the ants that visit a nest know whether it has attained a quorum population. From the perspective of transition dynamics, an ant that has perceived a quorum is in a different state than an ant that has not, but the two ants are otherwise identical. Therefore, the quorum condition does not violate the Markov property of the model.

3 Macro-continuous Model

Our model of ant house hunting behavior is an extension of the one presented in [1], which was constructed from experimental observations of *Temnothorax albipennis*. Although we try to reflect ant behavior as accurately as possible, our main goal is not to create a new description of ant house hunting, which has already been modeled in considerable detail [15]. Instead, our objective is to make the original model in [1] realizable on the microscopic level, with the ultimate purpose of synthesizing robot controllers that will produce ant-like activity.

The model consists of a set of coupled delay differential equations whose state variables represent population fractions that are physically located at the home nest or one of the M potential home sites. The time delays are averages of navigation times between sites from the microscopic simulation described in section 5.2. Each ant has knowledge of at most two sites, one of which is its home. A colony of N ants is divided into a fraction p of active ants and a remainder of passive ants. The active ant fraction is divided among the following state variables. Naive ants, Y_i, reside at site i, which they consider their home; they leave this site to search for a new nest. Assessing ants, Z_{ij}, regard site i as their home and are evaluating site j as a potential new home. Recruiting ants, $Y_{ij,n}$, are located at site $n \in \{i, j\}$ and leave to bring other ants from i to j. The method of recruitment of $Y_{ij,j}$ ants depends on the population fraction located at site j, P_j. If P_j has not reached a quorum Q, then $Y_{ij,j}$ ants still consider site i to be their home, and they limit themselves to using tandem runs to lead fellow active ants in one of b_{tand} states, Y_i and $Z_{k,i}$ $(k \neq i,j)$, to assess site j. If $P_j \geq Q$, then site j becomes their home and they use transports to carry the passive ants at site i, B_i, to site j. $Y_{ij,i}$ ants always recruit via transports. When $Y_{ij,n}$ ants realize that there are no B_i ants left to transport, they "forget" site i and become naive ants at site j, Y_j.

The rates in the model were experimentally derived [16]. Naive ants discover site i at per capita rate μ_i. Assessors become recruiters to site i at per capita rate k_i, which is directly related to the quality of the site. λ_i and ϕ_i are the per capita rates at which recruiters perform tandem runs and transports to site i, respectively. ρ_{ij} is the per capita rate at which assessors and recruiters at site i encounter site j and switch their allegiance by becoming assessors of that site.

The model is defined by equations (1)-(5). For a variable X, $X = X(t)$ and $X[\tau_{ij}] = X(t - \tau_{ij})$. The time delay τ_{ij} represents the time taken to travel from site i to site j; $\tau_{ji+ij} = \tau_{ji} + \tau_{ij}$. If i and j are in bold, unitalicized font, then the trip is a tandem run. To illustrate the state transitions, the flowchart in Figure 2 diagrams the model with all time delays set to zero.

$$\dot{Y}_i = \sum_{\substack{j=0 \\ j \neq i}}^{M}[\phi_i J_A(P_i[\tau_{ij+ji}], B_j[\tau_{ji}])Y_{ji,i}[\tau_{ij+ji}] + \phi_i(1 - H(B_j[\tau_{ji}]))Y_{ji,j}]$$
$$- \sum_{\substack{j=0 \\ j \neq i}}^{M}[\lambda_j I(P_j[\tau_{ji}], Y_i)Y_{ij,j}[\tau_{ji}] + \mu_j Y_i] \tag{1}$$

$$\dot{Z}_{ij} = \mu_j Y_i[\tau_{ij}] - (k_i + k_j)Z_{ij} + \sum_{\substack{k=0 \\ k \neq i,j}}^{M}[\rho_{kj}Z_{ik}[\tau_{kj}] - \rho_{jk}Z_{ij}]$$
$$+ \sum_{\substack{k=0 \\ k \neq i,j}}^{M}[\rho_{ij}(1 - G(P_i[\tau_{ij}]))Y_{ki,i}[\tau_{ij}] + \rho_{kj}G(P_k[\tau_{kj}])Y_{ik,k}[\tau_{kj}]]$$
$$+ \sum_{\substack{k=0 \\ k \neq i,j}}^{M}[\lambda_j I(P_j[\tau_{jk+\mathbf{kj}}], Z_{ik}[\tau_{\mathbf{kj}}])Y_{kj,j}[\tau_{jk+\mathbf{kj}}] - \lambda_k I(P_k[\tau_{kj}], Z_{ij})Y_{jk,k}[\tau_{kj}]]$$
$$+ \lambda_j I(P_j[\tau_{ji+\mathbf{ij}}], Y_i[\tau_{\mathbf{ij}}])Y_{ij,j}[\tau_{ji+\mathbf{ij}}] \tag{2}$$

$$\dot{Y}_{ij,i} = k_j Z_{ji} - \phi_j Y_{ij,i} \tag{3}$$

$$\dot{Y}_{ij,j} = k_j Z_{ij} + b_{tand}[-\lambda_j G(P_j)Y_{ij,j} + \lambda_j G(P_j[\tau_{ji+\mathbf{ij}}])Y_{ij,j}[\tau_{ji+\mathbf{ij}}]]$$
$$- \phi_j(1 - G(P_j))Y_{ij,j} + \phi_j J_B(P_j[\tau_{ji+ij}], B_i[\tau_{ij}])Y_{ij,j}[\tau_{ji+ij}]$$
$$+ \phi_j H(B_i[\tau_{ij}])Y_{ij,i}[\tau_{ij}] - \sum_{\substack{k=0 \\ k \neq i,j}}^{M} \rho_{jk}Y_{ij,j} \tag{4}$$

$$\dot{B}_i = \sum_{\substack{j=0 \\ j \neq i}}^{M}[\phi_i J_B(P_i[\tau_{ij+ji}], B_j[\tau_{ji}])Y_{ji,i}[\tau_{ij+ji}] + \phi_i H(B_j[\tau_{ji}])Y_{ji,j}[\tau_{ji}]]$$
$$- \sum_{\substack{j=0 \\ j \neq i}}^{M}[\phi_j J_B(P_j[\tau_{ji}], B_i)Y_{ij,j}[\tau_{ji}] + \phi_j H(B_i)Y_{ij,i}] \tag{5}$$

$$P_j = Y_j + B_j + \sum_{\substack{i=0 \\ i \neq j}}^{M}[Y_{ij,j} + Y_{ji,j} + Z_{ij}]$$

$G(P) = 1$ if $P < Q$; 0 otherwise

$H(B) = 1$ if $B > 0$; 0 otherwise

$I(P, X) = 1$ if $P < Q$ and $X > 0$; 0 otherwise

$J_A(P, B) = 1$ if $P \geq Q$ and $B = 0$; 0 otherwise

$J_B(P, B) = 1$ if $P \geq Q$ and $B > 0$; 0 otherwise

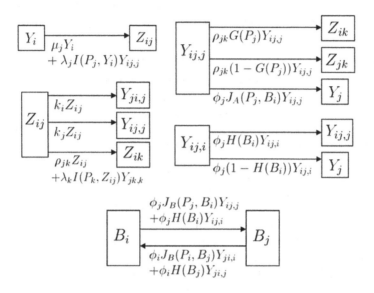

Fig. 2. Flowchart for ant house hunting dynamics without time delays

4 Reachability Analysis

4.1 Algorithm

The MARCO reachability algorithm [2] is written in Matlab and uses the Multi-Parametric Toolbox (MPT) for polyhedral operations. The algorithm, which generates reachable sets of a hybrid system H_p in the state space X_p, was developed to compute more precise and accurate reachable sets than an existing method [17], particularly for systems with multi-affine dynamics. The algorithm begins by initializing a list of reachable modes with the modes that contain the initial set. These modes are identified as members of generation 0. The portion of the initial set that each mode contains is considered its first "footprint." For each mode, a truncated cone is defined as the convex hull of the origin and the state derivatives at the mode vertices. The cone is scaled, added to the mode's footprint via a Minkowski sum, and bounded by the mode facets. The resulting set of states represents an overapproximation of the paths that all points in the footprint can traverse within the mode. Next, each neighboring mode with a facet that intersects this reached set is added to the list of reachable modes, and the intersection is designated as the footprint of that mode. These modes are identified as members of the next generation.

The algorithm repeats the reachable set overapproximation and footprint identification for modes in each consecutive generation. If a mode has multiple footprints, the union of their conical reached sets is the total reachable set within the mode. The algorithm terminates when the reachable set for each mode in a generation is a subset of the set already computed for these modes. It may also terminate if there are no new modes in the current generation, which occurs when the reachable set hits the boundary of X_p.

4.2   Application to the House-Hunting Model

We applied our algorithm to the macro-continuous model in [1] to identify sets of initial conditions that guarantee that a particular nest site reaches a quorum before the other site. This model is a special case of the model (1)–(5) and does not include time delays due to navigation. There are three nest sites, labeled 0, 1, and 2. Site 0 is the home nest, which has been destroyed and therefore does not attract recruitment. P_i is equal to the number of recruiters to site i, $Y_{0i,i}$. There are five active ant state variables $(Y_0, Y_{01,1}, Y_{02,2}, Z_{01}, Z_{02})$, which are decoupled from the three passive ant state variables (B_0, B_1, B_2). Thus, after eliminating Y_0 through the active ant conservation constraint, the full analysis region is the four-dimensional state space $\{Y_{01,1}, Y_{02,2}, Z_{01}, Z_{02} \geq 0, Y_{01,1} + Y_{02,2} + Z_{01} + Z_{02} \leq p\}$.

The state space is divided into modes by the hyperplanes $P_1 = Q$ and $P_2 = Q$, the quorum switches. The analysis focuses on a portion of the mode that is bounded by these hyperplanes. The analysis region is set to $Y_{01,1}, Y_{02,2} \in [0, 0.0481]$, $Z_{01}, Z_{02} \in [0, 0.0721]$ and divided into modes of dimension $0.0120 \times 0.0120 \times 0.0144 \times 0.0144$ for refinement of the reachable set. Initial box A is defined as $Y_{01,1} \in [0.0337, 0.0385]$, $Y_{02,2} \in [0, 0.00481]$, $Z_{01}, Z_{02} \in [0.0288, 0.0337]$; initial box B is $Y_{01,1} \in [0, 0.00481]$, $Y_{02,2} \in [0.0240, 0.0288]$, $Z_{01}, Z_{02} \in [0.0288, 0.0337]$.

In Figure 3, the unions of gray polygons are two-dimensional projections of the reachable set from each initial box. The computation took 33.5 minutes and consisted of 8 generations for box A and 22.3 minutes, 9 generations for box B. Each four-dimensional box has 16 vertices, which are projected onto the $Y_{01,1} - Y_{02,2}$ plane. The black lines are the solutions of the continuous model starting at these vertices. As shown by comparison with these solutions, both reachable sets correctly predict the first site to achieve a quorum of 0.0481. The reachability results show that all system trajectories starting inside box A and box B will first cross the quorum for site 1 and site 2, respectively. The algorithm guarantees this without computing any of the actual trajectories.

5   Simulation

5.1   Algorithms

Macro-Continuous Level. The system of equations (1)–(5) can be numerically integrated using standard techniques such as the Runge-Kutta method.

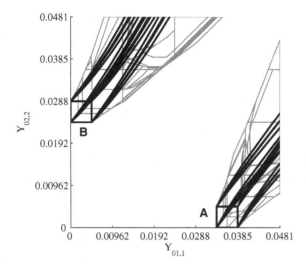

Fig. 3. Two-dimensional projection of reachable sets; $p = 0.25$, $Q = 0.0481$, $\mu_1 = \mu_2 = 0.013$, $\lambda_1 = \lambda_2 = 0.033$, $\rho_{12} = 0.004$, $k_1 = 0.019$, $k_2 = 0.020$ (values are from [1], [16])

Macro-Discrete Level. Gillespie's Direct Method [9] was used to perform a stochastic simulation of the system that is represented deterministically by the macro-continuous model. This method was originally devised to numerically calculate the time evolution of chemical reactions. Like a system of reactions, the macro-continuous model (1)–(5) is described by a set of coupled differential equations. Consider the model without time delays in Figure 2. Each of the S possible transformations of x_i into x_j, the population fractions in task states i and j, respectively, is governed by a term of the form $k_{s0}f(P_q, x_r)x_m$. The fraction x_i is analogous to the molecular concentration of a chemical species, and k_{s0} is analogous to a deterministic reaction-rate constant. When $m \neq i$, m is a recruiter state. $f(P_q, x_r) = 1$ when the transformation is not governed by a switch. Otherwise, it is 0 or 1 depending on P_q, the population fraction at the site containing ants in state m, and/or x_r, the fraction of ants in a recruitee state r. We can remove the switch dependence on x_r, since an ant that decides to recruit does not immediately know about the availability of recruitees. This dependence is replaced with a deterministic state transition of the recruiter based on the presence of recruitees once the recruiter reaches their site.

To construct a stochastic formulation of the system, we convert the macro-continuous model into a set of unidirectional "reactions" with one "reactant ant" X_i and one "product ant" X_j. These reactions describe individual state transitions. The transition is enabled only when $f(P_q) = 1$. Like a chemical reaction, each transition is characterized by a parameter c_s such that $c_s dt$ is the average probability that a particular ant in state i will undergo transition s in the next time interval dt. Since each transition has only one "reactant ant," $c_s = k_s$ [9]. The parameter c_s for transition s is computed by setting the original term

$k_{s0}x_m = c_{s0}x_m$ equal to a new term $c_s x_i$. In this way, we generate S transitions $X_i \rightarrow X_j$ with parameter $c_s = c_{s0}x_m/x_i$.

The propensity a_s is defined such that $a_s dt$ is the probability that transition s will occur in the next time interval dt. It is the product of c_s with h_s, the current number of distinct "reactant ant" combinations that can undergo the transition. Because each transition has only one "reactant ant" X_i, h_s is the number of ants in state i, $n_i = x_i N$ [9]. Thus, $a_s = c_s n_i = c_{s0}n_m$. The propensity a_s is zero if $n_m = 0$ or if transition s is disabled by a switch term $f(P_q)$.

The Direct Method is implemented in the following way. First, the number of ants in each state is initialized in a counter and the S propensities are calculated. The next state transition is selected according to a uniform probability distribution over the propensities, and the time until its occurrence, $\Delta\tau$, is computed from an exponential distribution with $\sum_s a_s$ as its parameter. The time is advanced by $\Delta\tau$ and the transition is effected. If $m = i$ for the transition, then n_i is decremented and n_j is incremented either immediately, as in the the transition from assessor to recruiter, or at a deterministic time in the future that represents the completion of the ant's navigation between sites. When $m \neq i$, then n_m, the number of ants in a recruiter state, is decremented to reflect the start of a tandem run or transport. If any recruitees are available at the time when the recruiter is expected to arrive at their site, then their population is decremented in the state counter. At the end of the recruiter's round-trip journey, the counter is updated to reflect the recruiter's success or failure at bringing another ant to the site. Whenever the counter is updated, the propensities must be recalculated and a new transition and $\Delta\tau$ are computed.

Microscopic Level. At the microscopic level, each ant is represented as an individual entity that stores knowledge of its task state, home nest, another nest site, position, speed, type of ant it is recruiting (if any), and whether it is navigating to a site. The stochastic simulation method described in the previous section is used to generate state transitions and their times. At this level, the simulation runs in time steps Δt to implement the ants' incremental navigation through their environment. As a result, the completion of inter-site navigation is checked at the beginning of every time step rather than acknowledged at the exact time it happens, and transitions at time τ are initiated when $t \leq \tau \leq t + \Delta t$.

When a transition is generated, a random ant in the appropriate task state that is not already en route to a site is selected to attempt recruitment or change state, either immediately or after traveling. Navigation functions [14] are used to generate ant trajectories that mimic the behavior of traveling between sites while avoiding obstacles. A navigation function provides a form for a feedback controller that guides an agent to a goal, the unique minimum of the function, while preventing collisions with obstacles. It can be defined on any environment that is deformable to one with a spherical boundary and disjoint, spherical obstacles.

In the simulation, ants and their destinations are represented as points, and obstacles are circular. The position r of an ant is updated at each time step by numerically integrating the equation

$$\dot{r} = -v\nabla\varphi_\kappa(r, r_d)/\parallel \nabla\varphi_\kappa(r, r_d) \parallel , \tag{6}$$

where v is the ant's speed and $\varphi_\kappa(r, r_d)$ is the navigation function with the ant's current destination r_d. The φ of each ant share a common parameter κ, which was selected empirically. Various combinations of v and r_d are used to produce different agent controllers; for example, one $l \in L_a$ would be navigating from site 0 to site 1 at the tandem-running speed.

The microscopic simulation uses a centralized approach, since a "global planner" initiates transitions. However, the simulation has a decentralized equivalent: it produces transition times according to the same probability distribution as a strategy in which each ant, at every time step Δt, independently undergoes one of its possible transitions s with probability $c_s \Delta t$. To determine whether it can execute switch-dependent transitions, an ant only needs to know whether the population at its current site, P_q, exceeds a quorum. In a robotic system, this estimate can be achieved through local sensing. The advantage of the centralized simulation is its speed; unlike the decentralized approach, it does not require looping through all ants at each time step.

5.2 Application to the House-Hunting Model

We implemented macro-continuous, macro-discrete, and microscopic simulations in Matlab of the model (1)–(5). The model is reduced to the scenario of a destroyed home and two available new nests, although it is more detailed than the model in [1]. All ants are initially located at site 0, and all active ants begin as naive ants. The rate units are $\min^{-1}$. The nests are 65 cm apart, the inter-site distance used in experiments to derive the site discovery and recruitment rates [16].

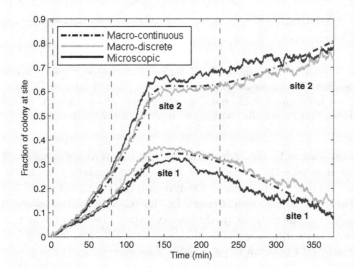

Fig. 4. Population fractions at sites 1 and 2; $p = 0.25$, $Q = (10/208)N$, $\mu_1 = \mu_2 = 0.013$, $\lambda_1 = \lambda_2 = 0.033$, $\rho_{12} = 0.008$, $k_1 = 0.016$, $k_2 = 0.020$, $\phi_1 = \phi_2 = 0.099$ (values are from [1], [16]); $\rho_{21} = 0.002$, $\kappa = 2.7$. Dashed vertical lines correspond to the times of the snapshots in Figure 5.

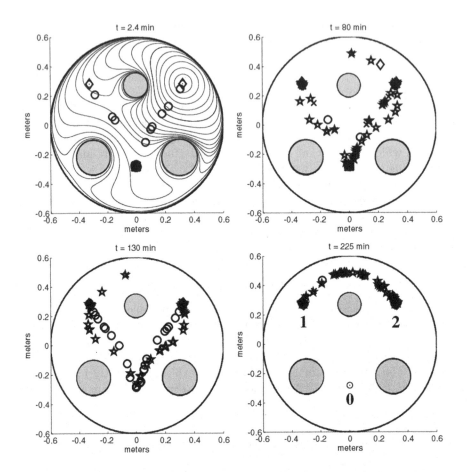

Fig. 5. Agent simulation snapshots ($\bigcirc$ = *naive*; $\Diamond$ = *assessor*; $\bigstar$ = *recruiter*; $\times$ = *passive*) showing the colony at (a) 2.4 min (top left); (b) 80 min (top right); (c) 130 min (bottom left); and (d) 225 min (bottom right). The navigation function that corresponds to an agent controller with r_d at site 2 is shown at the top left.

Each nest is represented as a circle of radius 0.02 m; an ant is considered inside the nest once it enters the circle. Ants performing tandem runs move at 1.5 mm/sec, while all other ants move at 4.6 mm/sec, the transport speed [1]. There are three obstacles in the environment. In the macro-continuous and macro-discrete simulations, the time delays due to navigation, measured from the microscopic simulation, are $\tau_{01} = \tau_{02} = 6$ min, $\tau_{01} = \tau_{02} = 2.2$ min, $\tau_{10} = \tau_{20} = 2.5$ min, $\tau_{12} = \tau_{21} = 7.84$ min, and $\tau_{12} = \tau_{21} = 2.48$ min.

Figure 4 displays the population fractions at sites 1 and 2 from the macro-continuous model solution and from macro-discrete and microscopic simulations with $N = 832$, $\Delta t = 0.05$ min. The two simulations match the macro-continuous model fairly well. Although not shown, it has been verified that the macro-discrete simulation approaches the macro-continuous model as N increases. In all plots, both sites achieve a quorum prior to 30 min and initially experience population growth. Site 2 outpaces site 1 in growth because ants commit to site 2 more quickly ($k_2 > k_1$) and are more willing to switch allegiance from site 1 to 2 than vice versa ($\rho_{12} > \rho_{21}$). By ~130 min, all passive ants have been transported from site 0, and recruiters "forget" this site. The newly naive ants at site 1 or 2 repeat the process of finding, assessing, and recruiting to the other potential home site; however, now they can recruit *from* the site as well. Assessors at either site are more likely to recruit to the site of higher quality, which results in a net transport of passive ants to site 2. By ~376 min in the macro-continuous and microscopic models, all passive ants at site 1 have been removed to be reunited with those at site 2; only active ants remain at site 1. Due to stochastic fluctuations, some passive ants still remain at site 1 in the macro-discrete model.

Figure 5 shows snapshots of the microscopic simulation at times indicated by the vertical lines in Figure 4. Nest sites are labeled in Figure 5d; gray circles denote obstacles. The curvature in the ant trajectories is due to the shape of the navigation functions, one of which is displayed in Figure 5a. The snapshots correspond to the initial searching and assessing phase (5a), the period of transport from site 0 (5b), the realization that site 0 contains no passive ants (5c), and the period of transport between sites 1 and 2 (5d).

6   Conclusion

We have described abstractions of a robotic swarm at three different levels and presented a methodology for synthesizing behaviors for individual robotic agents. Our behavioral synthesis at the highest level was derived from a mathematical model of an ant population. The macro-continuous model was reduced to a macro-discrete model to account for an integer number of agents. The macro-scopic behaviors were then further realized by behaviors for individual agents. The components of the methodology have been illustrated through the analysis and simulation of nest site population growth in a model of ant house hunting.

We are interested in designing macroscopic swarm behaviors that are more relevant to multi-robot applications such as surveillance, sampling, and search-and-rescue. We want to determine parameter ranges and/or control terms that produce a desired group objective by using reachability analysis and control synthesis at the macro-continuous level. Here the methodology of [13] can be used to synthesize macro-continuous behaviors, which can be translated to macro-discrete level and then to microscopic level behaviors. We have begun this investigation in [18], where we adapt the house hunting model to a robot deployment task in which the swarm splits between two sites in a predefined ratio.

Acknowledgements. We are grateful for the support of NSF grants CCR02-05336 and IIS-0427313, and ARO Grants W911NF-05-1-0219 and W911NF-04-1-0148. We thank the workshop organizers and attendees for their helpful comments.

References

1. Franks, N., Pratt, S., Mallon, E., Britton, N., Sumpter, D.: Information flow, opinion polling and collective intelligence in house-hunting social insects. Phil Trans Roy Soc London B **357** (2002) 1567–1584
2. Berman, S., Halász, Á., Kumar, V.: MARCO: A reachability algorithm for multi-affine systems with applications to biological systems. Accepted to HSCC'07, Pisa, Italy, April 2007.
3. Bonabeau, E., Dorigo, M., Theraulaz, G.: Swarm Intelligence: From Natural to Artificial Systems. Oxford University Press, New York (1999)
4. Belta, C., Kumar, V.: Abstraction and control for groups of robots. IEEE Transactions on Robotics **20:5** (2004) 865–875
5. Martinoli, A., Easton, K., Agassounon, W.: Modeling of swarm robotic systems: a case study in collaborative distributed manipulation. Special issue on Experimental Robotics, Int. Journal of Robotics Research **23**(4) (2004). B. Siciliano (ed.) 415–436
6. Agassounon, W., Martinoli, A., Easton, K.: Macroscopic modeling of aggregation experiments using embodied agents in teams of constant and time-varying sizes. Autonomous Robots **17**(2-3) (2004). M. Dorigo, E. Sahin (eds.) 163–191
7. Lerman, K., Jones, C., Galstyan, A., Mataric, M.: Analysis of dynamic task allocation in multi-robot systems. Int. J. of Robotics Research, **25**(4) (2006) 225–242
8. Lerman, K., Martinoli, A., Galstyan, A.: A review of probabilistic macroscopic models for swarm robotic systems. In *Swarm Robotics Workshop: State-of-the-art Survey*, LNCS **3342** (2005). E. Sahin, W. Spears (eds.) 143–152
9. Gillespie, D.: A general method for numerically simulating the stochastic time evolution of coupled chemical reactions. J Comp Physics **22** (1976) 403–434
10. Crespi, V., Galstyan, A., Lerman, K.: Comparative analysis of top-down and bottom-up methodologies for multi-agent systems. Proc 4th Int'l Conf on Autonomous Agents and Multi Agent Systems (AAMAS'05), Utrecht, The Netherlands
11. Julius, A., Halász, Á., Kumar, V., Pappas, G.: Finite state abstraction of a stochastic model of the lactose regulation system of *Escherichia coli*. IEEE Conf on Decision and Control, San Diego, CA, December 2006. To appear.
12. Heylighen, F.: The science of self-organization and adaptivity. In The Encyclopedia of Life Support Systems, EOLSS Publishers Co. Ltd. (2003)
13. Habets, L., and van Schuppen, J.: A control problem for affine dynamical systems on a full-dimensional polytope. Automatica **40** (2004) 21–35
14. Rimon, E., Koditschek, D.: Exact robot navigation using artificial potential functions. IEEE Transactions on Robotics and Automation **8**(5) (1992) 501–518
15. Pratt, S., Sumpter, D., Mallon, E., Franks, N.: An agent-based model of collective nest choice by the ant *Temnothorax albipennis*. Animal Behav **70** (2005) 1023–1036
16. Pratt, S., Mallon, E., Sumpter, D., Franks, N.: Quorum sensing, recruitment, and collective decision-making during colony emigration by the ant Leptothorax albipennis. Behav Ecol Sociobiol **52** (2002) 117–127
17. Belta, C., Finin, P., Habets, L., Halász, A., Imielinski, M., Kumar, V., Rubin, H.: Understanding the bacterial stringent response using reachability analysis of hybrid systems. HSCC '04, Philadelphia. LNCS **2993**. R. Alur, G. J. Pappas (eds.) 111–125
18. Berman, S., Halász, A., Kumar, V., Pratt, S.: Bio-inspired group behaviors for the deployment of a swarm of robots to multiple destinations. Accepted to ICRA'07, Rome, Italy, April 2007.
19. Parrish, J., Hamner, W. (eds.): Animal Groups in Three Dimensions. Cambridge University Press, New York (1997)

Coordination and Control of Multi-agent Dynamic Systems: Models and Approaches*

Veysel Gazi[1] and Barış Fidan[2]

[1] TOBB University of Economics and Technology, Department of Electrical and Electronics Engineering, Söğütözü Cad., No: 43, Söğütözü, 06560 Ankara, Turkey
[2] National ICT Australia Ltd. and The Australian National University – Research School of Information Sciences & Engineering, Canberra, Australia

Abstract. The field of multi-agent dynamic systems is an inter-disciplinary research field that has become very popular in the recent years in parallel with the significant interest in the practical applications of such systems in various areas including robotics. In this article we give a relatively short review of this field from the system dynamics and control perspective. We first focus on mathematical modelling of multi-agent systems paying particular attention on the agent dynamics models available in the literature. Then we present a number of problems on coordination and control of multi-agent systems which have gained significant attention recently and various approaches to these problems. Relevant to these problems and approaches, we summarize some of the recent results on stability, robustness, and performance of multi-agent dynamic systems which appeared in the literature. The article is concluded with some remarks on the implementation and application side of the control designs developed for multi-agent systems.

1 Introduction

The field of coordinated multi-agent dynamic systems including swarms and swarm robotics is a relatively new field that has become popular in recent years. Since the pioneering work by Reynolds [1] on simulation of a flock of birds in flight using a behavioral model based on few simple rules and only local interactions, the field has witnessed many developments. Currently, there is significant interest in the applications of the field in various areas involving teams of manned or unmanned aerial, ground, space or underwater vehicles, robots, mobile sensors, etc. [2, 3, 4, 5, 6, 7, 8].

Because of the interdisciplinary nature of the field, the literature on coordinated multi-agent dynamic systems has a moderately wide spectrum of perspectives. This article focuses on the system dynamics and control perspective. Noting that it is by no means a complete survey on the topic, even from this particular perspective, the aim of the article is to present a short review on mathematical modelling, coordination and control of multi-agent dynamical systems.

* The work of V. Gazi is supported by the Scientific and Technological Research Council of Turkey (TÜBİTAK) under grant 104E170. The work of B. Fidan is supported by National ICT Australia, which is funded by the Australian Government's Department of Communications, Information Technology and the Arts and the Australian Research Council through the Backing Australia's Ability Initiative.

E. Şahin et al. (Eds.): Swarm Robotics Ws, LNCS 4433, pp. 71–102, 2007.

The rest of the article is organized as follows: In Section 2, we briefly review the terminology and mathematical models used in the field of coordinated multi-agent dynamic systems and introduce the main elements of these models. Among these elements, the agent dynamics is further elaborated in Section 3, presenting the main mathematical models available in the literature for agent dynamics. In Section 4, we present a number of problems on coordination and control of multi-agent systems which have gained significant attention recently. Various approaches to these problems are reviewed in Section 5. The main results on stability, robustness, and performance of multi-agent dynamic systems, which are obtained in the studies on the problems and approaches of Sections 4 and 5 are summarized in Section 6. The article is concluded with some remarks on the implementation and application side of the control designs developed for multi-agent systems given in Section 7.

2   Multi-agent Dynamic Systems, Formations, and Swarms

A *multi-agent dynamic system*, in general, can be defined as a network of a number of loosely coupled dynamic units that are called agents. In real-life, each agent can be a robot, a vehicle, or a dynamic sensor, etc. The main purpose of using multi-agent systems is to collectively reach goals that are difficult to achieve by an individual agent or a monolithic system. Sometimes, if the main dynamic action of interest is motion, the term *swarm* or sometimes *formation* are used in place of *multi-agent dynamic system*.

In this article we use mostly the term *swarm* for a collection of (physical) agents moving in real 2- or 3- dimensional space to fulfill certain mission requirements, noting that in some particular cases the effective motion space of interest can be 1-dimensional. The distinction between the terms *formation* and *swarm* is not clearly formulated or stated in the systems and control literature,[1] although in some places *swarm* is preferred to indicate that the corresponding collection of agents is less structured, the number of agents is larger, or the motion of each agent has higher uncertainty as opposed to *formation* indicating a well-structured collection of a relatively small number of agents with more deterministic dynamics. Using this convention, a *swarm* can be thought as a multi-agent dynamic system that can form various types of *formations*. In this article we use both of these two terms interchangeably with the term *multi-agent dynamic systems* without making any distinction although sometimes when necessary for the context we also try stick to the above conventions.

Note also that *swarm robotic systems* are a particular kind of *swarms* as we mean it here (and therefore they are also a particular kind of multi-agent dynamic systems as well). Typically, since they are inspired by natural systems they are much more constrained than many other multi-agent dynamic systems. In particular, usually they are minimalist, agents have very limited capabilities and only very limited local knowledge, are totally distributed and operate asynchronously, whereas in some other multi-agent dynamic systems it is possible to have global knowledge and centralized hierarchical control structure. Nevertheless, much of the recent work on multi-agent dynamic

---

[1] One exception is the work by Erol Şahin in [9] where the author formally defines properties that a *swarm robotics* system should possess.

systems in the systems and control literature (and all the work we describe here) has been focusing on decentralized or distributed algorithms for swarm coordination and control.

An important property of swarm robotic systems (and more general in swarms) is the property of *emergence*. Usually coordination in these systems is a property that emerges through the local interactions between the agents. It is difficult to study emergence from both modeling and design perspectives. In other words, given a desired emergent property or behavior usually it is difficult to specify the local interaction rules that will lead to that desired property or behavior. There has not been much work on modeling of emergence in the multi-agent dynamic systems literature (one exception is the work by Kubik in [10]) and it remains an important open problem.

The main elements of a swarm (or a formation) are the agents and the information (i.e. sensing, control, and communication) links among these agents, assuming that the individual dynamics of the agents are uncoupled or loosely coupled. For formations where the individual agent dynamics are coupled, the dynamic interactions among the agents need to be considered as well.

2.1 Formation Control Graphs and Underlying Graphs

The main mathematical tools used in representing swarms, beside differential or difference equations describing agent dynamics, are directed and undirected graphs and their geometric representations in the particular motion space, e.g. $\Re^2$ or $\Re^3$ [11, 12, 13, 14, 15, 16, 17, 18, 19, 20, 21, 22]. Using these tools, each swarm S is represented by a weighted graph $\bar{G}_S = (V_S, E_S, D_S)$ with a *vertex (node) set V_S*, an *edge set $E_S \subseteq V_S \times V_S$*, and a *weighting set D_S*, where each element (*weight*) in D_S is a positive real number and $|D_S| = |E_S|$, $|\cdot|$ denoting the number of elements in the corresponding set. In this representation, each *vertex (node) $i \in V_S$* represents an agent A_i in S and each *edge $(i, j) \in E_S$* represents an information link between a pair (A_i, A_j) of agents. Any pair of agents (A_i, A_j) that are linked by an information link, i.e. that satisfies $(i, j) \in E_S$, is called a *neighbor agent pair*. Each weight $d_{ij} \in D_S$ represents a control objective or a set point corresponding to the link between the neighbor agent pair, e.g. the desired value of the distance between A_i, A_j.[2] In the literature, the weighted graph $\bar{G}_S$ and the unweighted graph $G_S = (V_S, E_S)$ are respectively called the *formation control graph* and the *underlying graph* of the swarm S [15, 18, 19, 20, 21, 22]. As implied above, these graphs represent the *communication, information flow* or *interaction topology* in a swarm.

The underlying graph G_S for a particular swarm S can be directed or undirected depending on the properties of information links of S. Usually, directed graphs are used if the directions of the information links are important, e.g. the information flows or the inter-agent constraints corresponding to the links are unidirectional, and undirected graphs are used otherwise. For example, in a swarm where it is required to maintain the distance between each neighbor agent pair (A_i, A_j) at a desired value d_{ij}, one may use two types of control structures: Symmetric and asymmetric [20, 21, 22]. In the symmetric case, the distance maintenance requirement for each neighbor agent pair (A_i, A_j) is

---

[2] Depending on the application *distance* could also be *physical distance* or *weighted or Hamming distance* between the neighboring agents.

addressed via a joint effort of both A_i and A_j to simultaneously and actively maintain their relative positions and the associated underlying graph is undirected. On the other hand, in the asymmetric case the associated underlying graph is directed and only one of the agents in each neighbor agent pair (A_i, A_j), e.g. agent A_i, actively maintains its distance to agent A_j at the desired value d_{ij}. Hence, in the latter case, only A_i needs to sense the position of A_j and it can make decisions on its own. This is indicated in the directed underlying graph $G_S = (V_S, E_S)$ by assigning the direction of the edge (i, j) from vertex i to vertex j. The structure and properties of G_S can also be dictated by the hardware (and software) capabilities of the agents. For example, if the agents in the swarm S are very simple and do not have information exchange capability except the ability to myopically sense relative positions, then a directed underlying graph G_S may be needed to represent the agent interactions in S.

In a swarm S with directed underlying graph G_S, an agent A_i is said to be *connected* to another agent A_j if there is a directed path from i to j in G_S, i.e. a sequence of arcs (directed edges) $\overrightarrow{(i_1, i_2)}, \overrightarrow{(i_2, i_3)}, \dots, \overrightarrow{(i_{p-1}, i_p)}$ in G_S such that $i = i_1$ and $j = i_p$. If there is a (directed) path from every i to every j in G_S, then both S and G_S are said to be *strongly connected*. A *directed tree* is a directed graph in which every vertex, except a specific one, which is called the *root*, has exactly one incoming edge (arc). If a tree graph G_T connects all the vertices of the underlying graph G_S, then it is called a spanning tree of G_S. Note that if G_S has a *spanning tree*, then there is at least one agent in S which is connected to all the other agents in S.

2.2   Rigidity and Persistence

In Section 2.1, an example was given about swarms where it is required to maintain the distance between each neighbor agent pair constant. Such requirements are widely encountered in swarm and formation control applications where it is required to maintain the shape or structure of the formation during operation [18, 19, 20, 21, 22]. The notions of *rigid* and *persistent* formations are introduced to construct a mathematical framework for formal analysis and design for such applications [18, 19, 20, 21].

A swarm S with an underlying graph $G_S = (V_S, E_S)$ is called *rigid* if by explicitly maintaining distances between all the neighbor agent pairs, the distances between all other pairs of agents in S are consequentially held fixed as well, and hence S can move as a cohesive whole [18, 20, 21, 22]. In a geometric representation of the underlying graph G_S, explicit maintenance of the distance between a neighbor agent pair (A_i, A_j) corresponds to keeping the length of the edge $(i, j) \in E_S$ constant, e.g. at a desired value $d_{ij} \in D_S$.

Note here that the notion of *rigidity* introduced above is an undirected one, i.e. in the above definition of *rigidity*, the requirement of maintaining the distance between each neighbor agent pair is not assigned to a particular agent and no directional specification is made about the corresponding link to meet this requirement. Hence, although we can use *rigidity* for swarms with symmetric control structures as it is, for a swarm S with asymmetric control structure we need to introduce two further notions to address the issue of assigning the distance maintenance task. If each agent in S is able to satisfy all the distance maintenance constraints on it provided that all other agents within S satisfy as many of their constraints as possible, then S is called *constraint-consistent*. A swarm (a formation) that is both rigid and constraint-consistent is called *persistent* [20, 21]. In a persistent formation, provided that all the agents satisfy as many of their constraints as possible, they can in fact satisfy all the constraints and, consequently, the shape of the formation is preserved, i.e., when the formation moves, it necessarily moves as a cohesive whole.[3] Note that the above definitions of *rigidity*, *constraint-consistence*, and *persistence* are all intuitive. Formal definitions of these notions as well as fundamental characteristics of *rigid*, *constraint-consistent*, and *persistent* formations can be found in [18, 19, 20, 21, 22, 23].

2.3 Neighborhood

As can be deduced from the discussions above, the graphical structure and the information architecture of a swarm corresponds to *neighborhood map* (or *proximity net*) of agents within the swarm, where *neighborhood* (or *proximity*) of and agent A_i is intuitively defined as the set of *neighbors* of A_i, i.e. the set of agents A_j such that (A_i, A_j) is a neighbor agent pair, together with the information links between A_i and each of these neighbor agents. There are different ways to formally define and classify *neighborhoods* (or *communication topologies*) in a swarm, based on the assumed characteristics of the information links. Two different types of neighborhoods commonly used in the literature are *fixed neighborhood* (neighborhood that is predefined and does not change with time) and *dynamic neighborhood* (neighborhood that can change with time). A subclass of the fixed neighborhood topology that was used in the initial studies on multi-agent dynamic systems (see for example [24, 25, 26]) is the *fully interconnected topology* or *basic neighborhood topology*, viz. a neighborhood topology in which every agent is a neighbor of every other agent. In addition to these, there exist other studies in the literature on fixed topologies that are not fully/completely connected as well (see for example [27, 28, 29, 30]).

The *dynamic neighborhood topology* can be defined using different methods such as ad-hoc, probabilistic, or nearest-neighbor rules. A commonly used dynamic neighborhood topology definition is based on the assumption of a fixed range $\delta > 0$ of communication (information exchange), in which the neighborhood $\mathcal{N}_i(t)$ of an agent A_i at time t is defined as

$$\mathcal{N}_i(t) = \{A_j \mid j \neq i, \ \|p_i(t) - p_j(t)\| \leq \delta\} \tag{1}$$

for some δ, where p_i denotes the position of agent A_i in the assumed coordinate system ($\mathfrak{R}^2$ or $\mathfrak{R}^3$). This definition is found realistic and useful for many applications, since sensing and communication ranges for the agents are usually bounded and agent interactions can take place within these bounded ranges.

3   Mathematical Models for Agent Dynamics

In Section 2 we have briefly introduced the main elements of mathematical swarm models. In this section, we focus on a particular element among those, the agents and modelling of their dynamics. We briefly summarize some of the mathematical models for

---

[3] This statement is valid for all the 2 and 3-dimensional swarms except a particular small class of swarms in $\mathfrak{R}^3$. The details about this exceptional class can be found in [23].

agent/vehicle dynamics considered in the systems and control literature on multi-agent dynamic systems (or swarms). We consider a swarm consisting of N individuals/agents moving in an n-dimensional Euclidean space and unless otherwise stated denote with $x_i \in \mathbb{R}^n$ the state vector and with $u_i \in \mathbb{R}^m, m \leq n$ the control input of agent i. Depending on the context, the state vector x_i may denote (a collection of) the position, orientation, synchronization frequency, information to be agreed upon, etc. The dimensions of the state and control spaces (i.e. the values of n and m) change depending on the context as well.

3.1   Higher-Level (Single Integrator) Model

The simplest mathematical model considered in the literature for studying swarm behavior is the so-called *higher-level* or *kinematic* or *single integrator* model in which the agent motions are given by

$$\dot{x}_i = u_i, i = 1, \ldots, N, \tag{2}$$

where x_i is the state of agent A_i, u_i is its control input, and the *dot* represents the derivative (the change) with respect to time. As mentioned above, depending on the context the state x_i can represent the position p_i, the orientation angle or synchronization frequency θ_i, or other variables (or collection of those).

We refer to this model as a *higher-level* or *kinematic* model since it ignores the lower-level vehicle dynamics of the individual agents (e.g., robots). However, it is a relevant and useful model since it can be used for studying higher level algorithms independent of the agent/vehicle dynamics and obtaining "proof of concept" type results for swarm behavior. Moreover, in certain control tasks involving path planning, the trajectories generated using the *higher-level* agent models can be used as reference trajectories for the actual agents to track. Furthermore, (2) is a realistic simplified kinematic model for a class of *omni-directional* mobile robots with so-called *universal* (or *Swedish*) *wheels* [31, 32, 33]. Nevertheless, in implementations of the results obtained for (2) with real-life agents/robots it may be necessary to consider the effects of the actual agent dynamics. As example works using the agent model in (2) the reader may refer to [2, 15, 22, 24, 25, 26].

3.2   Point Mass (Double Integrator) Model

Another dynamic model which is commonly used in the multi-agent coordination and control literature is the *point mass* or *double integrator* model given by

$$\dot{p}_i = v_i,$$
$$\dot{v}_i = \frac{1}{m_i} u_i, i = 1, \ldots, N, \tag{3}$$

where p_i is the position, v_i is the velocity, m_i is the mass of the agent, and u_i is the force (control) input (and the state of the systems can be defined as $x_i^\top = [p_i^\top, v_i^\top]$). The *higher-level* model in (2) can be viewed also as a special case of the point mass model (3) under the assumption that the motion environment is very viscous, that $m_i \approx 0$ (as is the case for some bacteria), and the control input is taken as

$$u_i = -k_v v_i + \bar{u}_i$$

with the velocity damping coefficient $k_v = 1$, and the control term $\bar{u}_i$ corresponding to u_i of (2) [26]. However, in general for many biological and engineering systems this assumption is not satisfied and the point mass model in (3) becomes more relevant. It is an alternative model that can be used for analyzing swarm behavior and has been considered in [34, 35, 30, 36, 37, 14].

3.3 Fully Actuated Model with Uncertainty

A more realistic model for agent/vehicle dynamics (compared to the higher-level and the point mass models) is the *fully actuated model*

$$M_i(p_i)\ddot{p}_i + f_i(p_i, \dot{p}_i) = u_i, 1 \leq i \leq N, \tag{4}$$

where p_i represents the position or configuration (and as above we have $x_i^\top = [p_i^\top, v_i^\top]$), $M_i(p_i) \in \mathbb{R}^{n \times n}$ is the mass or inertia matrix, $f_i(p_i, \dot{p}_i) \in \mathbb{R}^n$ represents the centripetal, Coriolis, gravitational effects and additive disturbances. It is a realistic model for fully actuated omni-directional mobile robots or for some fully actuated manipulators [31, 32, 33]. What makes the model even more realistic is that it is assumed that (4) contains uncertainties and disturbances. In particular, it is assumed that

$$f_i(p_i, \dot{p}_i) = f_i^k(p_i, \dot{p}_i) + f_i^u(p_i, \dot{p}_i), 1 \leq i \leq N,$$

where $f_i^k(\cdot, \cdot)$ represents the *known* part and $f_i^u(\cdot, \cdot)$ represents the *unknown* part. The unknown part is assumed to be bounded with a known bound, i.e.,

$$\|f_i^u(p_i, \dot{p}_i)\| \leq \bar{f}_i(p_i, \dot{p}_i), 1 \leq i \leq N,$$

where $\bar{f}_i(p_i, \dot{p}_i)$ are known for all i. Moreover, besides the additive disturbances and uncertainties, it is assumed that for all i the mass/inertia matrix is unknown but is non-singular and lower and upper bounded by known bounds. In other words, the matrices $M_i(p_i)$ satisfy

$$\underline{M}_i\|y\|^2 \leq y^\top M_i(p_i)y \leq \bar{M}_i\|y\|^2, 1 \leq i \leq N,$$

where $y \in \mathbb{R}^n$ is arbitrary and $\underline{M}_i$ and $\bar{M}_i$ are known and satisfy $0 < \underline{M}_i < \bar{M}_i < \infty$. These uncertainties provide an opportunity for developing algorithms that are robust with respect to above type of realistic uncertainties and disturbances. This model was considered, e.g., in [38, 39].

3.4 Non-holonomic Unicycle Model

Another realistic agent dynamics model commonly considered in the systems and control literature (for motion in a 2-dimensional space) is the unicycle model

$$\dot{p}_{ix} = v_i \cos(\theta_i),$$
$$\dot{p}_{iy} = v_i \sin(\theta_i),$$
$$\dot{\theta}_i = \omega_i,$$
$$\dot{v}_i = \frac{1}{m_i} F_i,$$
$$\dot{\omega}_i = \frac{1}{J_i} \tau_i, 1 \leq i \leq N, \tag{5}$$

where p_{ix} and p_{iy} are the Cartesian (x and y, respectively) coordinates (on the 2-dimensional motion space), θ_i is the steering angle (or orientation), v_i is the translational (linear) speed, and ω_i is the rotational (angular) speed of each agent A_i. The quantities m_i and J_i are positive constants and represent the mass and the moment of inertia of each agent, respectively. The control inputs to the system are the force input F_i and the torque input τ_i. Many mobile robots used for experimentation in the laboratories (e.g., robots with one castor and two differentially driven wheels) obey the model in (5).

It is possible to consider only the kinematic part of the dynamics in (5) consisting of only the first three equations as was done in [40, 3, 15, 22, 41, 42], four-state part of the model [43], or the complete five state model [44]. Furthermore, by adding one more integrator to the force input terminal of the model it can be extended to a six state model which, under certain conditions, can be completely linearized via the feedback linearization method [45].

It is well known that for the dynamics in (5) the position $p_i = (p_{ix}, p_{iy})$ and the orientation θ_i of the robot cannot be simultaneously stabilized by a continuous static (time-invariant feedback) [46]. In order to avoid this problem one may, for some $d_i > 0$, define

$$z_i = \left[p_{ix} + d_i \cos(\theta_i),\; p_{iy} + d_i \sin(\theta_i) \right]^\top \tag{6}$$

as the output of the system and set the control objective based on the position of that output. This output may represent the position of a gripper at the end of a hand of length d_i or a sensor positioned in front of the robot. With respect to that output the system is input-output feedback linearizable with a well defined relative degree equal to two [44]. The drawback is that under the feedback linearizing controller the zero dynamics of the system are only marginally stable, which may lead to instability in the internal unobservable dynamics during tracking of certain trajectories [44, 45]. This may not be a problem in some applications since internal unobservable dynamics constitutes of the orientation angle θ_i. Nevertheless, one is not required to use a feedback linearizing controller and the above problem may probably be avoided by using other types of controllers.

3.5 Dubins' Vehicle Model

In a recent work [47], a special case of the non-holonomic unicycle model (5) in which the translational speeds of the agents are fixed to a constant value was considered for studying the connection between oscillator synchronization and collective motions. This model is given by

$$\begin{aligned} \dot{p}_i &= e^{j\theta_i} \\ \dot{\theta}_i &= u_i \end{aligned} \tag{7}$$

where the vector $p_i \in C \approx \mathbb{R}^2$ denotes the position of agent/particle i (in complex notation) whereas the angle θ_i denotes its orientation. In this model the agents are assumed to move with a constant speed with normalized magnitude $v = 1$. Note that the (unit) velocity vector of the agent is given by $e^{j\theta_i} = \cos(\theta_i) + j \sin(\theta_i)$ (here $j = \sqrt{-1}$).

An equivalent (or slightly more general) form of (7) that is widely used in the literature is the so-called *Dubins' vehicle model* [48, 49, 42] given by

$$
\begin{aligned}
\dot{p}_{ix} &= v\cos(\theta_i), \\
\dot{p}_{iy} &= v\sin(\theta_i), \\
\dot{\theta}_i &= \omega_i, 1 \le i \le N,
\end{aligned} \tag{8}
$$

where p_{ix} and p_{iy} are the Cartesian (x and y, respectively) coordinates, θ_i is the steering angle, v is the constant translational speed, and ω_i is the rotational speed of each agent A_i.

The Dubins' vehicle model (8) is found useful in various studies where each vehicle of interest is required to move with a constant translational speed because of dynamic constraints (such as the ones for flight of certain unmanned aerial vehicles (UAVs) at a specified altitude) [49, 50] or optimality considerations (such as using the maximum available speed of each vehicle) [49, 51].

3.6 Self-propelled Particle Model

The terms self-propelled or self-driven particles are mostly used by physicists [52]. In [52], the following discrete-time *self-propelled particle* model is used to study the effects of noise on the complex dynamic particle systems and phase transition from disordered to ordered states:

$$
\begin{aligned}
p_{ix}(t+1) &= p_{ix}(t) + v\cos(\theta_i(t+1)), \\
p_{iy}(t+1) &= p_{iy}(t) + v\sin(\theta_i(t+1)), i = 1, ..., N,
\end{aligned} \tag{9}
$$

where p_{ix} and p_{iy} are the Cartesian coordinates, v is the translational speed, and θ_i is the steering angle of a particle with index i.

The model (9), a more general form of which can be found in [1], is later adapted to model the dynamics of an agent (A_i) in a swarm in a number of studies on the coordination of groups of mobile agents [13, 14, 12]. In the studies mentioned above, it is assumed that the translational speed v is constant and equal for all agents. In other words, it is assumed that all the agents move with the same constant speed in possibly different directions. The directions of motion are updated at each step based on

$$
\theta_i(t+1) = \omega_i(t), i = 1, ..., N, \tag{10}
$$

where the control (new direction) input $\omega_i(t)$ is calculated based on the current direction of the agent and the direction of its neighbors with some additive noise.

Note that the self-propelled particle model in (9)-(10) is the discrete time equivalent of the Dubins' vehicle model in (8).

4 Swarm Coordination and Control Problems

There exist a number of different swarm coordination and control tasks investigated in the systems and control literature. In this section, we briefly present some of the main ones among these tasks, namely aggregation and foraging, flocking, rendezvous, formation stabilization, formation acquisition, formation reconfiguration, formation maintenance, agreement, cohesive motion and cooperation.

4.1 Aggregation and Social Foraging

Aggregation (or gathering together) is a basic behavior that many swarms in nature exhibit. Moreover, many of the collective behaviors seen in biological swarms and some behaviors to be possibly implemented in engineering multi-agent dynamic systems emerge in aggregated swarms. Therefore, developing mathematical models for swarm aggregations and studying the dynamics and properties of these models are important. Initial studies on mathematical modeling and simulation of aggregation in biological swarms were performed by biologists [53, 54, 55, 56]. Inspired by the work of biologists, two recent studies [24, 25] provided a rigorous analysis of an artificial potential function based model of swarm aggregations and some corresponding convergence results, assuming discrete time swarm models with synchronous motion dynamics. The asynchronous counterpart of the analysis and the results are also provided in the literature [27, 28, 29].

In a recent work [57], Soysal and Şahin perform a systematic study of the aggregation behavior in a robotic swarm acting probabilistically based on few simple rules/behaviors. Similarly, in [58] Bahçeci and Şahin study the use and effectiveness of evolutionary methods for developing neural network based controllers for the agents in an aggregative swarm robotic system.

Aggregation in biological swarms usually occurs during *social foraging*. Social foraging has many advantages such as increasing probability of success for the individuals [59, 60]. Therefore, social foraging is an important problem since swarm studies in engineering may benefit from similar advantages. For example, the study and bio-mimicry of foraging behavior in ant colonies has led to development of the popular *ant colony optimization* method [61]. Similarly, the *particle swarm optimization* method [62, 63] is another optimization method which is inspired by social foraging in swarms.

In social foraging the environment affects the motion or behavior of the agents. The environment may have favorable regions (representing food or nutrients in biological swarms or targets or goals in engineering applications) to which the agents may want/need to move and unfavorable regions (representing toxic or hazardous substances in biological swarms or threads or obstacles in engineering applications) which the agents may want/need to avoid. Therefore, the studies on social foraging usually incorporate determining strategies to move towards and achieve aggregation in the favorable regions while avoiding unfavorable ones. Example studies on the topic include [26, 37].

4.2 Flocking and Rendezvous

Flocking, in general, can be defined as collective motion behavior of a large number of interacting agents with a common group objective. The work by Reynolds [1] is the first extensive study in the literature on flocking. This work has proposed three simple rules to implement a flocking behavior, namely (i) separation, (ii) alignment, and (iii) cohesion. These rules have been used to develop realistic computer simulations of the flocking behavior of animal swarms.

A simplified and special form of the Reynolds' model [1] of flocking is proposed in [52] based on the *self-propelled particle* model (introduced in Section 3.6) to study the effects of noise on the complex dynamic particle systems and phase transition from disordered to ordered states. The study in [52] has also provided simulation results that make use of a so-called "nearest neighbor rule" (where the agents adjust their motion based only on their nearest neighbors) and eventually all the agents (particles) move in the same direction despite the absence of centralized coordination and time-varying nature of neighborhoods. In other words, coordination (which is in the form of motion in a common direction) emerges from the local interactions of the agents in the swarm.

A mathematical analysis of achieving common orientation during the flocking behavior based on "nearest neighbor rules" is provided and some corresponding convergence results are established in [12]. Recent empirical studies in [64,65] study the effect of neighborhood size and asynchronism [64] and the turning angle restrictions (a type of non-holonomic constraint) [65] on the flocking behavior of the system in [52]. It is observed in [65] that for a synchronous system under high restrictions on the turning angle the averaging rule for determining the direction of motion by the agents considered in [52, 12] may hinder the flocking behavior and result in oscillatory dynamics while the asynchronous system may not result in such dynamics.

Another pioneer attempt to rigorously model and analyze flocking behavior was performed by Tanner and coworkers in [30, 36] for systems with point mass dynamics and in [43] for agents with non-holonomic unicycle dynamics. In [43], the speeds and attitudes of the agents converge asymptotically to the same value and collisions between the agents are avoided. Due to this convergence, the agents move in a particular direction with a constant speed.

In a more recent work [14], Olfati-Saber considers stable flocking of agents with point mass dynamics as in (3). He considers "nearest neighbor rules" and uses potential functions for aggregation and alignment. Several algorithms are proposed and analyzed with and without group objective and is shown that under certain conditions flocking will be achieved and the flock will have a lattice-type structure. Moreover, the author argues that his model incorporates the rules of the model of Reynolds [1] (which he expresses as flock centering, collision avoidance, and velocity matching rules) and his model is more general than the model of Reynolds. Olfati-Saber studies the dynamics/performance of several different algorithms including ones with and without common group objective. Another contribution of the paper is determination/specification of finite range and relatively smooth (differentiable everywhere) potential functions.

Rendezvous can be thought as a specific form of flocking where the task is meeting of agents at a point or a small region [66]. In the rendezvous problem, each agent is assumed be able to continuously track the positions of all its neighbors, where neighborhood is defined as in (1). The individual controllers of the agents are required to be "local", i.e. not to actively communicate with any other agent. A solution to this problem is provided in [67, 68], where a decentralized control strategy is developed for a group of agents to meet at an unspecified location. The synchronous and asynchronous settings for the solution are described in [67] and [68], respectively. Another relevant study focusing on the behavior of swarms under cyclic pursuit (i.e., swarms where each agent follows (only) another one) is presented in [42, 69].

4.3   Formation Stabilization and Acquisition

In *formation stabilization*, the task is convergence of a group of agents that are initially at random positions asymptotically (or exponentially) to a particular geometrical configuration, thereby construction of a structured formation, not necessarily matching a pre-defined geometric pattern. Note that the rendezvous problem introduced in the previous subsection is a special formation stabilization problem, by definition.

A study on formation stabilization of agents for non-holonomic agent dynamics is presented in [41]. In the same work, a feasibility problem of achieving a stable formation of a group of unicycles with certain specified geometries is investigated. In [70] formation stabilization of autonomous agent formations with undirected underlying graphs is investigated using potential functions derived from the underlying graph. Formation stabilization of swarms under cyclic pursuit is considered in [42].

If in a particular *formation stabilization* task it is also required that the final shape of the swarm matches a pre-defined geometric pattern, then the task is further called *formation acquisition* or *formation achievement*. In a *formation acquisition* task, the scale of the pre-defined geometric pattern (i.e., the distances between the nodes in the geometric pattern indicating the desired final positions of agents relative to each other) may or may not be specified. Examples of *formation acquisition* studies can be seen in [71, 72, 73].

4.4   Formation Maintenance and Cohesive Motion Control

Formation maintenance and *cohesive motion control* problems focus on maintenance of an achieved formation structure of a swarm during any continuous motion of the swarm. In [72], the task of following a prescribed trajectory for swarms without breaking the formation topology is discussed. In this work however there is a flexibility in the shape of the formation as no constraint is introduced on the inter-agent distances. Similarly, in [39] the problem of a swarm of agents to capture/enclose and track a moving target in a formation using artificial potentials and sliding mode control is investigated.

In a slightly different context, in [22], the problem of moving a persistent swarm with specified initial position and orientation to arbitrary desired final position and orientation without deforming the shape of the swarm is introduced under the name *cohesive motion control* problem. In [22], a class of decentralized controllers are proposed for the solution of this problem as well.

4.5   Formation Reconfiguration and Switching

For swarms in the form of structured formations it is of interest to maintain certain properties of this structure during various types of structure break-downs. Maintenance of rigidity and persistence during certain changes or operations on the formation structure is considered in [18, 19, 74, 75]. The three key categories of formation operations considered in these studies are *merging, splitting,* and *agent loss.* Merging is combining of two formations via some information links in between to form a single post-merged rigid formation. Splitting is the "reverse" of merging, i.e. division of a pre-split formation into two post-split smaller formations via breaking some of the information links. In agent loss, one or more agents together with the attached information links are lost. The corresponding *rigid* (or resp. *persistent*) *merging*, *splitting*, and *closing ranks* problems, respectively, are the tasks of maintaining rigidity (or resp. persistence) during these operations via establishing some new information links between some of the existing agent pairs.

In *formation switching*, the swarm changes from one shape to another, usually as a reaction to environmental changes. In [76], a paradigm is presented for switching between simple decentralized controllers that allows for changes in formation. Using this approach a triangular formation switches to a linear formation to avoid obstacles. Similar work can be found in [77] where maneuvers such as group translation, rotation, expansion and contraction are considered.

4.6 Distributed Agreement Problems

At different stages of swarm studies there may arise situations in which the agents may need to agree on some information which could be agent position, velocity, oscillation phase, decision variable, etc. Such a phenomenon can be seen also in nature in, for example, distributed synchronization of the flashing of fireflies (or coupled oscillators in more general terms), distributed decision making in swarm of bees during nest site selection and others. The corresponding tasks of developing distributed or decentralized control strategies for agreement are called *distributed agreement problems*. A recent survey on distributed agreement problems can be found in [78]. Note that the problem of distributed agreement is sometimes called *distributed consensus seeking* as well. It is said that *agreement* or *consensus* is achieved if the corresponding states of all agents converge to the same value. Related problems are the problems of rendezvous or gathering [78]. However, they are also little bit different then the consensus seeking problems in that there the agents have to arrive to the same state in a finite time [67, 68,79,80]. Note also that the distributed agreement problem is very similar to finding a fixed point of a function in parallel and distributed computing systems [81].

Synchronization of Coupled Nonlinear Oscillators and the Kuramoto Model. A good example of distributed synchronization (a type of distributed agreement) in nature is the synchronization of the flashing of fireflies [82]. More generally this phenomenon can be viewed as distributed synchronization of coupled oscillators which mathematically is usually represented by the Kuramoto model [47, 83]

$$\dot{x}_i = \omega_i + \sum_j u_{ij}(x_j - x_i) \tag{11}$$

where x_i is the oscillation phase of the $i'th$ individual and ω_i is the oscillation frequency. Moreover, usually researchers take $u_{ij}(x_j - x_i) = \frac{1}{N}\sin(x_j - x_i)$. Note that this model is a special case of the *kinematic* model (2) with the control input taken as $u_i = \omega_i + \sum_j u_{ij}(x_j - x_i)$.

The control strategies or update rules that lead to agreement are usually called *consensus protocols* in the literature. Both continuous-time and discrete-time update rules or consensus protocols have been considered in the literature. The equation in (11) is an example of a continuous-time consensus protocol. Other examples are described below.

Continuous-Time Consensus Protocol. The model of the continuous-time consensus protocol considered in the literature (see for example [84, 13, 12, 17]) can be summarized as [78]

$$\dot{x}_i(t) = - \sum_{j \in \mathcal{N}_i(t)} \alpha_{ij}(t)(x_i(t) - x_j(t)), \tag{12}$$

where $\mathcal{N}_i(t)$ represents the set of neighbors of agent i at time t or basically the set of agents whose information is available to agent i at time t and $\alpha_{ij}(t) > 0$ denote positive time-varying weighting factors. In other words, the information state of each agent is driven toward the states of its (possibly time-varying) neighbors at each time. Note that some agents may not have any information exchange with other agents during some time intervals.

Discrete-Time Consensus Protocol. The discrete-time consensus protocol considered in [12, 16, 17] (see also [78]) can be summarized as

$$x_i(t+1) = \sum_{j \in \mathcal{N}_i(t) \cup i} \beta_{ij}(t)x_j(t), \tag{13}$$

where $\sum_{j \in \mathcal{N}_i(t) \cup i} \beta_{ij}(t) = 1$ and $\beta_{ij}(t) > 0$ for all $j \in \mathcal{N}_i(t) \cup i$. In other words, the next state of each agent is updated as the weighted average of its current state and the current states of its (possibly time-varying) neighbors. Note that an agent simply maintains its current state if it has no information exchange with other agents at a certain time step.

A special case of the discrete-time consensus protocol in (13) is the model for the orientation dynamics of the discrete-time self-propelled particles systems in (10) which is usually taken as

$$\theta_i(t+1) = \frac{1}{1 + |\mathcal{N}_i(t)|} \left(\theta_i(t) + \sum_{j \in \mathcal{N}_i(t)} \theta_j(t) \right), i = 1, ..., N, \tag{14}$$

where $\mathcal{N}_i(t)$ is the current set of neighbors of agent/particle i and $|\mathcal{N}_i(t)|$ is the number of agents in this set. This is the model considered also in [52] with also additive noise included. This model is based on the assumption that the agents update their orientation based on its own orientation and the orientation of its neighbors and tries to reorient itself in the average direction of motion of its neighbors (including its own current direction). Analysis of the convergence properties of (14) is performed in [12].

4.7   Cooperative Control

A different aspect in swarm coordination and control is cooperative operations of a collection of dynamical objects which communicate and cooperate in order to achieve a common or shared objective. Various examples of this, including surveillance, sweeping and coverage tasks, can be found in the literature, e.g. [76, 85, 86, 87, 88].

5   Approaches to Modeling and Coordination and Control of Swarms

A common requirement in most of the swarm coordination and control tasks is developing decentralized controllers for individual agents, instead of a centralized control scheme. The main concerns leading to this requirement are complexity and computational cost, sensitivity to loss of certain agents, (e.g., a central commander), communication delays between the commander agent and the other agents, and feasibility concerns regarding processing of local information by a central control unit, etc. in a possible central control scheme.

Beside the general property of being decentralized, the coordination and control schemes developed in the literature have a large variety in terms of the approaches and techniques used to develop them as well as particular specifications of the swarm of interest and the mathematical models assumed for the swarm structure and the agent dynamics. There exist various studies, e.g. based on the higher level model (2) using potential functions [24,25,26], the point mass dynamics (3) using potential functions [70], the non-holonomic dynamics in (5) using Lyapunov analysis [3, 40] and feedback linearization [44], the fully actuated uncertain dynamics in (4) using potential functions and sliding mode control [38], etc. Some of these studies impose certain underlying graph/information architecture structures (such as the leader-follower structure [15], minimum number of communication links [3], etc.) while some other do not.

The approaches for swarm coordination and control considered in the literature include those based on *artificial potential functions*, *Lyapunov analysis* and other nonlinear control techniques, *sliding mode control* and *feedback linearization*, *neuro-fuzzy* techniques, *behavior modelling*, *probabilistic* and *evolutionary* methods, etc. as well as hybrid approaches combining two or more of these techniques. Next, we briefly discuss some main ones among these approaches.

In our discussion we assume that the control inputs are typically of the form

$$u_i = u_{pi} + u_{vi} + u_{oi} \tag{15}$$

where u_{pi} is agent position (relative to each other or within the environment) based term, u_{vi} is the velocity based term (velocity damping, velocity matching or velocity consensus term), and u_{oi} is a navigational feedback or general control term corresponding to a group objective.

5.1 Potential Function Based Approaches

Artificial potential functions have been extensively used for robot navigation and control [89, 90]. In recent years the researchers started applying them also for specifying inter-individual interactions in a group of robots. One of the first works in this area is the work on *social potential fields* method by Reif and Wang [91].

By defining the inter-individual interactions and the interactions between the individuals and the environment (or basically the control inputs u_i) using artificial potential functions one can construct a potential function based swarm model. Consider the *higher-level* agent model (2), in which the lower-level vehicle dynamics of the individuals (i.e., robots) has been ignored. One can define a higher-level swarm model by choosing the control inputs $u_i \in \mathbb{R}^n$ so that the agents move along the negative gradient of the artificial potential or basically in the control input (15) we have $u_{vi} = 0$, $u_{oi} = 0$, and

$$u_i = u_{pi} = -\nabla_{x_i} J(x), i = 1, \ldots, N, \tag{16}$$

where $x = [x_1^\top, \dots, x_N^\top]^\top$ is the vector of the positions of all the agents in the swarm, and $J : \mathbb{R}^{nN} \to \mathbb{R}$ is the *potential function*.

The potential function $J : \mathbb{R}^{nN} \to \mathbb{R}$ may represent only the inter-agent interactions as in [24, 25] or may include also environmental effects as in [2, 26, 35, 37] or may be defined for some other purpose. Typical potential functions have the form

$$J(x) = \sum_{i=1}^{N} J_{env}(x_i) + \sum_{i=1}^{N-1} \sum_{j=i+1}^{N} J_{ij}(\|x_i - x_j\|), \tag{17}$$

where $J_{ij} : \mathbb{R}^+ \to \mathbb{R}$ is the interaction potential between i and j and can be different for different pairs and $J_{env} : \mathbb{R}^n \to \mathbb{R}$ is the "resource profile" modeling/representing the environment. Usually, it is assumed that the potentials $J_{ij}(\|x_i - x_j\|)$ are: (i) symmetric and satisfy $\nabla_{x_i} J_{ij}(\|x_i - x_j\|) = -\nabla_{x_j} J_{ij}(\|x_i - x_j\|)$; (ii) its gradient at y is along y or basically there exist function $g_{ij} : \mathbb{R}^+ \to \mathbb{R}$ such that $\nabla_y J_{ij}(\|y\|) = y g_{ij}(\|y\|)$; (iii) it is attractive at long distances and repulsive at short distances and there is a unique distance at which the attraction and repulsion balance, or basically there exist *unique distances* δ_{ij} at which we have $g_{ij}(\delta_{ij}) = 0$ and $g_{ij}(\|y\|) > 0$ for $\|y\| > \delta_{ij}$ and $g_{ij}(\|y\|) < 0$ for $\|y\| < \delta_{ij}$.

In the context of biological swarms, the resource profile $J_{env}(\cdot)$ can be a profile of nutrients or some attractant or repellent substances (e.g., food/nutrients, pheromones laid by other individual, or toxic chemicals). For example, $J_{env}(y) < 0$ may represent attractant or nutrient rich, $J_{env}(y) = 0$ may represent a neutral, and $J_{env}(y) > 0$ may represent a noxious environment at y, respectively. In the context of multi-agent (i.e., multi-robot) systems the resource profile $J_{env}(\cdot)$ models the environment containing obstacles or threats to be avoided (analogous to toxic substances) and targets or goals to be caught or moved towards (analogous to nutrients). Typical resource profiles studied in the literature include plane, quadratic, Gaussian, and multi-modal Gaussian profiles [2, 26, 35, 37].

A disadvantage of potential function based approaches is that the potential may have many local minima (especially if it is based only on relative distances) leading to only local results, while an advantage is that potential function based controllers are very easy to implement.

Usage of potential functions is not limited to the *higher level* model and they are used with other agent dynamics models as well. For the *point mass (double integrator)* model (3), besides the position based term u_{pi}, usually the other two terms u_{vi} and u_{oi} are chosen to be non-zero as well. An example is the work in [37] which considers social foraging of agents with point mass dynamics in a noisy environment including uncertainties (or, as called in [37], additive noise) in sensing of the environment (i.e., the resource profile) as well as the relative positions of the other agents (or basically the inter-individual distances) and determines conditions for the cohesiveness of the swarm as well bounds on the swarm size.

The approach there is also based on artificial potential functions (meaning that the control input or the inter-agent interactions and the interactions between the individual agents and the environment are determined by potential functions) and Lyapunov methods are used for analysis. Moreover, each agent tries to move towards the center of the swarm and match its velocity with the average velocity of the group. Stable foraging is shown despite the uncertainties in the sensing/measurements. Moreover, it is shown via simulation that social foraging is more advantageous in a noisy environment compared to individual foraging due to its averaging effect supporting the principle of Grünbaum observed in chemotaxis of bacteria [59, 60]. The equation of the control input used in [37] is

$$u_i = -m_i k_{pi}(x_i - \bar{x} - d_{pi}) - m_i k_{vi}(v_i - \bar{v} - d_{vi}) - m_i k v_i - m_i \nabla_{x_i} J(x), i = 1, \ldots, N, \quad (18)$$

where $\bar{x}$ is the center and $\bar{v}$ is the average velocity of the swarm, and $\nabla_{x_i} J(x)$ is a noisy gradient. The constants k_{pi}, k_{vi}, and k are the controller gains and m_i is the mass of the corresponding agent. The terms d_{pi} and d_{vi} represent the measurement errors (additive disturbances). Note that the velocity term here is given by

$$u_{vi} = -m_i k_{vi}(v_i - \bar{v} - d_{vi}) - m_i k v_i, i = 1, \ldots, N, \quad (19)$$

where as stated above $\bar{v}$ is the average velocity of the swarm and d_{vi} is a disturbance (uncertainty) term. Other velocity terms u_{vi} used in the literature are terms which consist of just the velocity matching term of the form [14]

$$u_{vi} = -m_i \sum_{j \in \mathcal{N}_i(t)} k_{vij}(v_i - v_j), i = 1, \ldots, N. \quad (20)$$

The group objective term for each agent can be represented in the form [14]

$$u_{oi} = -m_i k_1(x_i - x_r) - m_i k_2(v_i - v_r), i = 1, \ldots, N. \quad (21)$$

where x_r is the position and v_r the velocity of a reference agent (virtual leader) that guides the swarm to a common goal point.

Artificial potential functions are being used for swarm aggregations, formation stabilization and acquisition, and some other multi-agent coordination and control tasks. For example, in [24, 25, 26] attraction/repulsion functions have been used for swarm aggregations while in [34, 35] similar potentials have been used for control of a group of point-mass agents. Similarly, in [40, 70] potential functions are used for formation stabilization, while in [2], they are used for generating hunting behavior in fully actuated robot troops. Although the agent dynamics in the above articles are not all in the same form and hence the agents in each study may be concerned with different problems, the desired "structure" of the swarm of agents can be defined in terms of the system or environment potential.

Defining the inter-agent interactions and the interactions of the agents with the environment using artificial potentials, the researchers investigate variety of issues including the cohesiveness of the group and establishing bounds on the swarm size, the motion of the group in the environment (the resource profile), the ultimate dynamics of the group and whether it will perform the desired behavior, the achievement of the desired formation (or basically many of the swarm coordination and control problems and related issues are addressed). Lyapunov-like methods are usually used for analysis resulting in conservative bounds/results.

Some of the works address directly the issues of collisions between the agents, while some do not. One approach to avoid collisions using artificial potentials may be to use unbounded repulsion functions to guarantee collision avoidance (preventing two individuals from occupying the same space) [25, 34].

In the analysis, in some of the studies [24, 25, 26] it is assumed that each individual agent knows the *relative* position of *all* the other agents (i.e., a fully connected communication graph is assumed) which is a shortcoming of the approach. In biological swarms, often each individual can see (or sense) only the individuals in its neighborhood because its sensing range is limited. This phenomenon is one of the main reasons of the wide use of dynamic neighborhood definition based on inter-agent distances, e.g. (1), in the literature.

5.2 Sliding Mode Control

The *higher-level* agent dynamics model (2) has the shortcoming of not realistically representing actual agent dynamics. Still, the results obtained for it are of value since given particular agent dynamics one may design controllers so as to obey the higher-level model. This was shown in [38] for the realistic fully actuated model with model uncertainties in (4) using the sliding mode control method.

The sliding mode control method [92] is a method in which a switching controller with high enough gain is applied to suppress the effects of modelling uncertainties and disturbances, and the agent dynamics are forced to move along a stabilizing manifold called *sliding manifold*. The value of the gain is computed using the known bounds on the uncertainties and disturbances.

Given the agent dynamics in (4), using the sliding mode control technique, it is possible to design each of the control inputs u_i to enforce satisfaction of the trajectories generated by the *higher-level* model and therefore recover from the deficiencies due to mismatches between the actual and modelled agent dynamics [38]. This can be done by defining the n-dimensional sliding manifold for agent i as

$$s_i = \dot{p}_i + \nabla_{p_i} J(p) = 0, i = 1, \ldots, N, \tag{22}$$

where $p^\top = [p_1^\top, \ldots, p_N^\top]$. Then by choosing the control input as

$$u_i = -u_{i0}(p) sign(s_i) + f_i^k(p_i, \dot{p}_i), \tag{23}$$

where $sign(s_i) = [sign(s_{i1}), \ldots, sign(s_{in})]^\top$ and the gain $u_{i0}(p)$ of the control input is "high enough", i.e. satisfies

$$u_{i0}(p) > \bar{M}_i \left(\frac{1}{\underline{M}_i} \bar{f}_i(p_i, \dot{p}_i) + \bar{J}_i(p) + \varepsilon_i \right), \tag{24}$$

where $\bar{M}_i$, $\underline{M}_i$, and $\bar{f}_i(p_i, \dot{p}_i)$ are the known bounds on the uncertainties and disturbances, $\bar{J}_i(p)$ is the computable bound on the potential function derivative, and $\varepsilon_i > 0$ is an arbitrary constant, one can guarantee that

$$s_i^\top \dot{s}_i < -\varepsilon_i \|s_i\|$$

is satisfied and that sliding mode occurs. In other words, it is guaranteed that $s_i = 0$ is achieved in finite time resulting in $\dot{p}_i = -\nabla_{p_i} J(p)$ which is exactly the model in (2) with the control input in (16). Therefore, all the results obtained for the dynamics in (2)-(16) are recovered for the fully actuated model in (4) as well.

The main advantage of the sliding mode approach is that the above achievement is performed in the existence of uncertainties and the disturbances in the agent/vehicle dynamics in (4) - issues not considered often. This is mainly because of the suppression and robustness properties of the sliding mode control method. The shortcomings (of the raw form of the sliding mode control scheme) on the other hand are the so-called chattering effect and possible generation of high-magnitude control signals. Note that these shortcomings may possibly be avoided or relaxed via integration and some filtering techniques. Application of the sliding mode approach with complex agent dynamics models such as the non-holonomic unicycle model (5) is currently being investigated by the authors.

5.3 Feedback Linearization

Consider the non-holonomic dynamics in (5) with the output defined as in (6). Differentiating the output z_i twice, one can easily show that

$$\ddot{z}_i = A_i + B_i \bar{u}_i, \tag{25}$$

where $\bar{u}_i = \begin{bmatrix} F_i, \tau_i \end{bmatrix}^\top$ and

$$A_i = \begin{bmatrix} -v_i w_i \sin(\theta_i) - d_i(w_i)^2 \cos(\theta_i) \\ v_i w_i \cos(\theta_i) - d_i(w_i)^2 \sin(\theta_i) \end{bmatrix}, \text{ and } B_i = \begin{bmatrix} \frac{1}{m_i}\cos(\theta_i) & -\frac{d_i}{J_i}\sin(\theta_i) \\ \frac{1}{m_i}\sin(\theta_i) & \frac{d_i}{J_i}\cos(\theta_i) \end{bmatrix},$$

respectively. By choosing

$$\bar{u}_i = B_i^{-1}\left[-A_i + u_i\right] \tag{26}$$

where $u_i = [u_{i1}, u_{i2}]^\top$, we obtain

$$\ddot{z}_i = u_i.$$

Note that the matrix B_i is always invertible, since its determinant is given by $\frac{d_i}{m_i J_i}$, which implies that the linearizing controller always exists. The unobservable states (rendered by the particular feedback linearizing controller) are given by

$$\dot{\theta}^i = -\frac{1}{d_i}\dot{z}_{i1}\sin(\theta_i) + \frac{1}{d_i}\dot{z}_{i2}\cos(\theta_i). \tag{27}$$

Note that the zero dynamics of the system are marginally stable since when $z_i = \dot{z}_i = 0$ we have $\dot{\theta}_i = 0$.

After linearizing the system from input-output point of view using the above approach, one can design the controller using linear or other techniques. This approach has been used in [44] and in [93] for developing algorithms for formation stabilization. An important issue that one needs to be careful about in this approach is that the zero dynamics of the system are only marginally stable (i.e. not asymptotically or exponentially stable). This, under some conditions, may lead to the unobservable dynamics being unstable and therefore resulting in undesired behavior. To avoid this problem, it may be required to add one more integrator to the force input terminal of the dynamics in (5) and fully linearize the system (i.e., both input-output and input-state). However, application of this technique has not been investigated in detail in the literature.

5.4 Lyapunov Analysis and Other Nonlinear Control Techniques

As can be deduced from the above discussions, asymptotic stability and convergence properties in coordination and control of swarms are usually analyzed employing *Lyapunov* or *Lyapunov-like* functions and performing so-called Lyapunov(-like) analysis (see, e.g. [12, 13, 14, 15, 24]). Beside these, there also exist studies in the literature in which Lyapunov techniques, particularly the so called *control Lyapunov functions* (*CLFs*) are used at the controller design stage, e.g. [94].

Beside the Lyapunov-based ones, there exist a number of other nonlinear control and mathematical tools employed in the swarm coordination and control literature. A particular nonlinear control design for formation acquisition and maintenance with the non-holonomic unicycle agent dynamics model, which involves geometric and inverse kinematic considerations, is presented in [3,72,73]. The corresponding control schemes are called the *separation - separation* and *separation - bearing* controllers, and used for maintaining the desired inter-agent distance and bearing angle, respectively. A relevant mathematical tool, used particularly in formation acquisition and maintenance, is the concept of *virtual leader*, i.e. moving reference point that influences vehicles in its neighborhood, which is also considered in Section 5.1 [22, 34, 95]. Another particular nonlinear control tool used in [22] for avoiding chattering phenomena in positioning as well as implementing the changes among a number of control actions smoothly is *continuous switching*.

Beside the works mentioned above, there exist a number of other studies in the literature on applications of various nonlinear control frameworks, such as *neural networks*, *dynamic inversion*, *backstepping*, *adaptive control*, *output regulation* etc. to different swarm coordination and control problems. Examples of these studies can be found in [85, 86, 87, 88, 96] and the references therein.

5.5 Behavior Based and Evolutionary Approaches

Another common approach for coordinating groups of robots is the *behavior based* approach. One of the first studies on swarm coordination using behavior based approach is the work by Reynolds [1] discussed earlier. In a more recent study in [97] Balch and Arkin present and evaluate a reactive behavior based approach for formation stabilization and acquisition in multi-robot teams. They also integrate the formation behaviors with other navigational behaviors such as avoiding collisions with obstacles and other robots, reaching goals/targets, etc. The integration allows the system to reach navigational goals and avoid collisions while simultaneously maintaining the geometric formation structure. Besides the simulation studies, they also describe implementation of the algorithm on real-life vehicles and integration of the behaviors with available robot control architectures.

In [97], several different formation patterns are considered for a team of four robots including *line* (robots travelling in a line parallel to each other), *column* (robots travelling behind each other), *diamond* (robots travelling in a diamond shaped formation), and *wedge* (robots travelling in a V shaped formation).

In the algorithm considered in [97], each robot computes its desired position in the formation based on the locations of the other robots. Three techniques are considered in this study for formation position determination:

(i) *Unit Center Referencing*: The unit (swarm) center is computed independently by each robot by averaging the positions of all the robots involved in the formation and each robot determines its own formation position relative to that center.

(ii) *Leader Referencing*: Each robot determines its formation position with respect to the leader. In this approach the leader does not attempt to maintain formation, the other robots are responsible for formation maintenance.

(iii) *Neighbor Referencing*: Each robot maintains a position relative to one other pre-assigned robot.

Above, the orientation of the formation is defined by a line from the center of the group to the next navigational waypoint. Several basic behaviors are defined and implemented including *move-to-goal, avoid-static-obstacle, avoid-robot*, and *maintain-formation*. Using these behaviors the robots move to a goal location while avoiding obstacles and collisions with other robots and maintaining the formation.

Behavior based approaches have also been used for studying aggregation strategies in swarm robotic systems. Two recent studies are the works by Soysal and Şahin in [57] and Bahçeci and Şahin in [58]. In [57] the authors determine three basic behaviors namely, *approaching, repelling*, and *waiting* together with *obstacle avoidance* and arbitrate the behavior using a finite state machine with different probabilities for the switching behavior. They perform a systematic study of aggregation behavior based on the values of the control parameters. They investigate also the effects of the size of the arena and the simulation time. The metrics used for determining the performance of the system (the quality of aggregation) for a swarm S with N agents (here robots) $A_1, \ldots, A_N$ are the *expected cluster size*

$$ECS = \frac{1}{n} \sum_{i=1}^{N} size^2(A_i), \tag{28}$$

where $size(A_i)$ is the number of agents in the cluster[4] that A_i belongs to, and the total distance (TD)

$$TD = - \sum_{i=1}^{N} \sum_{j=i+1}^{N} \|p_i - p_j\|, \tag{29}$$

where p_i, p_j denote the positions of A_i, A_j, respectively, as before.

As a separate study, in [58] neural network controllers for generating aggregation behavior are considered. The parameters of the neural network controllers are tuned (determined) using evolutionary strategies (genetic algorithms) and their performance and scalability are evaluated. In other words, the performance of a simulated swarm robotic system controlled by neural network controllers tuned by genetic algorithms is systematically studied with different parameter settings. In particular, they consider four experiments by varying some of the parameters, and derive rules of thumb which can be of guidance to the use of evolutionary methods for generating other swarm robotic behaviors (beside the aggregation behavior).

---

[4] A cluster is defined as the group of agents which are connected to (meaning are neighbors of) each other either directly or indirectly through other agents.

An interesting study is also the work in [98] where the authors consider the application of Lyapunov stability techniques to the design of motor schema for behavior-based systems. While the paper is originally intended for the design of single complex agents, the methods can be easily applied to the design of swarm agents as well.

5.6 Artificial Physics

An important approach that can be thought as a subclass of the potential function based approaches is the *artificial physics* based approach introduced by Spears and Gordon in [99] (obtained independently from the work of Reif and Wang in [91]). It is a method based on the fundamental laws of physics, particularly mechanics, such as the Newton's laws of motion. Since then Spears and coworkers have addressed many of the problems mentioned in the preceding section within their framework and have combined the approach with other methods [100, 101, 102, 103, 104, 105, 106, 107]. In particular, they have addressed the problems of formation stabilization, acquisition, maintenance, formation and cohesion during motion. They have addressed also formation switching and reconfiguration (in case of loss of agents) and have implemented their method asynchronously on several (inexpensive) robots. They use novel methods of analysis (which differ from Lyapunov based methods) that allow them to set parameters a priori. Furthermore, compared to the behavior-based approaches they have looked at obstacle avoidance problems with higher numbers of robots and higher obstacle densities.

Another important swarm task that they have analyzed extensively in simulation and implementation on real robots is the problem of chemical plume tracing [103, 106]. In cases in which analytical analysis is intractable they apply evolutionary methods to learn parameter settings of the system. Moreover, they've developed an online learning algorithm that adjusts the system parameters in real-time in dynamic environments.

Finally, it warrants mention that Spears and coworkers have implemented a physics-based (not potential-based) model based on kinetic theory which is useful for tasks such as surveillance, sweep or coverage of an area.

5.7 Asynchronous Swarm Models

Multi-agent dynamic systems are naturally distributed systems which naturally act in asynchronous manner and in general it is difficult to implement synchronous motion in them. Still many of the models and approaches considered in the systems and control literature are synchronous. We believe that the reason for that is tractability for analysis. In other words, analyzing the dynamics of asynchronous systems is more difficult compared to their synchronous counterparts, in general. Nevertheless, in addition to the synchronous swarm models there are also studies in the literature which consider asynchronous modeling of multi-agent systems [27, 28, 29, 108, 109].

The work by Beni and Liang in [108] is one of the first studies on the stability of asynchronous swarm systems in which the authors determine sufficient conditions for the asynchronous convergence of a linear swarm to a synchronously achievable configuration.

In [27, 28] Liu and Passino study the stability of one-dimensional and m-dimensional asynchronous swarms incurring also time delays in communication or sensing. In [28] the stability of both one-dimensional stationary and mobile swarms is studied. For the stationary case the authors determine asymptotic convergence (to the desired configuration) under *total asynchronism* conditions (i.e., asynchronism in which the time delay in sensing/communication and the time intervals between two consequent updates can become arbitrarily large) and finite time convergence under *partial asynchronism* conditions (i.e., asynchronism in which there is a bound on the maximum possible time delay in sensing/communication and the time between two consecutive updates). For the mobile swarm case they prove that cohesion will be preserved during motion under conditions expressed as bounds on the maximum possible time delay. In [27] multi-dimensional swarms with a specific class of communication topologies (i.e., leader-follower structure) are studied. In this work, it is proven that cohesion will be preserved during motion (therefore extending the work in [28]) by imposing special constraints on the "leader" movements expressed as bounds on the maximum possible time delay.

In [29], Gazi and Passino consider asynchronous swarms in one-dimensional space with different rules for inter-individual interactions (compared to those in [28]), and using results on contractive mappings developed for parallel and distributed computation in computer networks in [81], show that swarm stability or convergence to a *comfortable position* will be obtained under assumptions of the sector boundedness of the attraction/repulsion function and *total asynchronism* in the motion of the agents. Similar approach is taken also in [110] for showing convergence of asynchronous cyclic pursuit. Note here that multi-agent systems (such as swarms of robots, flocks of birds, schools of fish) are naturally parallel and distributed computing systems and results obtained for parallel and distributed computation in computer networks are very relevant in the study of the dynamics of such systems.

In [109], Beni shows that asynchronous swarms may converge in cases in which synchronous swarms may not. In particular, he shows that asynchronous swarms converge to the same fixed points as their synchronous counterparts and moreover the asynchronous systems may reach fixed points that are unreachable for the synchronous ones. Furthermore, [109] argues that achieving an order from disordered actions is a basic characteristic of swarms.

Some other recent (empirical) studies on the flocking behavior of asynchronous multi-agent systems are the works by Şamiloğlu, Gazi, and Koku in [64, 65]. In [64], the effects of the level of asynchronism and size of neighborhood on the clustering performance of a swarm of self-propelled particles are studied. In [65], on the other hand, rotation angle restrictions (a type of non-holonomic constraint) are imposed on the self-propelled particles and their effect on the performance of the system is investigated.

5.8 Probabilistic Approaches

Non-spatial or probabilistic approaches and Markov models are also being used in the literature for modeling of swarm behavior. Usually in these approaches the population level swarming dynamics are described in a non-spatial way in terms of frequency distributions of groups of various size. Then usually it is assumed that groups of various sizes split or merge probabilistically into other groups based on the inherent group dynamics, environmental conditions, and encounters of other groups. An example work on this approach from the biological literature is the article in [111] where the authors present a general continuous model for animal group size distribution (a non-spatial patch model). Also an interesting comparative study from the biological literature is presented by Durrett and Levin in [112], where they compare four different approaches to modeling the dynamics of spatially distributed systems by using three different examples, each with different realistic biological assumptions. They show that the solutions of all the models do not always agree, and argue in favor of the discrete (individual based) models that treat the space explicitly.

A recent article from the swarm robotics literature considering probabilistic model is the work by Matinoli and coworkers in [113]. Also recent review describing probabilistic approaches is the article by Lerman and coworkers in [114] where the authors consider a discrete-time, non-spatial, macroscopic models able to capture the dynamics of collective aggregation experiments using groups of embodied agents endowed with reactive controllers. They perform several experiments with teams with various sized and show that their models can deliver both qualitatively and quantitatively correct predictions and they represent a useful tool for generalizing the dynamics of such swarm-robotic systems (which are as the authors state highly stochastic, asynchronous, nonlinear systems, often outperforming intuitive reasoning).

One of the most recent studies on probabilistic approaches is the work by Soysal and Şahin in [115] where the authors investigate the aggregation behavior in an enclosed environment where the perception range of robots is much smaller than the size of the environment. In particular they consider a discrete-time non-spatial macroscopic markov model for probabilistic aggregation under some simplifying assumptions. The evolution of the swarm during aggregation is modeled with geometric approximations and case by case analysis supported with number theory. The effects of probabilistic parameters and size of environment are investigated using the model and a sensor-based simulation.

6   Stability, Performance, and Robustness

Stability is an essential control theoretical concept that dynamical systems are usually required to satisfy. In the context of multi-agent dynamical systems, *stability* may be defined in different ways depending on the particular problem or behavior being studied, although one common requirement is state-boundedness, i.e., using the previous notations in the article, the boundedness of the state x_i (e.g. the position p_i) of each agent A_i in the swarm S of interest.

For example, in *aggregation* studies, a widely used stability criterion for a swarm S, is its *asymptotic cohesiveness*, which may be formulated as

$$\lim_{t \to \infty} x_i(t) \in B_\varepsilon(\bar{x}(t)), \ \forall i \in \{1, \dots, N\}$$

where $\bar{x} = \frac{1}{N}\sum_{i=1}^{N} x_i$ is the *centroid* of the swarm and $B_\varepsilon(\bar{x}(t)) = \{y(t) : \|y(t) - \bar{x}(t)\| \leq \varepsilon\}$ is the ε-neighborhood of $\bar{x}$ [24, 26, 25]; whereas in *agreement* problems the stability criterion becomes the convergence of the states of the agents to a common value, which may be formulated as

$$\lim_{t \to \infty} \|x_i(t) - x_j(t)\| = 0, \tag{30}$$

for any pair $i, j \in \{1, \ldots, N\}$ such that $i \neq j$. In *rendezvous* problems, the stability criterion is a more restricted form of (30), i.e. it is satisfaction of the convergence (30) in finite time (instead of being satisfied asymptotically).

In *formation acquisition* and *maintenance* studies, one essential stability criterion is the ability of the swarm S to achieve and maintain the desired or predefined geometrical or topological formation structure. In *social foraging* studies, on the other hand, the main criterion is ability of the swarm S to converge to a favorable region (e.g. a region with food, targets or goals). Note that in order to meet the stability criterion, S needs to be able to avoid sticking into any unfavorable region (e.g. any region with toxic substances, threads or obstacles) in the environment as well.

As demonstrated above, the stability criteria differ for different classes of swarm coordination and control problems. Note here that, in most of the swarm coordination and control studies mentioned in this article, stability of the swarm system of interest is discussed either via some formal mathematical analysis or using some experimental or simulation results. This is expected, as stability is the most important property to check in a control design and it is impossible to consider the *performance* or *effectiveness* of the control system if it is unstable (implying that, at least for some very likely cases, the control goal or objective can not be achieved). Nevertheless, there exist studies in the literature that mainly focuses on stability of swarm systems in various contexts of coordination and control that are briefly introduced in Section 4 [15, 16, 24, 26, 27, 28, 29, 45, 116, 117]. The details of these studies, however, are not discussed in this article mainly due to space considerations.

Performance of a dynamical system is related to how different the actual behavior of the system is than its desired or ideal behavior. A dynamical system whose behavior is closer to the ideal is said to have a better performance. In order to quantify the performance, one needs to define a set of quantitative *performance indices* that depend on another set of quantitative indices for the "ideal behavior". As in the case with *stability*, depending on the particular problem and control tasks, the performance indices for a multi-agent dynamical system can be defined in different ways.

For example, in the case of aggregation or flocking behavior metrics like *speed of convergence, the size of the swarm* (in terms of the region occupied by the swarm), *the number of clusters in the swarm* [24, 25, 26, 57, 58, 64, 65], and others can be defined as *performance criteria*. Equations (28) and (29) are examples of such criteria considered in [57, 58]. The studies on the performance of swarm systems are usually done in two different ways: *analytical* and *empirical/simulation*. The analytical studies (e.g. [24, 25, 26]) appear as a companion on the studies on stability analysis and derive explicit theoretical parameters quantifying performance such as theoretical bounds on the swarm size or time of convergence. The empirical studies (e.g. [57, 58, 64, 65]) usually derive conclusions about the swarm performance through large number of independent simulations.

A third essential system theoretical concept for a dynamical systems, accompanying *stability* and *performance* is *robustness*. Many swarm systems that are stable and that work perfectly with high performance under ideal conditions may lose these properties in the existence of some perturbations, i.e. disturbances or uncertainties, even if they are very small. *Robustness* of a swarm system in terms of a particular property (e.g. stability or performance) can be thought as the ability of the system to preserve this property in the presence of uncertainties and disturbances whose magnitudes are less than a certain acceptable bound. The corresponding *robustness level* of the swarm system quantifies the maximum magnitude of disturbances and/or uncertainties this system can tolerate without losing the corresponding property (e.g. stability or performance).

Robustness issues in the swarm studies have not been considered on a satisfactory level in the control systems literature so far. Exception studies include the work by Olfati-Saber and Murray in [13] where they consider continuous time consensus protocols in systems with time delay. Another work is the study in [37] where measurement uncertainties are considered and foraging controllers are developed. The sliding mode control method [38, 92] also provides a level of robustness against certain type of disturbances and model uncertainties. Nevertheless, comprehensive robustness studies are still needed.

7   Concluding Remarks

In this article we have presented a summary of the main models, problems, and approaches for coordination and control of multi-agent dynamical systems (or swarms) that have been considered in the systems and control literature. As can be deduced from this summary, the studies in the field are fairly extensive and diverse, the scientific achievement is significant, and the results obtained are important. However, there are still a number issues to be investigated.

First, it is worth to note that there still exist a number of open problems related to each of the coordination and control tasks introduced in Section 4. Details of these open problems, which are mostly of theoretical nature, can be found in the corresponding references. A particular issue is the issue of asynchronism. Since the operation of most of the multi-agent systems is naturally asynchronous, we believe that more attention should be paid to asynchronous models and results obtained for synchronous models should be verified against asynchronous counterparts as well. Moreover, communication and sensing delays are present in many multi-agent systems. Therefore, studies of systems with delay needs more attention and results obtained for models with no delay should be verified against delayed ones as well, noting that the results incorporating delays are currently very few. Two further future research topics based on the above is the formal analysis of the effect of asynchronism and time delays on the performance of swarm systems and development of algorithms robust to delay and asynchronism of a ceratin extent.

Another important issue, that is being overlooked in the systems and control literature, is the implementation and testing. Usually the theoretical findings are being verified through computer simulations (using Matlab or other software); however, for practical applications this may not be sufficient. Hence, there is a need for extensive experimental studies in the fields as well.

References

1. Reynolds, C.W.: Flocks, herds, and schools: A distributed behavioral model. Comp. Graph. **21**(4) (1987) 25–34
2. Yamaguchi, H.: A cooperative hunting behavior by mobile-robot troops. The International Journal of Robotics Research **18**(8) (1999) 931–940
3. Desai, J.P., Ostrowski, J., Kumar, V.: Modeling and control of formations of nonholonomic mobile robots. IEEE Trans. on Robotics and Automation**17**(6) (2001) 905–908
4. Fowler, J., D'Andrea, R.: A formation flight experiment. IEEE Control Systems Magazine **23**(5) (2003) 35–43
5. Ren, W., Beard, R.: A decentralized scheme for spacecraft formation flying via the virtual structure approach. AIAA Journal of Gudiance, Control and Dyanmics **27**(1) (2004) 73–82
6. Stilwell, D., Bishop, B., Sylvester, C.: Redundant manipulator techniques for partially decentralized path planning and control of a platoon of autonomous vehicles. IEEE Transactions on Systems Man and Cybernetics Part B-Cybernetics **35**(4) (2005) 842–848
7. Cortes, J., Martinez, S., Karatas, T., Bullo, F.: Coverage control for mobile sensing networks. IEEE Trans. on Robotics and Automation**20**(2) (2004) 243–255
8. Akyildiz, I.F., Su, W., Sankarasubramniam, Y., Cayirci, E.: A survey on sensor networks. IEEE Commununications Magazine **40**(8) (2002) 102–114
9. Sahin, E.: Swarm robotics: From sources of inspiration to domains of application. In Sahin, E., Spears, W., eds.: Swarm Robotics: State-of-the-art Survey. Lecture Notes in Computer Science (LNCS 3342). Springer-Verlag, Berlin Heidelberg (2005) 10–20
10. Kubik, A.: Towards a formalization of emergence. Artificial Life **9** (2003) 41–65
11. Godsil, C., Royle, G.: Algebraic Graph Theory. Volume 207 of Graduate Texts in Mathematics. Springer-Verlag, New York (2001)
12. Jadbabaie, A., Lin, J., Morse, A.S.: Coordination of groups of mobile autonomous agents using nearest neighbor rules. IEEE Trans. on Automatic Control**48**(6) (2003) 988–1001
13. Olfati-Saber, R., Murray, R.M.: Consensus problems in networks of agents with switching topology and time-delays. IEEE Trans. on Automatic Control**49**(9) (2004) 1520–1533
14. Olfati-Saber, R.: Flocking for multi-agent dynamic systems: Algorithms and theory. IEEE Trans. on Automatic Control**51**(3) (2006) 401–420
15. Tanner, H., Pappas, G.J., Kumar, V.: Leader-to-formation stability. IEEE Trans. on Robotics and Automation **20**(3) (2004) 443–455
16. Moreau, L.: Stability of multiagent systems with time-dependent communication links. IEEE Trans. on Automatic Control**50**(2) (2005) 169–182
17. Ren, W., Beard, R.W.: Consensus seeking in multi-agent systems under dynamically changing interaction topologies. IEEE Trans. on Automatic Control**50**(5) (2005) 655–661
18. Anderson, B., Yu, C., Fidan, B., Hendrickx, J.: Control and information architectures for formations. In: Proc. IEEE Conference on Control Applications (Joint CCA/CACSD/ISIC). (2006)
19. Eren, T., Anderson, B., Morse, A., Whiteley, W., Belhumeur, P.: Operations on rigid formations of autonomous agents. Communications in Information and Systems **3**(4) (2004) 223–258
20. Hendrickx, J., Anderson, B., Blondel, V.: Rigidity and persistence of directed graphs. In: Proc. 44th IEEE Conference on Decision and Control and the European Control Conference 2005. (2005) 2176 – 2181
21. Hendrickx, J., Fidan, B., Yu, C., Anderson, B., Blondel, V.: Rigidity and persistence of three and higher dimensional formations. In: Proc. 2nd Int. Conf. on Informatics in Control, Automation & Robotics (ICINCO) - 1st Int. Workshop on Multi-Agent Robotic Systems (MARS). (2005) 39–46

22. Sandeep, S., Fidan, B., Yu, C.: Decentralized cohesive motion control of multi-agent for-
    mations. In: Proc. 14th Mediterranean Conference on Control and Automation, Ancona,
    Italy (2006)
23. Yu, C., Hendrickx, J., Fidan, B., Anderson, B.: Structural persistence of three dimensional
    autonomous formations. In: Proc. 2nd Int. Conf. on Informatics in Control, Automation &
    Robotics (ICINCO) - 1st Int. Workshop on Multi-Agent Robotic Systems (MARS). (2005)
    47–55
24. Gazi, V., Passino, K.M.: Stability analysis of swarms. IEEE Trans. on Automatic Con-
    trol**48**(4) (2003) 692–697
25. Gazi, V., Passino, K.M.: A class of attraction/repulsion functions for stable swarm aggre-
    gations. Int. J. Control**77**(18) (2004) 1567–1579
26. Gazi, V., Passino, K.M.: Stability analysis of social foraging swarms. IEEE Trans. on
    Systems, Man, and Cybernetics: Part B **34**(1) (2004) 539–557
27. Liu, Y., Passino, K.M., Polycarpou, M.M.: Stability analysis of m-dimensional asyn-
    chronous swarms with a fixed communication topology. IEEE Trans. on Automatic Con-
    trol**48**(1) (2003) 76–95
28. Liu, Y., Passino, K.M., Polycarpou, M.M.: Stability analysis of one-dimensional asyn-
    chronous swarms. IEEE Trans. on Automatic Control**48**(10) (2003) 1848–1854
29. Gazi, V., Passino, K.M.: Stability of a one-dimensional discrete-time asynchronous swarm.
    IEEE Trans. on Systems, Man, and Cybernetics: Part B **35**(4) (2005) 834–841
30. Tanner, H.G., Jadbabaie, A., Pappas, G.J.: Stable flocking of mobile agents, part i: Fixed
    topology. In: Proc. of Conf. Decision Contr., Maui, Hawaii (2003) 2010–2015
31. Guldner, J., Utkin, V.I.: Sliding mode control for gradient tracking and robot navigation
    using artificial potential fields. IEEE Trans. on Robotics and Automation**11**(2) (1995) 247–
    254
32. Campion, G., Bastin, G., Dandrea-Novel, B.: Structural properties and classification of
    kinematic and dynamicmodels of wheeled mobile robots. IEEE Tr. on Robotics and Au-
    tomation **12**(1) (1996) 47–62
33. Yi, B.J., Kim, W.: The kinematics for redundantly actuated omnidirectional mobile robots.
    Journal of Robotic Systems **19**(6) (2002) 255–267
34. Leonard, N.E., Fiorelli, E.: Virtual leaders, artificial potentials and coordinated control of
    groups. In: Proc. of Conf. Decision Contr., Orlando, FL (2001) 2968–2973
35. Bachmayer, R., Leonard, N.E.: Vehicle networks for gradient descent in a sampled envi-
    ronment. In: Proc. of Conf. Decision Contr., Las Vegas, Nevada (2002) 112–117
36. Tanner, H.G., Jadbabaie, A., Pappas, G.J.: Stable flocking of mobile agents, part ii: Dynamic
    topology. In: Proc. of Conf. Decision Contr., Maui, Hawaii (2003) 2016–2021
37. Liu, Y., Passino, K.M.: Stable social foraging swarms in a noisy environment. IEEE Trans-
    actions on Automatic Control **49**(1) (2004) 30–44
38. Gazi, V.: Swarm aggregations using artificial potentials and sliding mode control. IEEE
    Trans. on Robotics**21**(6) (2005) 1208–1214
39. Yao, J., Ordonez, R., Gazi, V.: Swarm tracking using artificial potentials and sliding mode
    control. In: Proc. of Conf. Decision Contr., San Diago, CA, USA (2006)
40. Egerstedt, M., Hu, X.: Formation constrained multi-agent control. IEEE Trans. on Robotics
    and Automation**17**(6) (2001) 947–951
41. Lin, Z., Francis, B., Maggiore, M.: Necessary and sufficient graphial conditions for forma-
    tion control of unicycles. IEEE Trans. on Automatic Control**50**(1) (2005) 121–127
42. Marshall, J., Broucke, M., Francis, B.: Formations of vehicles in cyclic pursuit. IEEE Trans.
    on Automatic Control **49**(11) (2004) 1963–1974
43. Tanner, H.G., Jadbabaie, A., Pappas, G.J.: Flocking in teams of nonholonomic agents. In
    V.J. Kumar, N.L., Morse, A., eds.: Cooperative Control. Volume 309 of Lecture Notes in
    Control and Information Sciences., Springer-Verlag (2005) 229–239

44. Lawton, J.R.T., Beard, R.W., Young, B.J.: A decentralized approach to formation maneuvers. IEEE Trans. on Robotics and Automation**19**(6) (2003) 933–941
45. Gazi, V.: Stability Analysis of Swarms. PhD thesis, The Ohio State University (2002)
46. Brockett, R.W.: Asymptotic stability and feedback stabilization. In Millman, R.S., Sussmann, H.J., eds.: Differential Geometric Control Theory. Birkhauser (1983) 181–191
47. Sepulchre, R., Palay, D., Leonard, N.E.: Collective motion and oscillator synchronization. In Kumar, V.J., Leonard, N.E., Morse, A.S., eds.: Cooperative Control: 2003 Block Island Workshop on Cooperative Control. Volume 309 of Lecture Notes in Control and Information Sciences., Springer-Verlag (2005)
48. Dubins, L.: On curves of minimal length with a constraint on average curvature and with prescribed initial and terminal positions and tangents. American Journal of Mathematics **79** (1957) 497–516
49. Savla, K., Bullo, F., Frazzoli, E.: On traveling salesperson problems for Dubins' vehicle: stochastic and dynamic environments. In: Proc. 44th IEEE Conference on Decision and Control and the European Control Conference 2005. (2005) 4530–4535
50. Tomlin, C., Mitchell, I., Ghosh, R.: Safety verification of conflict resolution manoeuvres. IEEE Tr. on Intelligent Transportation Systems **2**(2) (2001) 110–120
51. Boscain, U., Piccoli, B.: Optimal Syntheses for Control Systems on 2-D Manifolds. Springer Verlag, New York, NY (2004)
52. Vicsek, T., Czirok, A., Ben-Jacob, E., Cohen, I., Shochet, O.: Novel type of phase transition in a system of self-driven particles. Physical Review Letters**75**(6) (1995) 1226–1229
53. Breder, C.M.: Equations descriptive of fish schools and other animal aggregations. Ecology **35**(3) (1954) 361–370
54. Okubo, A.: Dynamical aspects of animal grouping: swarms, schools, flocks, and herds. Advances in Biophysics **22** (1986) 1–94
55. Warburton, K., Lazarus, J.: Tendency-distance models of social cohesion in animal groups. Journal of Theoretical Biology**150** (1991) 473–488
56. Grünbaum, D., Okubo, A.: Modeling social animal aggregations. In: Frontiers in Theoretical Biology. Volume 100 of Lecture Notes in Biomathematics. Springer-Verlag, New York (1994) 296–325
57. Soysal, O., Sahin, E.: Probabilistic aggregation strategies in swarm robotic systems. In: Proc. of the IEEE Swarm Intelligence Symposium, Pasadena, California (2005)
58. Bahceci, E., Sahin, E.: Evolving aggregation behaviors for swarm robotic systems: A systematic case study. In: Proc. of the IEEE Swarm Intelligence Symposium, Pasadena, California (2005)
59. Grünbaum, D.: Schooling as a strategy for taxis in a noisy environment. In Parrish, J.K., Hamner, W.M., eds.: Animal Groups in Three Dimensions. Cambridge Iniversity Press (1997) 257–281
60. Grünbaum, D.: Schooling as a strategy for taxis in a noisy environment. Evolutionary Ecology **12** (1998) 503–522
61. Bonabeau, E., Dorigo, M., Theraulaz, G.: Swarm Intelligence: From Natural to Artificial Systems. Oxford University Press, New York (1999)
62. Kennedy, J., Eberhart, R.C.: Swarm Intelligence. Morgan Kaufmann Publisher (2001)
63. Clerc, M., Kennedy, J.: The particle swarm—explosion, stability, and convergence in a multidimensional complex space. IEEE Trans. on Evolutionary Computation**6**(1) (2002) 58–73
64. Şamiloglu, A.T., Gazi, V., Koku, A.B.: Effects of asynchronism and neighborhood size on clustering in self-propelled particle systems. In Levi, A., et al., eds.: Proc. of International Symposium on Computer and Information Sciences (ISCIS06). Lecture Notes in Computer Science (LNCS) 4263. Springer Verlag (2006) 665–676

65. Şamiloglu, A.T., Gazi, V., Koku, A.B.: An empirical study on the motion of self-propelled particles with turn angle restrictions. In Şahin et al., E., ed.: Proc. of SAB06 Workshop on Swarm Robotics. Lecture Notes in Computer Science (LNCS). Springer Verlag (2006)

66. Ando, H., Oasa, Y., Suzuki, I., Yamashita, M.: Distributed memoryless point convergence algorithm for mobile robots with limited visibility. IEEE Transactions on Robotics and Automation **15**(5) (1999) 818–828

67. Lin, J., Morse, A.S., Anderson, B.D.O.: The multi-agent rendezvous problem. In: Proc. of Conf. Decision Contr., Maui, Hawaii, USA (2003) 1508–1513

68. Lin, J., Morse, A.S., Anderson, B.D.O.: The multi-agent rendezvous problem - the asynchronous case. In: Proc. of Conf. Decision Contr., Atlantis, Paradise Island, Bahamas (2004) 1926–1931

69. Marshall, J.A., Broucke, M.E., Francis, B.A.: Pursuit formations of unicycles. Automatica **42**(1) (2006) 3–12

70. Olfati-Saber, R., Murray, R.M.: Distributed cooperative control of multiple vehicle formations using structural potential functions. In: Proc. IFAC World Congress, Barcelona, Spain (2002)

71. Lin, Z., Broucke, M., Francis, B.: Local control strategies for groups of mobile autonomous agents. IEEE Trans. on Automatic Control **49**(4) (2004) 622–629

72. Das, A., Fierro, R., Kumar, V.: Control graphs for robot networks. In Butenko, S., Murphey, R., Pardalos, P., eds.: Cooperative Control: Models, Applications and Algorithms, Kluwer Academic (2003) 55–73

73. Fierro, R., Song, P., Das, A., Kumar, V.: Cooperative control of robot formations. In Murphey, R., Pardalos, P., eds.: Cooperative Control and Optimization, Kluwer Academic (2002) 73–94

74. Yu, C., Fidan, B., Anderson, B.: Persistence acquisition and maintenance for autonomous formations. In: Proc. 2nd Int. Conf. on Intelligent Sensors, Sensor Networks and Information Processing (ISSNIP). (2005) 379 – 384

75. Yu, C., Fidan, B., Anderson, B.: Principles to control autonomous formation merging. In: Proc. American Control Conference. (2006) 762 – 768

76. Das, A., Fierro, R., Kumar, V., Ostrowski, J.: A vision-based formation control framework. IEEE Trans. on Robotics and Automation **18**(5) (2002) 813–825

77. P. Ögren, Fiorelli, E., Leonard, N.E.: Formations with a mission: Stable coordination of vehicle group maneuvers. In: Symposium on Mathematical Theory of Networks and Systems. (2002)

78. Ren, W., Beard, R.W., Atkins, E.M.: A survey of consensus problems in multi-agent coordination. In: Proc. American Control Conf., Portland, OR, USA (2005) 1859–1864

79. Gordon, N., Wagner, I.A., Bruckstein, A.M.: Gathering multiple robotic a(ge)nts with limited sensing capabilities. In Dorigo, M., Birattari, M., Blum, C., Gambardella, L.M., Mondada, F., Stützle, T., eds.: Proceedings of ANTS 2004 – Fourth International Workshop on Ant Colony Optimization and Swarm Intelligence. Volume 3172 of Lecture Notes in Computer Science., Brussels, Belgium, Springer Verlag (2004) 142–153

80. Flocchini, P., Prencipe, G., Santoro, N., Widmayer, P.: Gathering of autonomous mobile robots with limited visibility. In: Proc. 18th International Symposium on Theoretical Aspects of Computer Science (STACS 2001). Volume 2010 of Lecture Notes in Computer Science., Dresden, Germany, Springer Verlag (2001) 247–258

81. Bertsekas, D.P., Tsitsiklis, J.N.: Parallel and Distributed Computation: Numerical Methods. Athena Scientific, Belmont, MA (1997)

82. Strogatz, S.H., Stewart, I.: Coupled oscillators and biological synchronization. Scientific American (1993) 102–109

83. Strogatz, S.H., Mirollo, R.E., Matthews, P.C.: Coupled nonlinear oscillators below the synchronization threshhold: Relaxation by generalized landau damping. Physical Review Letters **68**(18) (1992) 2730–2733
84. Fax, J.A., Murray, R.M.: Information flow and cooperative control of vehicle formations. IEEE Trans. on Automatic Control**49**(9) (2004) 1465–1476
85. Butenko, S., Murphey, R., Pardalos, P., eds.: Cooperative Control: Models, Applications and Algorithms. Kluwer Academic (2003)
86. Murphey, R., Pardalos, P., eds.: Cooperative Control and Optimization. Kluwer Academic (2002)
87. Kumar, V.J., Leonard, N.E., Morse, A.S., eds.: Cooperative Control: 2003 Block Island Workshop on Cooperative Control. Volume 309 of Lecture Notes in Control and Information Sciences. Springer-Verlag (2005)
88. Pettersen, K., 'and H. Nijmeijer, J.G., eds.: Group Coordination and Cooperative Control. Volume 336 of Lecture Notes in Control and Information Sciences. Springer-Verlag (2006)
89. Khatib, O.: Real-time obstacle avoidance for manipulators and mobile robots. The International Journal of Robotics Research **5**(1) (1986) 90–98
90. Rimon, E., Koditschek, D.E.: Exact robot navigation using artificial potential functions. IEEE Trans. on Robotics and Automation**8**(5) (1992) 501–518
91. Reif, J.H., Wang, H.: Social potential fields: A distributed behavioral control for autonomous robots. Robotics and Autonomous Systems**27** (1999) 171–194
92. Utkin, V.I.: Sliding Modes in Control and Optimization. Springer Verlag, Berlin, Heidelberg (1992)
93. Gazi, V.: Formation control of mobile robots using decentralized nonlinear servomechanism. In: 12'th Meditteranean Conference on Control and Automation, Kusadasi, Turkey (2004)
94. Ögren, P., Egerstedt, M., Hu, X.: A control Lyapunov function approach to multi-agent coordination. IEEE Trans. on Robotics and Automation**18**(5) (2002) 847–851
95. P. Ögren, Fiorelli, E., Leonard, N.E.: Cooperative control of mobile sensor networks: Adaptive gradient climbing in a distributed environment. IEEE Trans. on Automatic Control**49**(8) (2004) 1292–1302
96. Wu, H., Jagannathan, S.: Adaptive neural network control and wireless sensor network-based localization for UAV formation. In: Proc. 14th Mediterranean Conference on Control and Automation, Ancona, Italy (2006)
97. Balch, T., Arkin, R.C.: Behavior-based formation control for multirobot teams. IEEE Trans. on Robotics and Automation**14**(6) (1998) 926–939
98. Harper, C.J., Winfield, A.F.T.: A methodology for provably stable intelligent control. Robotics and Autonomous Systems **54**(1) (2006) 52–73
99. Spears, W.M., Gordon, D.F.: Using artificial physics to control agents. In: Proceedings of the IEEE International Conference on Information, Intelligence, and Systems. (1999) 281–288
100. Gordon, D.F., Spears, W.M., Sokolsky, O., Lee, I.: Distributed spatial control, global monitoring and steering of mobile agents. In: Proceedings of the IEEE International Conference on Information, Intelligence, and Systems. (1999) 681–688
101. Gordon-Spears, D.F., Spears, W.M.: Analysis of a phase transition in a physics-based multiagent system. In Hinchey, M.G., Rash, J.L., Truszkowski, W., Rouff, C., Gordon-Spears, D.F., eds.: FAABS. Volume 2699 of Lecture Notes in Computer Science., Springer (2002) 193–207
102. Spears, W.M., Spears, D.F., Hamann, J.C., Heil, R.: Distributed, physics-based control of swarms of vehicles. Auton. Robots **17**(2-3) (2004) 137–162
103. Zarzhitsky, D., Spears, D.F., Spears, W.M., Thayer, D.R.: A fluid dynamics approach to multi-robot chemical plume tracing. In: AAMAS. (2004) 1476–1477

104. Spears, W.M., Heil, R., Spears, D.F., Zarzhitsky, D.: Physicomimetics for mobile robot formations. In: AAMAS. (2004) 1528–1529
105. Spears, W.M., Spears, D.F., Heil, R.: A formal analysis of potential energy in a multi-agent system. In: FAABS. (2004) 131–145
106. Zarzhitsky, D., Spears, D.F., Thayer, D.R., Spears, W.M.: Agent-based chemical plume tracing using fluid dynamics. In: FAABS. (2004) 146–160
107. Spears, W.M., Spears, D.F., Heil, R., Kerr, W., Hettiarachchi, S.: An overview of physicomimetics. In: SAB. (2004) 84–97
108. Beni, G., Liang, P.: Pattern reconfiguration in swarms—convergence of a distributed asynchronous and bounded iterative algorithm. IEEE Trans. on Robotics and Automation **12**(3) (1996) 485–490
109. Beni, G.: Order by disordered action in swarms. In Sahin, E., Spears, W.M., eds.: Proc. SAB 2004 International Workshop on Swarm Robotics. Lecture Notes in Computer Science (LNCS 3342). Springer Verlag (2004) 153–171
110. Şamiloglu, A.T., Gazi, V., Koku, A.B.: Asynchronous cyclic pursuit. In et al., S.N., ed.: Proc. of 9'th Conference on Simulation of Adaptive Behavior (SAB06). Lecture Notes in Artificial Intelligence (LNAI) 4095. Springer Verlag (2006) 667–678
111. Gueron, S., Levin, S.A.: The dynamics of group formation. Mathematical Biosciences **128** (1995) 243–264
112. Durrett, R., Levin, S.: The importance of being discrete (and spatial). Theoretical Population Biology **46** (1994) 363–394
113. Agassounon, W., Martinoli, A., Easton, K.: Macroscopic modeling of aggregation experiments using embodied agents in teams of constant and time-varying sizes. Autonomous Robots **17**(2-3) (2004) 163–192
114. Lerman, K., Martinoli, A., Galstyan, A.: A review of probabilistic macroscopic models for swarm robotic systems. In Sahin, E., Spears, W., eds.: Swarm Robotics: State-of-the-art Survey. Lecture Notes in Computer Science (LNCS 3342), Berlin Heidelberg, Springer-Verlag (2005) 143–152
115. Soysal, O., Sahin, E.: A macroscopic model for probabilistic aggregation in swarm robotic systems. In Şahin et al., E., ed.: Proc. of SAB06 Workshop on Swarm Robotics. Lecture Notes in Computer Science (LNCS). Springer Verlag (2006)
116. Baillieul, J., Suri, A.: Information patterns and hedging Brockett's theorem in controlling vehicle formations. In: Proc. IEEE Conf. on Decision and Control. (2003) 556–563
117. Arcak, M.: Passivity as a design tool for group coordination. In: Proc. American Control Conf. (2006) 29–34

Communication in a Swarm of Miniature Robots: The e-Puck as an Educational Tool for Swarm Robotics

Christopher M. Cianci, Xavier Raemy, Jim Pugh, and Alcherio Martinoli

Swarm-Intelligent Systems Group
École Polytechnique Fédérale de Lausanne
CH-1015 Lausanne, Switzerland
{chris.cianci,xavier.raemy,jim.pugh,alcherio.martinoli}@epfl.ch

Abstract. Swarm intelligence, and swarm robotics in particular, are reaching a point where leveraging the potential of communication within an artificial system promises to uncover new and varied directions for interesting research without compromising the key properties of swarm-intelligent systems such as self-organization, scalability, and robustness. However, the physical constraints of using radios in a robotic swarm are hardly obvious, and the intuitive models often used for describing such systems do not always capture them with adequate accuracy. In order to demonstrate this effectively in the classroom, certain tools can be used, including simulation and real robots. Most instructors currently focus on simulation, as it requires significantly less investment of time, money, and maintenance—but to really understand the differences between simulation and reality, it is also necessary to work with the real platforms from time to time. To our knowledge, our course may be the only one in the world where individual students are consistently afforded the opportunity to work with a networked multi-robot system on a tabletop. The e-Puck,[1] a low-cost small-scale mobile robotic platform designed for educational use, allows us bringing real robotic hardware into the classroom in numbers sufficient to demonstrate and teach swarm-robotic concepts. We present here a custom module for local radio communication as a stackable extension board for the e-Puck, enabling information exchange between robots and also with any other IEEE 802.15.4-compatible devices. Transmission power can be modified in software to yield effective communication ranges as small as fifteen centimeters. This intentionally small range allows us to demonstrate interesting collective behavior based on *local* information and control in a limited amount of physical space, where ordinary radios would typically result in a completely connected network. Here we show the use of this module facilitating a collective decision among a group of 10 robots.

1 Introduction

One of the aspects of swarm intelligence that makes it so exciting is that it involves an entirely different approach to problem solving than is intuitive to

---

[1] http://www.e-puck.org/

E. Şahin et al. (Eds.): Swarm Robotics Ws, LNCS 4433, pp. 103–115, 2007.

most people [4]. Therefore, the fact that many students may not be accustomed to these different types of thinking and analysis should come as no surprise. The challenge to us is to provide them with the tools, materials, and guidance necessary to help them understand the principles of swarm intelligence and how they can be applied to an embedded real-time system such as a multi-robot swarm or a sensor network.

Our course, "Swarm Intelligence,"[2] includes weekly laboratory exercises (Figure 1) in which the students themselves use a combination of real robots and simulations to test and verify the topics and theories presented in lecture; this also allows them the opportunity to explore other possibilities that might not have been previously discussed. In doing so, the students are better able to assimilate theoretical concepts and understand the difficulties of implementing them. This also helps them understand the differences between various types of implementation levels; for example realistic simulation and real experiments.

Unfortunately, it seems that courses of this kind are rare; indeed, in the area of swarm intelligence, ours is the only one we know of to date. This is likely due in large part to the overhead of acquiring and maintaining enough hardware to provide individual students with a sufficient amount of direct contact with the equipment. Size is also a major concern specific to multi-robot systems, as it is necessary to simultaneously have several robots on a desk or tabletop. Simulation is occasionally used in courses as a substitute for real systems, but we find this to be a shame as well, since the two are not interchangeable, but rather complementary.

 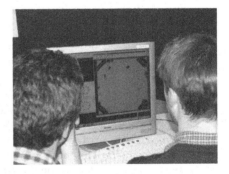

Fig. 1. Students using real and simulated e-Pucks during a laboratory exercise for the course "Swarm Intelligence" at EPFL, Fall 2005

2   Tools and Methods for Swarm Robotics

Certain tools can be extremely effective in helping one understand the principles behind swarm robotics; chief among them are naturally real robots and

---

[2] http://swis.epfl.ch/teaching/

simulations. However, we must respect the fact that they serve different, complementary purposes, and it is often precisely the interaction between them which can give us the greatest insight into the dynamics and subtle details of a system.

2.1   The e-Puck: An Educational Robot

A recent collaboration between the Autonomous Systems Laboratory (ASL),[3] the Swarm-Intelligent Systems group (SWIS),[4] and the Laboratory of Intelligent Systems (LIS)[5] at the École Polytechnique Fédérale de Lausanne (EPFL) has resulted in the creation of a new small-scale robotic platform for educational purposes. Central to the design of the core robot were Francesco Mondada and Michael Bonani (ASL), with some additional contributions to the base module from Xavier Raemy (SWIS), who also designed the radio communication board.

Fig. 2. The e-Puck: a small-scale robotic platform for education. Shown here with the radio communication board stacked between the basic module and the jumper board.

The e-Puck (Figure 2) was developed with five principle objectives in mind, for making it a high-quality teaching tool:

1. simple and sturdy electro-mechanical architecture
2. flexibility and variety in sensors, processing power, and extensions
3. minimum-hassle connectivity and usability
4. robustness sufficient to withstand use by students, and simple maintenance/ repair procedures
5. sufficiently inexpensive that large numbers can be obtained so as to allow individual students direct contact with the equipment

---

[3] http://asl.epfl.ch/
[4] http://swis.epfl.ch/
[5] http://lis.epfl.ch/

As a part of point 3, the e-Puck design includes several features which make it very well suited to multi-robot experimentation. There are no cables (programming or remote control with a computer is done via Bluetooth) and the battery is interchangeable (reducing downtime due to charging); these were the two principle drawbacks of the Khepera [17], the only previous robotic platform we know of with similar capabilities in a package this small, so as to allow the operation of at least three robots together on a portion of a desktop (the minimal number necessary for observing interesting collective effects).

Additionally, in the interest of education and knowledge sharing, the e-Puck is based on an "open source hardware"[6] model, whereby all documentation relating to it may be freely distributed under a license allowing anyone to use it and develop for it.

In December of 2005, 400 units were produced for use in various courses at EPFL and elsewhere, several of which were already underway during the academic year 2005-2006.

2.2   The Webots™ Simulation Environment

As mentioned above, simulation also has its place; it allows us to run experiments with many more robots (at a constant price, without having to buy and maintain hundreds of real robots) and greatly increases the speed and thoroughness with which theories can be tested. For much of our realistic simulation work, we run experiments in Webots, an embodied robotic simulation environment produced by Cyberbotics Ltd. [16].

 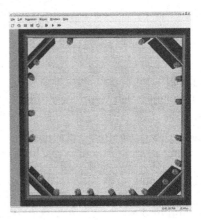

Fig. 3. (left) A simulated model of the e-Puck in Webots, and (right) a simulation of 20 e-Pucks in a setup similar to the collective decision experiment described in Section 5

Through a recent collaboration with Cyberbotics, we have established a preliminary framework for the integration of the open source network simulation

---

[6] http://www.e-puck.org/ → Project → License

engine OMNeT++ [20] into Webots as a modular plug-in to allow realistic modeling of radio communication channels between simulated robots (specifically utilizing a component we implemented containing the subset of the IEEE 802.15.4 and ZigBee protocols present in our physical modules for the robots, but the existing IEEE 802.11 components or any others written for use in OMNeT++ may be used as well). This work (and the related necessary verification) is on-going, and therefore is not yet ready to be presented in detail here.

2.3   Correspondence Between Reality and Simulation

One of the most important points that we try to teach our students is that simulation is a necessarily simplified representation of a system, but depending on the specifics of the system being considered, certain simplifications may be acceptable or even desirable. For example, if the simplified simulated model still produces results faithful to the behavior of the real system, one can say with reasonable confidence that the neglected parameters have little if any influence on the behavior being studied.

Used in this way, simulation then becomes a tool; one which can be extremely powerful when used properly in concert with real systems. Once we are confident that the simulation results accurately and precisely reproduce the outcomes of analogous experiments with real hardware, exploring the parameter space can be significantly easier and faster than performing similar experiments in reality. Finding this trade-off between realism and speed again requires careful consideration of the specific situation at hand to determine how much (or how little) realism is really necessary to achieve the desired results.

Taking this logic one step further, we can actually formalize the varying degrees of complexity possible; ranging from realistic simulation to mathematical macroscopic models [15]. Further details and examples of this multi-level approach can be found in [9,2].

3   Communication and Swarm Intelligence

Much of the previous work in swarm intelligence and swarm robotics has focused on so-called 'biologically inspired' mechanisms (some early definitions actually *limited* the definition of swarm intelligence to "algorithms or distributed problem-solving devices inspired by the collective behavior of social insect colonies and other animal societies." [5]). Consistent with this definition, [5] goes on to define self-organization and stigmergy as key mechanisms required in a swarm-intelligent system.

Stigmergy, or indirect communication via the environment, works well for insects, which are particularly adept in the area of mobility, but it seems clear that it is not always the most ideal communication channel for sharing information (it is typically slow, short range, untargetted, etc). Nonetheless, it has been used with some success in various robotic tasks (for example, [1]).

Self-organization is generally accepted to consist of four principle components:

Positive feedback: amplification, notably recruitment and reinforcement.

Negative feedback: the checks and balances for positive feedback mechanisms, i.e. saturation, exhaustion, and competition.

Randomness: unpredictability can be crucial for the explorative element of a self-organized system; the robustness often exhibited is a direct result of the sometimes seemingly inefficient behavior caused by reactions to noise in the environment.

Multiple interactions: for self-organization to occur, there must be at least a minimum number of mutually tolerant agents able to react to the presence or actions of the others.

While the application of these principles to multi-agent systems is relatively straightforward (take ACO [10], for instance), when we want to apply swarm-intelligent principles to embedded platforms we need to understand the differences between natural and artificial systems, and subsequently exploit the strengths that may be present in an artificial system, to minimize the impact of accompanying weaknesses. This represents a fundamental shift 'beyond bio-mimicry' [14], and one of the most obvious areas where this may be leveraged is with respect to communication. Though the caveat clearly remains that however we choose to utilize the radio channel (or any other addition to a swarm system), we must ensure that it does not affect the scalability of the system.

Direct, in this case radio, communication is simply a more sophisticated medium for achieving "multiple interactions." While one could argue that the inherent unreliability of communication vectors in natural systems is a large part of what forces the system to exhibit the robustness that swarm algorithms are renowned for, we believe that even using radio communication (which is not always reliable either), there remains sufficient noise in coordination and other parts of the system to provoke a collective response showing the appropriate balance of explorative and exploitative behavior for mitigating environmental unpredictability.

Without interference (be it physical or communication), the effects shown in [18] would not be possible; there would be no semblance of intelligent behavior emerging from the system. Despite the use of a decidedly non-natural element, such as radio communication, the swarm-intelligent nature of the resultant collective behavior is still utterly dependent on environmental uncertainty, noise, and self-organized coordination based on local interactions.

4   A Radio Communication Module for the e-Puck

To turn the e-Puck into a networked robotic system suitable for running experiments requiring local communication, we constructed a radio board (as shown in Figure 4.a) with the requirements that it be low power, as the e-Pucks run on batteries, and that it operate on standardized protocols, so as to be interoperable with our other existing robotic and sensor network platforms running TinyOS [12].

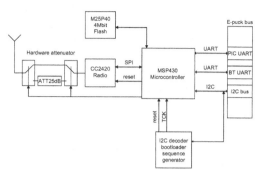

Fig. 4. (left) A stackable module for the e-Puck enabling local radio communication, and (right) a block diagram showing the principal components and functions of the same

4.1   Hardware Design and Structure of the Module

Figure 4.b includes a block diagram illustrating the basic structure of the radio board, which is based on a modified version of the Telos (rev. B) [19] schematics provided by MoteIV. The processor is a Texas Instruments MSP430F169 with 2kB of SRAM and 60kB of flash memory (program storage), selected for its attractive energy consumption profile and the existence of a functional TinyOS port to its architecture. The physical radio is a Chipcon CC2420, an IEEE 802.15.4 and ZigBee compliant transceiver, which allows us to take advantage of the partial implementation of the IEEE 802.15.4 and ZigBee extensions already present in TinyOS. This makes hybrid communication between this radio module and any of our other platforms trivial (we have previously constructed a similar module for the Alice [8,6], and also use a sensor network composed of MICAz [11] nodes). A software selectable custom attenuation circuit is added between the transceiver and the SMD antenna (Antenna Factor ANT-2.45-CHP), for range reduction (note that this affects both reception and transmission).

4.2   Software Control of the Radio Board

A firmware controller based on TinyOS was prepared to allow the module to act in accordance with high-level commands issued to it by the e-Puck via the I^2C bus. Appropriate primitives were then written and integrated into the e-Puck API for the sending and receiving of messages, as well as the modification of control parameters (such as the transmission power, etc).

   Existing modules were used wherever possible (i.e. `GenericBase`), and all of the necessary parameters were encapsulated to allow runtime modification from the e-Puck. However, as the implementation of the I^2C protocol [13] within the current distributed version of TinyOS only supports operating as a bus master, the slave layer had to be written and integrated so that the module could be properly accessed by the e-Puck. At present, since the radio functions as a slave, polling is necessary for message reception, but in the future, if a full implementation of the multi-master mode (as provided for in the I^2C specification) can be integrated into TinyOS, interrupts will be able to pass in both directions, easing the computational burden on the e-Puck and making control simpler and more intuitive.

4.3 Measurement of Physical Characteristics

A number of tests have been run for ascertaining the performance and limits of the device. Preliminary measurements of power consumption indicate that when not in use, the module draws less than 1.4mW, and with the radio on (ready to receive) and the processor under heavy load, approximately 76.2mW.

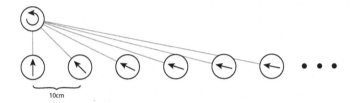

Fig. 5. Physical arrangement of robots for the range tests. Sixteen receivers are placed in a line at known distances from a transmitter, which is rotating to average out irregularities based on orientation.

The output transmission power of the CC2420 is specified by an integer register value between 3 and 31, minimum and maximum, respectively (these numbers are an artifact of the radio hardware; see the CC2420 datasheet [7] for more information). For measuring the effective transmission range at various power settings, 17 robots (1 emitter and 16 receivers each oriented towards the emitter) were arranged as shown in Figure 5. During each iteration, the emitter would spin in place (so as to average out any possible anomalous effects of orientation) while transmitting 250 packets. Each of the receivers would then count the number of packets received, yielding a reception rate at each receiver location (Figure 6.a), the collection of which was then fed into a sigmoidal regression to determine an approximate probability density function of distance (Figure 6.b). Fifteen such iterations were performed per experiment, one for each of the odd numbered transmission power settings in the set of allowed values (3–31). This experiment was repeated three times; with the hardware attenuator active on the sender, the receivers, and on both the sender and the receivers. Only the results from the symmetric case (both the sender and the receiver using the -25dB attenuator) are shown here, as it would not be possible to implement the case study presented in Section 5 with an asymmetric attenuator configuration.

Next, based on these results, three representative transmission power settings were selected (3, 7, and 31), and a more detailed test was performed, the results of which are shown for the value 7 in Figure 7 (the results of the remaining two

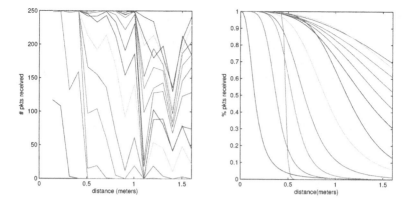

Fig. 6. (left) Raw received packet counts at each location for 15 different transmission powers, and (right) sigmoidal regression representing an approximate PDF. The apparent variance in sensitivity between nodes prompted the subsequent more specific tests, as illustrated in Figure 7.

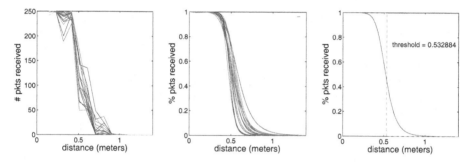

Fig. 7. (left) Raw received packet counts at each location at transmission power 7 for 16 different receiver orderings, (center) sigmoidal regressions for each of the 16 iterations, and (right) aggregate regression on all 256 data points, with corresponding Heaviside approximation (equal area under curve)

experiments are extremely similar in form to those shown, and therefore will be quoted numerically only).

Sixteen iterations were run using the same transmission power, but with each receiver eventually occupying every possible receiver location, to remove anomalous contributions from manufacturing heterogeneities in the hardware (which, as can be seen in Figure 7.a, are present, but do not shift the basic shape of the curve). The corresponding regressions were calculated (Figure 7.b), and all 256 data points were used to create a master regression, shown in Figure 7.c with its Heaviside approximation around the definite integral (from 0 to ∞), which can be used in geometric modeling as an estimated radius of communication.

For the three values tested in this manner, the associated approximate radii are 0.150987, 0.532884, and 4.84131 meters, respectively.

5   Case Study: Collective Decision

One of the most basic examples of swarm intelligence is the emergence of a consensus, or collective choice, in a distributed system. This fundamental question has recently been highlighted in the context of the European project LEURRE,[7] among others [3].

5.1   Experimental Setup

For testing our module in an experimental application, we have set up a simple environment in which independent robots, using only the local information available to them, interact in such a way as to exhibit convergence to a self-organized collective decision.

In a round arena approximately 1 meter in diameter, the robots each initially select at random to execute either left or right wall following, and periodically announce their current preference over the radio. Upon reception of one or more such messages, if the perceived majority opinion is not the same as the robot's current opinion, it makes a probabilistic decision to possibly change its current direction. This behavior will eventually cause the system to converge to a state where all the robots are traveling in the same direction (Figure 8.a). And as one might naturally imagine, given that the decisions to switch directions are based on partial perception, the time required for reaching convergence will depend on the accuracy with which the local perception reflects the global state of the system. Here, that translates directly to the range of communication.

Note that this setup displays all the habitual signatures of a self-organized system: multi-stability (system may converge to either left or right wall following), positive feedback (the number of neighbors influences the probability of being convinced to change direction), negative feedback (there are a limited number of robots; resource exhaustion), randomness (non-deterministic decisions, formation of local subgroups due to partial perception), and multiple interactions (radio messages and physical detection/avoidance/following).

5.2   Results

Sixteen experiments were run for each of three transmission powers: 3, 7, and 31 (48 runs in total). A nearby MICAz node acted as an eavesdropper (with its antenna, it was able to reliably overhear even the minimum power messages from the robots, so long as it was near the arena), and counted the time between the start signal and when all received messages from the robots indicated that they were traveling in the same direction. The mean and standard deviation of these completion times are shown in Figure 8. At first glance, the deviation may seem a little large, but is likely due to the random nature of the initial conditions and the interactions between the agents.

---

[7] http://leurre.ulb.ac.be/

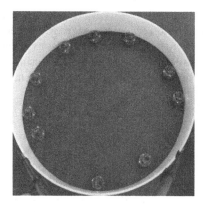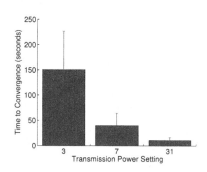

Fig. 8. (left) Overhead view of ten e-Puck robots after convergence to left wall-following, and (right) mean and standard deviation of convergence times for 48 experimental runs (16 each power)

5.3   Related Hybrid Network Example: Isolated Collective Decision

A similar setup which we presented to the students in a course laboratory exercise[8] involved a hybrid network, as pictured in Figure 9; each robot was isolated in its own miniature arena (still executing left or right wall following), but in one corner of its arena, it would be close enough to a fixed node in a sensor network

Fig. 9. Alternative setup to Figure 8: a hybrid network wherein isolated robots communicate via a sensor network backchannel

---

[8] http://swis.epfl.ch/teaching/swarm_intelligence/ay_2005-06/exercises/SI_05-06_labhwk10_assignment.pdf

which could act as a relay tower. Therefore, during a short section of its trip around the track, it had the opportunity to send and receive messages with other robots (which were also be close enough to their respective sensor nodes) via the 'backbone network' provided by the sensor nodes. While systematic testing is not shown here, this system also yielded convergence to a collective decision, in a network of 15 robot/node pairs.

6   Conclusion

Teaching and research activities in swarm intelligence and swarm robotics require tools; among these, we have found that simulation and physical hardware are both beneficial and mutually complementary in an educational setting. For reasons of accessibility (equally from the perspectives of cost, pedagogy, and usability), the e-Puck platform, particularly when equipped with our local communication module (range adjustable between about 15cm and 4.8m), promises to serve as a powerful addition to the toolset in this context. In the example scenario demonstrated here, collective decision occurs in groups of up to fifteen robots.

Acknowledgments

The authors are currently sponsored by a grant from the Swiss National Science Foundation (Contract Nr. PP002-68647). Additionally, portions of the works described received partial funding from the Fond d'Innovation pour la Formation (FIFO) and the School of Computer and Communication Sciences, both at EPFL. We would like to thank especially Francesco Mondada and Michael Bonani, ultimately responsible for the design and creation of the e-Puck, and also Olivier Michel, Yvan Bourquin, and Alexei Kounine, without whose assistance the modification and integration of the realistic network simulation engine OMNeT++ into Webots^{TM}would not have been possible. Inspiration for the experimental case study was initially seeded during an informal discussion between Alcherio Martinoli and Guy Theraulaz.

References

1. W. Agassounon and A. Martinoli. Efficiency and robustness of threshold-based distributed allocation algorithms in multi-agent systems. In *Proc. of the Int. Conf. on Autonomous Agents and Multi-Agent Systems (AAMAS)*, pages 1090–1097, Bologna, Italy, 2002. ACM Press.
2. W. Agassounon, A. Martinoli, and K. Easton. Macroscopic modeling of aggregation experiments using embodied agents in teams of constant and time-varying sizes. *Autonomous Robots*, 17(2–3):163–191, 2004.
3. J. M. Amé, J. Millor, J. Halloy, and J.-L. Deneubourg. Collective decision-making based on individual discrimination capability in pre-social insects. In *Proc. Simulation of Artificial Behaviour*, pages 700–711. Springer Verlag, Berlin, 2006.

4. G. Beni. From swarm intelligence to swarm robotics. In *Proc. of the SAB 2004 Workshop on Swarm Robotics, Santa Monica, CA, USA, July, 2004*, volume 3342, pages 1–9, 2005.
5. E. Bonabeau, M. Dorigo, and G. Theraulaz. *Swarm Intelligence: From Natural to Artificial Systems*. SFI Studies in the Science of Complexity, Oxford University Press, New York, NY, USA, 1999.
6. G. Caprari and R. Siegwart. Mobile micro-robots ready to use: Alice. In *Proc. of the IEEE/RSJ Int. Conf. on Intelligent Robots and Systems (IROS)*, pages 3295–3300, Canada, 2005.
7. CC2420: 2.4 GHz IEEE 802.15.4 / ZigBee-ready RF Transceiver, Chipcon Products from Texas Instruments. *http://www.chipcon.com/*, 2005.
8. N. Correll and A. Martinoli. Comparing coordination schemes for miniature robotic swarms: A case study in boundary coverage of regular structures. In *Proc. of the Int. Symp. on Experimental Robotics (ISER)*, Rio de Janeiro, Brazil, 2006. Springer Tracts for Advanced Robotics (STAR), to appear.
9. N. Correll and A. Martinoli. Modeling and optimization of a swarm-intelligent inspection system. In *Proc. of the Int. Symp. on Distributed Autonomous Robotic Systems (DARS)*, pages 369–378. Springer Distributed Autonomous Systems VI, 2006.
10. M. Dorigo and G. D. Caro. The ant colony optimization meta-heuristic. *New Ideas in Optimization*, pages 11–32, 1999.
11. J. Hill and D. Culler. Mica: A wireless platform for deeply embedded networks. *IEEE Micro*, 22(6):12–24, 2002.
12. J. Hill, R. Szewczyk, A. Woo, S. Hollar, D. Culler, and K. Pister. System architecture directions for network sensors. In *Architectural Support for Programming Languages and Operating Systems (ASPLOS)*, 2000.
13. The I2C-bus specification, version 2.1, Philips Electronics N.V. *http://www.semiconductors.philips.com/products/interface_control/i2c/index.html*, 2000.
14. IEEE Swarm Intelligence Symposium, Call for papers. *http://www.ieeeswarm.org/*, 2005.
15. A. Martinoli, K. Easton, and W. Agassounon. Modeling of swarm robotic systems: A case study in collaborative distributed manipulation. *Int. Journal of Robotics Research*, 23(4):415–436, 2004.
16. O. Michel. Webots: Professional mobile robot simulation. *Journal of Advanced Robotic Systems*, 1(1):39–42, 2004.
17. F. Mondada, E. Franzi, and P. Ienne. Mobile robot miniaturization: a tool for investication in control algorithms. In *Proc. of the Int. Symp. on Experimental Robotics (ISER)*, pages 501–513. Springer Verlag, Berlin, 1993.
18. J. Nembrini, A. Winfield, and C. Melhuish. Minimalist coherent swarming of wireless connected autonomous mobile robots. In *Proc. Simulation of Artificial Behaviour (SAB)*, pages 273–382, Edinburgh, 2002.
19. J. Polastre, R. Szewczyk, and D. Culler. Telos: Enabling ultra-low power wireless research. In *IEEE/ACM Int. Conf. on Information Processing in Sensor Networks (IPSN-SPOTS)*, 2005.
20. A. Varga. Software tools for networking: "OMNeT++". *IEEE Network Interactive*, 16(4), 2002.

UltraSwarm: A Further Step Towards a Flock of Miniature Helicopters

Renzo De Nardi and Owen Holland

Department of Computer Science
University of Essex
Colchester CO43SQ, United Kingdom
{rdenar, owen}@essex.ac.uk

Abstract. We describe further progress towards the development of a MAV (micro aerial vehicle) designed as an enabling tool to investigate aerial flocking. Our research focuses on the use of low cost off the shelf vehicles and sensors to enable fast prototyping and to reduce development costs. Details on the design of the embedded electronics and the modification of the chosen toy helicopter are presented, and the technique used for state estimation is described. The fusion of inertial data through an unscented Kalman filter is used to estimate the helicopter's state, and this forms the main input to the control system. Since no detailed dynamic model of the helicopter in use is available, a method is proposed for automated system identification, and for subsequent controller design based on artificial evolution. Preliminary results obtained with a dynamic simulator of a helicopter are reported, along with some encouraging results for tackling the problem of flocking.

1 Introduction

Swarm robotics is nowadays an established field of research; it offers the advantages of scalability, robustness through redundancy, flexibility, and reduced complexity of the individual robots. Within swarm intelligence, the topic of flocking deals with methods for controlling the motion of a group of agents (in real or virtual space) using rules directly inspired by ethological observations of real flocks of birds or schools of fish.

Since the seminal treatment of flocking developed by Reynolds [1] several researchers have explored the idea of flocking in real platforms or simulations. Most of the work involving flocking in real robots has concentrated on wheeled robots [2] [3] or airborne robots with limited dynamic capabilities [4]; due to the intrinsic dynamic and sensory limitations of the platforms used, none of these examples achieved really good-looking fluid flocking. Crowther addressed the problem of vehicles with more complex dynamics in his simulations of a flock of aircraft [5]. His research successfully demonstrated the potential usability of flocking as a decentralised traffic control method. In particular it showed that by simply changing the weights associated with Reynolds' rules, phase transitions appeared in the flock structure. However, omnidirectional perception was

E. Şahin et al. (Eds.): Swarm Robotics Ws, LNCS 4433, pp. 116–128, 2007.

assumed, and the presence of noise was neglected. Recently a development program carried out at the NASA Dryden Flight Research Center [6] demonstrated the coordination of two UAVs (in the form of two instrumented model aircraft) using Reynolds' flocking rules. GPS information was used to determine the relative positions of the aircraft, and this was sufficient to guarantee coordination. Unfortunately further details about this project are still unavailable. Another interesting application was developed by Atair Aerospace Inc. [7] in the domain of guided parafoils; a behaviour based algorithm inspired by flocking is used to ensure that all the payload-carrying parafoils will land together in the same area.

In the last few years, the problems of flocking and the distributed control of agents have gained popularity among the control system community [8][9][10]. The problems of stability, robustness, and the effects of sensing or communication delays are now being considered; see [11] for a more extensive review in the field. In a recent paper [12], Olfati Saber presents a theoretical approach to flocking; a single distance dependent potential function is defined to achieve both cohesion and separation. A particularly good definition of the potential function results in a smooth pairwise potential with a finite cut off that greatly simplifies the stability analysis. Since cohesion-separation and alignment can lead to fragmentation, an additional contribution to the control is added in the form of navigational feedback from progress towards a target point. The paper also presents an obstacle avoidance behaviour obtained by introducing fictitious agents near the obstacles.

Although the work of Olfati Saber addresses the problem of flocking using a simple point mass agent with double integrator dynamics, the results are supported by a sound theoretical analysis. It will be interesting to see if the same analysis can be extended to more dynamically complex vehicles. It is of course clear that extending this idea to highly nonlinear vehicles (e.g. helicopters) will constitute a big challenge in this respect. SamiloğluGazi et al. [13] give an example of how a simple physical constraint like a restriction on the turn angle may lead to oscillatory behaviours in the group.

2   The Idea

As we have clearly seen in the introduction, achieving the flocking or swarming of real vehicles with complex dynamics is still an unsolved problem. Our work addresses many of the issues involved in this area: we aim to build a flock of dynamically complex vehicles (i.e. microhelicopters) to perform flocking in a real world scenario where the dynamics of the vehicles and the noisy outputs of the sensors are not negligible. The use of an aerial robotic platform removes the two dimensional limitation to which most of the previous research has been constrained, allowing for a scenario more similar to the one normally experienced by fish or birds.

In order to reduce development time and research costs, we aim to leverage as much as possible of the technology available in the market place - in other words, to take a COTS (commercial-off-the-shelf) approach. This translates into selecting a suitable commercially available vehicle (see section 3) and fitting it with the necessary off-the-shelf components; however, some hardware will inevitably have to be designed (see section 3.1).

These helicopters are of course structurally identical, but differences in the electric motors, the trim of the blades and the swashplate mechanism, and deformation of the very flexible foam blades will result in quantitatively different dynamic properties. The design of our controller should take this variability into account, together with the changes that will be induced by different sensor instrumentations of the same helicopter. These considerations mean that it will be more appropriate to develop a general method for automated model identification and controller design that can then be applied to different individual helicopters with different dynamics. A method based on machine learning techniques and artificial evolution is proposed in 4.

3   The Helicopter Platform

The ability to move in three dimensions is deemed to be an essential requirement of our system, as well as the need to be usable indoors (for ease of development). Only a few platforms can fulfil those two constraints: lighter than air vehicles (e.g. small blimps), and miniature helicopters. Small aircraft and slowflyers are clearly not an option, since our research arena (a cylinder of 12m diameter and 6m height) is too small to accommodate a flock of them. The more favourable size to payload ratio when compared to blimps led us to settle for a rotary wing solution.

Every roboticist and aircraft model enthusiast knows that the lift and hovering capability typical of a helicopter come at the cost of reduced dynamic stability. The helicopter flight controller is therefore a key element of our system. After evaluating several other models, a helicopter with a counter rotating dual rotor configuration was chosen for this study [14] (see figure 1). The counter rotating

Fig. 1. Helicopter retrofitted with the new electronics, the Gumstix computer and the IMU

configuration is well known for delivering high efficiency as well as achieving excellent stability thanks to the direct compensation of the torque between the two rotors. The model we have selected uses a conventional fully controlled lower rotor, and an upper rotor fitted with a 45 degree stabilising bar. The stabilising bar exploits gyroscopic forces in order to counteract sudden changes in shaft inclination. This results in improved stability, but of course this comes at the cost of a reduced response to control commands. Testing by human pilots showed the model to be more stable and easier to fly than conventional single rotor helicopters; although not suitable for advanced aerobatic manoeuvres, the helicopter retains the manoeuvrability necessary to perform flocking.

Testing also established that the model can be flown with a payload of about 40g for about 15 minutes; we deem this sufficient to achieve the project's aims.

3.1   Electronics and Sensors

Since the helicopter is sold as a remotely controlled toy, the first step towards autonomy involved the complete redesign and replacement of the helicopter's electronics.

The bulk of the work on the platform involved the design and manufacture of an electronic board that interfaces a Gumstix SBC (single board computer) to the two main electric motors powering the rotors, and to the servos controlling the swashplate. The board was manufactured in surface mount technology, and is based around a low power 40 MHz ARM7 microcontroller. The microcontroller offers two serial ports for reflashing and for communication with the Gumstix, two i2c ports to interface to the ultrasonic sensors and the IMU (inertial measurement unit), and four PWM outputs to drive motors and servos. External interrupt inputs are also available to interface to two rotor speed encoders; an additional analogue input permits us to monitor the battery voltage. A second companion electronic board accommodates the power stabilisation circuitry and the highly efficient MOSFET motor drivers. The two electronic boards were specifically designed to fit within the original central housing of the helicopter in order to maintain all the moments of inertia as close as possible to those of the original helicopter.

The choice of having an additional low level microcontroller that directly interacts with the hardware was made to guarantee a high degree of reliability for the control system. The absence of an operating system allows a tighter coupling with the hardware, offering real-time execution of the critical code needed for helicopter stabilisation. The processing power of the Gumstix SBC will be entirely dedicated to the high level software (e.g. guidance and communication), where the use of the Linux operating system will allow for easy and fast development. Along with the electronics, a set of low level routines has been developed to allow the microcontroller to interact with the hardware and enable communication with the Gumstix SBC. Thanks to the Bluetooth wireless communication present on the Gumstix we are now at a stage in which it is possible to command all the helicopter flight controls from a remote computer. A simple yaw stabilization based on the IMU gyros has been implemented to aid during manual flight; being able to fly the helicopter manually by exploiting the Bluetooth connection is obviously important to test the helicopter hardware, but will be crucial during the process of data collection for modelling purposes. Previous work of the authors [15] with a similar helicopter and electronics showed how the delay introduced by the Bluetooth connection still allows for the full control of the flight machine. In the final system the communication delay will not be an issue since the control algorithm will run on board.

Ultrasonic sensors and an IMU are the crucial sensors for the control and stabilisation of the vehicle; however, for flocking, each helicopter also needs to determine the range and bearing of its nearby flockmates. Fortunately our indoor arena will shortly be provided with a state of the art 3D tracking system based on infrared markers that will be able to determine with great accuracy (i.e. to within a few millimetres) the position of each helicopter. The relative positions computed by a stationary computer can then be fed back to each of the helicopters through the wireless data link. This will enable us to test the basic flocking algorithm. Further research will investigate the direct sensing of relative position using RSSI (received-signal-strength-indication) from the communication channels, the use of onboard radio beacons, and also onboard vision.

3.2   State Estimation

A key problem is the need for the real-time computation of state estimation. This includes the helicopter's attitude (e.g. the Eulerian angles with reference to an Earth frame ϕ, θ, ψ), its rotational speeds (p, q, r), and its linear velocity and position (u, v, w and x, y, z). Attitudes and rotational speeds are needed for helicopter stabilisation; the position in the form of the relative distances between the members of the flock will be used for regulating flocking.

Given the reduced payload only a very light IMU can be carried on board. We have selected the Memsense nIMU [16] which includes three linear accelerometers, three gyros, and three magnetic field sensors. MEMS (Micro-Electro-Mechanical Systems) technology allows the production of inertial sensors of very compact size and reduced weight (the whole IMU has a weight of only 15g); however, their performance in terms of error and temperature bias tends to be significantly worse than alternative navigation grade solutions using optical methods. The dependency on temperature variation is already compensated within the IMU sensor, but the effects of noise and, more importantly, of the drift that affects gyros and accelerometers must still be compensated to allow sufficiently accurate data to be obtained.

The main inputs used for the state estimation are the measured rotational speed and linear acceleration; both are affected by noise, and by a time-variant bias. The magnetometer readings, the ultrasonic sensor values, and possibly the position obtained from the tracking system will be used to "correct" the inertial data. The magnetometers and ultrasonic sensors are not affected by time variant bias, and so have error characteristics complementary to those of the inertial sensor; the fusion of the two types of sensor data will allow us to improve the state estimation.

The most commonly used techniques for data fusion rely on Bayesian filtering techniques, among which the best known is probably the EKF (extended Kalman filter). Although it has been successfully applied to helicopter state estimation problems ([17] [18]) the EKF has some weaknesses when compared to other similar approaches. Van der Merwe and Wan conducted a comparison analysis between an EKF and a UKF (unscented Kalman filter) The analysis [19] shows that since the sensor model used in the filter is strongly nonlinear (due to the change of coordinates), the UKF can improve the estimation performance. In addition the implementation of the UKF is comparatively much simpler than that of the EKF since the there is no need to calculate the derivatives of the state equations. Given our limited computational power, it will also be interesting to explore the possibility of implementing the UKF in its square root form, [20] which presents improved numerical stability along with reduced computational complexity.

In order to limit the computational complexity, our system model is simply that of a 6DoF rigid body freely moving in a 3D space. Position, speeds, Euler angle and sensor bias constitute the state estimated by the filter. The system equations are represented by the classic equation of motion of a rigid body in a 3D space. The acceleration and rotational speed values coming from the IMU are used as control inputs to the model in order to propagate the system state. Readings from the ultrasonics sensors and the magnetometers constitute the measurements that will allow the correction, through the observation model, of the predicted state in the interactive prediction-correction fashion typical of Bayesian filtering.

The system model includes the update equations necessary to estimate the biases of the accelerometers and gyros, and so it will therefore allow them to be compensated.

4   An Automated Design Method

We already mentioned in section 2 the clear advantages offered by using an automated method to deal with the unknown dynamic differences between the aerial vehicles. Such an automated method will be useful in the future as well, as we plan to move the system outdoors, and therefore to use heavier and more complex helicopters.

Because of its complexity and severe nonlinearity, the understanding of helicopter aerodynamics is still relatively poor, and the direct estimation of model parameters from experimental flight data still remains the only effective way to accurately capture the dynamics of a vehicle with unknown characteristics.

4.1   Model Identification

The most common approach to model identification for small helicopters is simply a specialisation of the classical approach widely used for full scale vehicles.

Such models are based on a knowledge of aerodynamic principles, and the derived equations account for the lift and sideforce generated by the rotors, the effects of drag on the fuselage, the inertia and other effects of the stabilising bar, and the coupling between the major axes of the helicopter. This typically yields a very complicated model expressed in helicopter body coordinates, and with several tens of parameters. From a linearisation of this type of model, a state model can be derived; its free parameters can then be learned from flight data by using data association techniques in the frequency domain. By making provision for the selection of meaningful flight data, and by enabling the possibility of including several equilibrium points in the flight envelope, a sufficiently accurate helicopter model can be produced. Mettler *et al.* [21] and La Civita *et al.* [22] describe two successful applications of this technique.

A general weakness can be attributed to this method; since the model is ultimately linear, effects like inertia and gravity which involve the nonlinear contributions of velocity and angular rate are really hard to capture. To finesse this problem, Abbeel *et al.* [23] proposed an alternative approach to modelling based on acceleration prediction.

Physics tells us that the relationships between effects like inertia, gravity and acceleration are often straightforward, and so it is clear then that a model based on acceleration prediction could possibly be both simple and effective in describing these effects. Such a model will be expressed in acceleration terms, and so, in order to obtain the state vector, we will need to integrate the acceleration contributions at every timestep. Since the accelerations are expressed in body coordinates, and since the body reference frame changes at every timestep, a change of coordinates must be performed at every timestep before proceeding with the computation. Here we see that since the algorithm explicitly takes care of these changes of coordinates, the learning is greatly simplified since this highly nonlinear functional relationship does not need to be learned. (However, the model resulting from the integration of the acceleration prediction is still of course nonlinear).

The general model proposed by Abbeel represents a 6 DoF vehicle and deliberately avoids giving any aerodynamic meaning to the dynamic equations; the only system knowledge introduced is reflected in the choice of body-centred coordinates, and of the axes of symmetry. According to the authors, its generality means that the same model could also be used with minor changes for vehicles very different from a helicopter. Faced with the specific situation of learning a model of the helicopter used in our project, we can therefore see an excellent opportunity for the use of the technique proposed by Abbeel, since only a very limited knowledge of the vehicle is necessary.

It is necessary to point out that this type of model, although potentially very accurate, still has 15 parameters and is fairly computationally expensive. This is not a problem when we are evolving the controller off-line, but unfortunately it prevents us from using it real time in association with our Bayesian filtering algorithm. For this reason the simpler 6DoF model explained in 3.2 is used in the UKF.

4.2   Controller Design

The evolutionary design of controllers based on neural networks has proven to be an effective methodology for designing controllers for simple robotics problems [24], and also for agents in computer games [25] [26]. A controller based on neural networks with specific topologies has also been applied successfully to the domain of helicopter control [27] [28], although in this case the training was based on reinforcement learning. Building on this previous work we have developed a method for training a custom designed neural network using a form of neuroevolution [29].

The controllers (i.e. the neural networks) have a fixed topology and a fixed *tanh* activation function, and so a simple fixed length array of real numbers is sufficient to represent the genome of each of the controllers. A modular topology (see figure 2) inspired by the layout of a multiloop PID controller was chosen since it had been found to greatly improve evolvability .

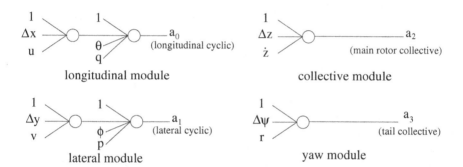

Fig. 2. Modular network used in the waypoint task. The same network topology was also used for the velocity task but the inputs $\Delta x, \Delta y$ ans Δz were substituted respectively by $\Delta u, \Delta v$ ans $\Delta \dot{z}$.

A variation of ES (Evolutionary Strategies), with a total population of 33 individuals and an elite of 10, is used to evolve the weights. The first population consists of neural networks with small random synaptic weights; each controller is then evaluated on the task at hand. This involves using the controller under test to fly the simulated helicopter model and try to achieve the desired task (e.g. flying a set of waypoints, or reaching a specific vectorial speed). Its fitness represents the ability demonstrated by the controller on the specific task used. The population is then sorted by fitness and the worst 23 individuals are replaced with mutated versions of the 10 best individuals (the elite). The algorithm does not apply recombination; the weights of the network are simply mutated by adding a random value (drawn from a Gaussian distribution with mean 0 and standard deviation 0.01). In this way, a new population is created, and the evolutionary process can then be repeated for the next generation.

The possibility of defining different tasks and the different fitness functions associated with them allows us to customise the helicopter controller to our needs. This constitutes a really valuable option, and offers clear advantages when compared to the traditional manual design of the controller.

As noted in section 3.2 our algorithms for state estimation and model identification have not yet been validated; this is due to a manufacturing problem with the IMU sensor that is currently being rectified. In the meantime, a freely available dynamic helicopter simulator with dynamics qualitatively similar to our helicopter [30] was used to test our approach to the evolution of the controller. This simulator accurately reproduces the dynamics of the XCell 60 model helicopter. Blade element theory is used as the basis for the computation of rotor thrust and drag forces, and the main rotor dynamics and stabilising bar are modelled as proposed in Mettler *et al.* [21]. Dynamic coupling and aerodynamics effects are also modelled. The simulator outputs the same state variables as will be available from the Hirobo helicopter, and accepts the same flight control inputs. Although qualitatively similar to the Hirobo in all essential respects, the simulated helicopter is much less stable[1], and so it definitely constitutes a challenging test bench for our design approach.

Two different tasks were devised to test the design method. In the first, the helicopter is commanded to perform a specific flight trajectory; this controller will be useful for testing autonomous flight. In the second, the controller is requested to fly the helicopter with a specific (vectorial) velocity; this controller gives a basis on top of which the classic Reynolds flocking rules could be applied.

In both tasks, there is an initial stage in which the controller is evolved for a few tens of generations using the heading error as the only fitness function. This evolution is very quick, and produces a minimal yaw stabilisation that enables the system to "bootstrap" the subsequent task evolution.

In the first task the controller is required to fly the helicopter along a predefined random generated set of waypoints. The fitness is based on progress along the path so defined; a waypoint was deemed to be visited when the centre of the helicopter approached within 1 foot of it. The waypoints were placed at a mean distance of 17.5 feet from each other. To encourage a straight path between the waypoint the fitness was reduced if the helicopter deviated from the path. Additional penalties were awarded for differences from the correct altitude and heading. The complete fitness function is this:

$$f = \frac{\sum_{i=0}^{N} (w_h P_{chain} \mid z - z_{next} \mid - \mid \psi - \psi_{ref} \mid)}{N}. \tag{1}$$

Where N is the number of timesteps allowed to execute the task (for evolution $N = 1000$ was used) and z_{next}, ψ_{ref} are respectively the altitude of the next waypoint, and the fixed reference heading. The factor w_h is equal to one if the helicopter is on the shortest path between waypoints and decays as the cube of the orthogonal distance from it.

---

[1] One of the authors, who can fly the Hirobo helicopter very competently, has consistently failed to control the simulated model for more than a few seconds of simulated time.

The input to the network are formed by the helicopter attitudes ϕ, θ, ψ, the rotational speeds p, q, r, the linear speeds u, v, w, and the relative distance to the next waypoint $\Delta x, \Delta y, \Delta z$ (both speeds are expressed in the helicopter body reference frame).

A sample of the trajectory flown by the best controller during a test run is shown in figure 3. As we can see, the evolved controller exhibits the ability to fly correctly through the predesigned waypoint chain. Regardless of the relative distance or the position between the waypoints, the path is very smooth.

A second task was devised with the Reynolds flocking rules in mind. At the beginning of the task the helicopter is started in a hovering position, and a randomly generated increment in velocity (expressed in the three helicopter frame of reference components) is requested. Each single velocity increment can have a value in the range $[-3.5 \div 3.5] ft/s$; if the sum of the current velocity and of the increment exceeds $10 ft/s$ a cut-off is applied to guarantee a requested speed consistent with the helicopter's capabilities. Along with the requested change in velocity, the required duration of the change is also specified. This is also a random value in the range $[12 \div 350]$ timesteps. The fitness is simply the squared magnitude of the error between the commanded and the instantaneous helicopter velocity:

$$f = \frac{\sum_{i=0}^{N} \|v(t) - v_c(t)\|_2^2}{N}. \tag{2}$$

Where N is the number of timesteps allowed to execute the task (for evolution $N = 1000$ was used), $v(t)$ is the velocity of the helicopter in the body frame coordinates at time t and $v_c(t)$ is the velocity commanded at the same time instant.

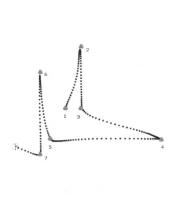

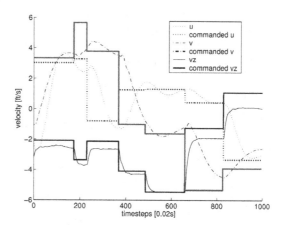

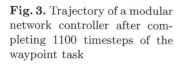

Fig. 3. Trajectory of a modular network controller after completing 1100 timesteps of the waypoint task

Fig. 4. Plot of the commanded speed vs the real helicopter speed for the best controller evolved with the velocity task

The inputs to the network are the helicopter attitudes ϕ, θ, ψ and rotational speeds p, q, r, the linear speeds in the body reference frame u, v, v_z, and the difference between the commanded speeds and the actual speeds $\Delta u, \Delta v, \Delta v_z$.

Sample plots of the difference between the commanded value of the velocity and the actual velocity are displayed in figure 4. It is clear that the helicopter speed varies in accordance with the request; unsurprisingly, a steady state error is present. It is noteworthy that the responses to the input steps do not show any signs of instability, and that a clear coupling between the longitudinal and lateral speeds is present. Future work will add complexity in the network structure to attempt to compensate for the coupling.

In the course of obtaining the results just described, various network topologies and incremental evolution approaches were investigated (for details see [29]). Without incorporating some domain knowledge into the evolutionary process, we were unable to evolve successful controllers. Domain knowledge was introduced in the form of the network topology, which neglects any coupling between the lateral, longitudinal, and vertical axes. Evolving the yaw controller first was also crucial for the evolutionary process, confirming the findings of other researchers about the nature and benefits of incremental evolution.

5 Future Work

In the immediate future we will implement and evaluate the approach of data collection, state estimation, system identification, and controller design on our model helicopter.

The first step will concentrate on the validation of the unscented Kalman filtering approach; the maximum update frequency and also the numerical robustness need to be determined. The performance of the filter algorithm in terms of noise and drift also needs to be tested to ensure that the data will be adequate for control.

Model identification based on recorded flight data will constitute the next step. By its very nature the system identification technique will provide us with a quantitative estimation of the error between the simulated and real trajectory. We expect that the simulator will not be able to predict the trajectory of the real helicopter for more then a short period of time, due to the accumulation of error. However, the dynamic response of the model to the control input, which is what is needed to evolve a controller, will always resemble that of the real helicopter.

Artificial evolution will then be applied to produce controllers tailored to our helicopter. Several controllers chosen from those with good fitness will than be evaluated directly on the real helicopter.

Finally, a controller will be implemented on board the helicopter and the sensor to motor action loop will be closed, allowing us to test autonomous flight.

The work will then proceed with the investigation of strategies for achieving flocking; these will initially be based on the classical rules of cohesion, separation, and velocity matching.

6   Concluding Remarks

The work presented here is clearly still in its early stages, but is following a clear path supported by existing research findings. The results achieved in the simulation and testing carried out so far are encouraging; we recognise however that porting the results obtained in simulation to a real system is very often problematical.

References

1. Reynolds, C.: Flocks, herds, and schools: A distributed behavioral model. In: Proceedings of the Conference on Computer Graphics (SIGGRAPH). Volume 21:4. (1987) 25–34
2. Mataric, M.: Interaction and intelligent behavior. PhD thesis, Massachusetts Institute of Technology, Cambridge, MA, USA (1995)
3. Kelly, I., Keating, D.: Flocking by the fusion of sonar and active infrared sensors on physical autonomous mobile robots. In: Proceedings of The Third Int. Conf. on Mechatronics and Machine Vision in Practice. Volume 1. (1996) 1–4
4. Welsby, J., Melhuish, C.: Autonomous minimalist following in three dimensions: A study with small-scale dirigibles. In: Proceedings of Towards Intelligent Mobile Robots Manchster. (2001)
5. Crowther, B., Riviere, X.: Flocking of autonomous unmanned air vehicles. In: Proceeding of the 17th UAV System conference, Bristol UK. (2002)
6. NASA, D.F.R.C.: New flight software allows UAVs to team up for virtual fire experiment. (http://www.nasa.gov/centers/dryden/news/NewsReleases/2005/05-12.html)
7. Calise, A., Preston, D.: Swarming/flocking and collision avoidance for mass airdrop of autonomous guided parafoils. In: AIAA Guidance, Navigation, and Control Conference and Exhibit. (2005)
8. Jadbabaie, A., Lin, J., Morse, A.: Coordination of groups of mobile autonomous agents using nearest neighbor rules. IEEE Trans. Automatic Control **48** (2003) 998–1001
9. Tanner, H., Jadbabaie, A., Pappas, G.: Stable flocking of mobile agents. part I: Static topology. In: Proceedings of the 42nd IEEE Conference on Decision and Control. (2003) 2010–2015
10. Tanner, H., Jadbabaie, A., Pappas, G.: Stable flocking of mobile agents. part II: Dynamic topology. In: Proceedings of the 42nd IEEE Conference on Decision and Control. (2003) 2016–2021
11. Gazi, V., Fidan, B.: Review of control and coordination of multi-agent dynamic systems: models and approaches. In Sahin, E., Spears, W., Winfield, A., eds.: Swarm Robotics Workshop (SAB06). Lecture Notes in Computer Science (2006)
12. Olfati-Saber, R.: Flocking for multi-agent dynamic systems: Algorithms and theory. IEEE Transaction on Automatic Control **51** (March 2006)
13. Samiloğlu, a., Gazi, V., Koku, B.: An empirical study on the motion of self-propelled particles with turn angle restrictions. In Sahin, E., Spears, W., Winfield, A., eds.: Swarm Robotics Workshop (SAB06). Lecture Notes in Computer Science (2006)
14. Hirobo Limited: XRB Lama helicopter. (http://model.hirobo.co.jp/products/0301-905/index.html)

15. Holland, O.E., Woods, J., De Nardi, R., Clark, A.: Beyond swarm intelligence: The UltraSwarm. In: Proceedings of the IEEE Swarm Intelligence Symposium (SIS2005), IEEE (2005)

16. Memsense: nIMU nano inertial measurement unit. (http://www.memsense.com/content/products/Datasheets/nIMUv1_92.pdf)

17. Jun, M., Roumeliotis, S., G.S., S.: State estimation via sensor modeling for helicopter control using an indirect kalman filter. In: IEEE/RSJ International Conference on Intelligent Robots and Systems. (1999)

18. Gavrilets, V.: Autonomous Aerobatic Manouvering of Miniature. PhD thesis, Massachusetts Institute of Technology (2003)

19. van der Merwe, R., Wan, E.A.: Sigma-point kalman filters for integrated navigation. In: 60th Annual Meeting of The Institute of Navigation (ION). (2004)

20. van der Merwe, R., Wan, E.A.: The square-root unscented kalman filter for state and parameter-estimation. In: International Conference on Acoustics, Speech, and Signal Processing. (2001)

21. Mettler, B., Tischler, M., Kanade, T.: System identification of a model-scale helicopter. Technical Report CMU-RI-TR-00-03, Robotics Institute, Carnegie Mellon University, Pittsburgh, PA (2000)

22. La Civita, M., Messner, W.C., Kanade, T.: Modeling of small-scale helicopters with integrated first-principles and system-identification techniques. In: American helicopter society 58th annual forum. (2002)

23. Abbeel, P., Ganapathi, V., Ng, A.Y.: Modeling vehicular dynamics, with application to modeling helicopters. In: Neural Information Processing Systems. (2005)

24. Nolfi, S., Floreano, D.: Evolutionary robotics. MIT Press, Cambridge, MA (2000)

25. Togelius, J., Lucas, S.M.: Evolving controllers for simulated car racing. In: Proceedings of the Congress on Evolutionary Computation. (2005)

26. Togelius, J., Lucas, S.M.: Forcing neurocontrollers to exploit sensory symmetry through hard-wired modularity in the game of cellz. In: Proceedings of the IEEE 2005 Symposium on Computational Intelligence and Games CIG05. (2005) 37–43

27. Ng, A., Kim, H., Jordan, M., Sastry, S., Ballianda, S.: Autonomous helicopter flight via reinforcement learning. Advances in Neural Information Processing Systems (2004)

28. Ng, A., Coates, A., Diel, M., Ganapathi, V., Schulte, J., Tse, B., Berger, E., Liang, E.: Autonomous inverted helicopter flight via reinforcement learning. In: Proceedings of the International Symposium on Experimental Robotics. (2004)

29. De Nardi, R., Togelius, J., Holland, O., Lucas, S.: Neural networks for helicopter control: Why modularity matters. In: IEEE Congress on Evolutionary Computation. (2006)

30. Autopilot: Do it yourself UAV. (http://autopilot.sourceforge.net)

Where Are You?

William M. Spears, Jerry C. Hamann, Paul M. Maxim, Thomas Kunkel,
Rodney Heil, Dimitri Zarzhitsky, Diana F. Spears, and Christer Karlsson*

Computer Science Department,
University of Wyoming, Laramie, WY, 82070, USA
wspears@cs.uwyo.edu
http://www.cs.uwyo.edu/~wspears

Abstract. The ability of robots to quickly and accurately localize their
neighbors is extremely important in swarm robotics. Prior approaches
generally rely either on global information provided by GPS, beacons,
and landmarks, or complex local information provided by vision systems.
In this paper we provide a new technique, based on trilateration. This
system is fully distributed, inexpensive, scalable, and robust. In addition,
the system provides a unified framework that merges localization with
information exchange between robots. The usefulness of this framework
is illustrated on a number of applications.

1 Goal of Our Work

Our goal is to create a new "enabling technology" for swarm robotics. Since the
concept of "emergent behavior" arises from the local interaction of robots with
their nearby neighbors, it is often crucial that robots know the location of those
neighbors. Because we do not want to impose a global coordinate system on the
swarm, this means that each robot must have its own local coordinate system,
and must be able to locate neighbors within that local coordinate frame. In contrast to the more traditional robotic localization that focuses on determining the
location of a robot with respect to the coordinate system imposed by an environment ("Where am I?"[1]), we focus on the complementary task of determining
the location of nearby robots ("Where are You?"), from an egocentric view.

Naturally, it is useful for robot 1 to know where robot 2 is. It is also useful
for robot 2 to send robot 1 some sensor information. Combining this knowledge
is imperative – e.g., robot 1 receives sensor information from robot 2 at location
(x, y) with respect to robot 1. With our technology this combination of knowledge
is provided very easily. By coupling localization with data exchange, we simplify
the hardware and algorithms needed to accomplish certain tasks.

It is important to point out that although this work was motivated by swarm
robotics, it can be used for many other purposes, including more standard collaborative robotics, and even with teams of humans and robots that interact with

---

* The chemical plume tracing application is supported by the National Science Foundation, Grant No. NSF44288.

E. Şahin et al. (Eds.): Swarm Robotics Ws, LNCS 4433, pp. 129–143, 2007.

each other. It is also not restricted to one particular class of control algorithms
– and in fact would be useful for behavior-based approaches[2], control-theoretic
approaches[3,4], motor schema algorithms[5], and physicomimetics[6].

The purpose of our technology is to create a plug-in hardware module that
provides the capability to accurately localize neighboring robots, without using global information and/or the use of vision systems. The use of this technology does not preclude the use of other technologies. Beacons, landmarks,
pheromones, vision systems, and GPS can all be added, if that is required. The
system described in this paper is intended for use in a 2D environment, however,
extension to 3D is readily achievable.

2   Localization

Two methodologies for robot localization are *triangulation* and *trilateration*.
Both methods compute the location of a point (in this case, the location of
a robot) in 2D space. In *triangulation*, the locations of two "base points" are
known, as well as the interior angles of a triangle whose vertices comprise the
two base points and the object to be localized. The computations are performed
using the Law of Sines. In 2D *trilateration*, the locations of three base points are
known as well as the distances from each of these three base points to the object
to be localized. Looked at visually, 2D trilateration involves finding the location
where three circles intersect.

Thus, to locate a remote robot using 2D trilateration the sensing robot must
know the locations of three points in its own coordinate system and be able to
measure distances from these three points to the remote robot. The configuration
of these points is an interesting research question that we examine in this paper.

2.1   Measuring Distance

Our distance measurement method exploits the fact that sound travels significantly more slowly than light, employing a Difference in Time of Arrival technique. The same method is used to determine the distance to a lightning strike
by measuring the time between seeing the lightning and hearing the thunder.

To tie this to 2D trilateration, let each robot have one radio frequency (RF)
transceiver and three ultrasonic acoustic transceivers. The ultrasonic transceivers
are the "base points." Suppose robot 2 simultaneously emits an RF pulse and
an ultrasonic acoustic pulse. When robot 1 receives the RF pulse (almost in-
stantaneously), a clock on robot 1 starts. When the acoustic pulse is received
by each of the three ultrasonic transceivers on robot 1, the elapsed times are
computed. These three times are converted to distances, according to the speed
of sound. Since the locations of the acoustic transceivers are known, as well as
the distances, robot 1 is now able to use trilateration to compute the location
of robot 2 (precisely, the location of the emitting acoustic transceiver on robot
2). Of the three acoustic transceivers, all three must be capable of receiving, but
only one of the three must be capable of transmission.

Measuring the elapsed times is not difficult. Since the speed of sound is roughly $1087'$ per second (at standard temperature and pressure), then it takes approximately 76 microseconds for sound to travel $1''$. Times of this magnitude are easily measured using inexpensive electronic hardware.

2.2   Channeling Acoustic Energy into a Plane

Ultrasonic acoustic transducers produce a cone of energy along a line perpendicular to the surface of the transducer. The width of this main lobe (for the inexpensive 40 kHz transducers used in our implementation) is roughly 30°. To produce acoustic energy in a 2D plane would require 12 acoustic transducers in a ring. To get three base points would hence require 36 transducers. This is expensive and is a large power drain. We took an alternative approach. Each base point is comprised of one acoustic transducer that is pointing down. A parabolic cone is positioned under the transducer, with its tip pointing up towards the transducer (see also Figure 3 later in this paper). The parabolic cone acts like a lens. When the transducer is placed at the virtual "focal point" the cone "collects" acoustic energy in the horizontal plane, and focuses this energy to the receiving acoustic transceiver. Similarly, a cone also functions in the reverse, reflecting transmitted acoustic energy into the horizontal plane. This works extremely well – the acoustic energy is detectable to a distance of about $7'$, which is more than adequate for our own particular needs. Greater range can be obtained with more power (the scaling appears to be very manageable).

2.3   Related Work

Our work is motivated by the CMU *Millibot* project. They also use RF and acoustic transducers to perform trilateration. However, due to the very small size of their robots, each Millibot can only carry one acoustic transducer (coupled with a right-angle cone, rather than the parabolic cone we use). Hence trilateration is a collaborative endeavor that involves several robots. To perform trilateration, a minimum of three Millibots must be stationary (and serve as beacons) at any moment in time. The set of three stationary robots changes as the robot team moves. The minimum team size is four robots (and is preferably five). Initialization generally involves having some robots make "L-shaped" maneuvers, in order to disambiguate the localization[7].

MacArthur[8] presents two different trilateration systems. The first uses three acoustic transducers, but without RF. Localization is based on the differences between distances rather than the distances themselves. The three acoustic transducers are arranged in a line. The second uses two acoustic transducers and RF in a method similar to our own. Unfortunately, both systems can only localize points "in front" of the line, not behind it.

In terms of functionality, an alternative localization method in robotics is to use line-of-sight IR transceivers. When IR is received, signal strength provides an estimate of distance. The IR signal can also be modulated to provide communication. Multiple IR sensors can be used to provide the bearing to the transmitting robot (e.g., see[9,10]). We view this method as complementary to our own, but that our method is more appropriate for tasks where greater localization accuracy is required. This will be especially important in outdoor situations where water vapor or dust could change the IR opacity of air. Similar issues arise with the use of cameras and omni-directional mirrors/lenses, which also requires far more computational power and a light source.

2.4 Trilateration Method I

As mentioned above, the location of the "base points" is a significant research issue. The intuitively obvious placement, due to symmetry considerations, is at the vertices of an equilateral triangle. This is shown in Figure 1. Two robots are shown. The two large circles represent the robots (and the small open circles represent their centers). Assume the RF transceiver for each robot is at its center. The acoustic transceivers are labeled **A**, **B**, and **C**. Each robot has an XY coordinate system, as indicated in the figure.

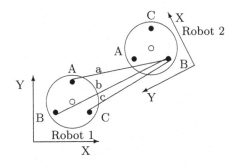

Fig. 1. Three base points in an equilateral triangle pattern

In Figure 1, robot 2 simultaneously emits an RF pulse and an acoustic pulse from its transceiver **B**. Robot 1 then measures the distances **a**, **b**, and **c**. Without loss of generality, assume that transceiver **B** of robot 1 is located at $(x_{1B}, y_{1B}) = (0,0)$[11]. Solving for the position of **B** on robot 2, with respect to robot 1, involves the simultaneous solution of three nonlinear equations, the intersecting circles with centers located at **A**, **B** and **C** on robot 1 and respective radii of **a**, **b**, and **c**:[1]

$$(x_{2B} - x_{1A})^2 + (y_{2B} - y_{1A})^2 = a^2 \tag{1}$$
$$(x_{2B} - x_{1B})^2 + (y_{2B} - y_{1B})^2 = b^2 \tag{2}$$
$$(x_{2B} - x_{1C})^2 + (y_{2B} - y_{1C})^2 = c^2 \tag{3}$$

---

[1] Subscripts denote the robot number and the acoustic transducer. The transducer **A** on robot 1 is located at (x_{1A}, y_{1A}).

The form of these equations allows for cancellation of the nonlinearity, and simple algebraic manipulation yields the following simultaneous linear equations in the unknowns:

$$\begin{bmatrix} x_{1C} & y_{1C} \\ x_{1A} & y_{1A} \end{bmatrix} \begin{bmatrix} x_{2B} \\ y_{2B} \end{bmatrix} = \begin{bmatrix} (b^2 + x_{1C}{}^2 + y_{1C}{}^2 - c^2)/2 \\ (b^2 + x_{1A}{}^2 + y_{1A}{}^2 - a^2)/2 \end{bmatrix}$$

With the base points at the vertices of an equilateral triangle, the coefficient matrix can be given by $\begin{bmatrix} 1/2 & \sqrt{3}/2 \\ 1/2 & -\sqrt{3}/2 \end{bmatrix}$. Unfortunately, the solution to these simultaneous trilateration equations are somewhat complex and inelegant. Also, the *condition number* of the coefficient matrix is $\sqrt{3}$. The condition number of a matrix is a measure of the sensitivity of the matrix to numerical operations. Since distance measurements are quantized and noisy, the goal is to have a condition number near the optimum, which is 1.0 (i.e., the matrix is *well-conditioned*).

2.5   Trilateration Method II

There is a better placement for the acoustic transducers (base points). Let **A** be at $(0, d)$, **B** be at $(0, 0)$, and **C** be at $(d, 0)$, where d is the distance between **A** and **B**, and between **B** and **C** (see Figure 2). Assume that robot 2 emits from its transducer **B**.

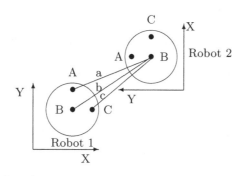

Fig. 2. Three base points in an XY coordinate system pattern

The trilateration equations turn out to be surprisingly simple (see[11]):

$$x_{2B} = \frac{b^2 - c^2 + d^2}{2d} \qquad\qquad y_{2B} = \frac{b^2 - a^2 + d^2}{2d}$$

A very nice aspect of these equations is that they can be simplified even further, if one wants to trilaterate purely in hardware. Since squaring (or any other kind of multiplication) is an expensive process in hardware, we can minimize the number of multiplications and divisions as follows:

$$x_{2B} = \left[\frac{(b+c)(b-c)}{d} + d \right] \gg 1 \qquad\qquad y_{2B} = \left[\frac{(b+a)(b-a)}{d} + d \right] \gg 1$$

where "$\gg 1$" is a binary "right-shift by 1".

With the base points in this configuration, the coefficient matrix is the identity matrix, and hence has a condition number of 1.0. Thus not only is the solution elegant, but the system is well-conditioned. Further analysis of our trilateration framework indicates that, as would be expected, error is reduced by increasing "base-line" distance d (our robots have d equal to 6″). Error can also be reduced by increasing the clock speed of our trilateration module (although range will decrease correspondingly, due to counter size).

By allowing robots to share coordinate systems, robots can communicate their information arbitrarily far throughout the swarm network. For example, suppose robot 2 can localize robot 3. Robot 1 can localize only robot 2. If robot 2 can also localize robot 1 (a fair assumption), then by passing this information to robot 1, robot 1 can now determine the position of robot 3. Furthermore, the orientations of the robots can also be determined. Naturally, localization errors can compound as the path through the network increases in length, but multiple paths can be used to alleviate this problem to some degree. Heil[11] provides details on these issues.

2.6 Trilateration Method II + Communication

Thus far we have only discussed issues of localization by using trilateration. Trilateration method II provides simplicity of implementation with robustness in the face of sensor noise. However, we have not yet discussed the issue of merging localization with data exchange. The framework makes the resolution of this issue straightforward. Instead of simply emitting an RF pulse that contains no information but serves merely to synchronize the trilateration mechanism, we can also append data to the RF pulse. With this simple extension, robot 2 can send data to robot 1, and when the trilateration is complete, robot 1 knows the location of robot 2, and has received the data from robot 2. Simple coordinate transformations allow robot 1 to convert the data from robot 2 (which is in the coordinate frame of robot 2) to its own coordinate frame, if this is necessary. Trilateration method II with communication is assumed throughout the remainder of this paper.

3 Trilateration Implementation

3.1 Trilateration Hardware

Figure 3 illustrates how our trilateration framework is currently implemented in hardware. The left figure shows two acoustic transducers pointing down, with reflective parabolic cones. The acoustic transducers are specially tuned to transmit and receive 40 kHz acoustic signals.

Figure 3 (middle) shows our in-house acoustic sensor boards (denoted as "XSRF" boards, for *Experimental Sensor Range Finder*). There is one XSRF board for each acoustic transducer. The XSRF board calculates the time difference between receiving the RF signal and the acoustic pulse. Each XSRF

Fig. 3. Important hardware components: (left) acoustic transducers and parabolic cones, (middle) the XSRF acoustic sensor printed circuit board, and (right) the completed trilateration module (beta-version top-down view)

contains 7 integrated circuit chips. A MAX362 chip controls whether the board is in transmit or receive mode. When transmitting, a PIC microprocessor generates a 40 kHz signal. This signal is sent to an amplifier, which then interfaces with the acoustic transducer. This generates the acoustic signal.

In receive mode a trigger indicates that an RF signal has been heard, and that an acoustic signal is arriving. When the RF signal is received, the PIC starts counting. To enhance the sensitivity of the XSRF board, three stages of amplification occur. Each of the three stages is accomplished with a LMC6032 operational amplifier, providing a gain of roughly 15 at each stage. Between the second and third stage is a 40 kHz bandpass filter to eliminate out-of-bound noise that can lead to saturation. The signal is passed to two comparators, set at thresholds of ± 2V. When the acoustic energy exceeds either threshold, the PIC processor finishes counting, indicating the arrival of the acoustic signal.

This timing count provided by each PIC (one for each XSRF) is sent to a MiniDRAGON[2] 68HC12 microprocessor. The MiniDRAGON performs the trilateration calculations. Figure 3 (right) shows the completed trilateration module, as viewed from above. The MiniDRAGON is outlined in the center.

3.2 Synchronization Protocol

The trilateration system involves at least two robots. One robot transmits the acoustic-RF pulse combination, while the others use these pulses to compute (trilaterate) the coordinates of the transmitting robot. Hence, trilateration is a one-to-many protocol, allowing multiple robots to simultaneously trilaterate and determine the position of the transmitting robot.

The purpose of trilateration is to allow all robots to determine the position of all of their neighbors. For this to be possible, the robots must take turns transmitting. For our current implementation we use a protocol that is similar to a token passing protocol. Each robot has a unique hardware encoded ID. When

---

a robot is transmitting it sends its own ID. As soon as the neighboring robots receive this ID they increment the ID by one and compare it with their own ID. The robot that matches the two IDs is considered to have the token and will transmit next. The other robots will continue to trilaterate. Each robot maintains a data structure with the coordinate information, as well as any additional sensor information, of every neighboring robot.

Although this current protocol is distributed, there are a few problems with it. First, it assumes that all robots know how many robots are in the swarm. Second, the removal or failure of a robot can cause all robots to pause, as they wait for the transmission of that robot. We are currently working on new protocols to rectify these issues.

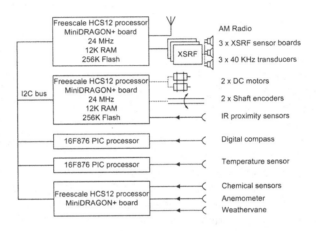

Fig. 4. The architecture of the Version 1.0 Maxelbot

4   The Maxelbot

Our University of Wyoming "Maxelbot" (named after the two graduate students that designed and built the robot) is modular. A primary MiniDRAGON is used for control of the robot. It communicates via an I^2C bus to all other peripherals, allowing us to plug in new peripherals as needed. Figure 4 shows the architecture. The primary MiniDRAGON is the board that drives the motors. It also monitors proximity sensors and shaft encoders. The trilateration module is shown at the top of the diagram. This module controls the RF and acoustic components of trilateration. Additional modules have been built for digital compasses and thermometers. The PIC processors provide communication with the I^2C bus. The last module is being built especially for the purpose of chemical plume tracing (i.e., following a chemical plume back to its source). It is composed of multiple chemical sensors, and sensors to measure wind speed and direction. Chemical plume tracing algorithms will run on the additional dedicated MiniDRAGON. The completed Maxelbot is shown in Figure 5.

Fig. 5. The Version 1.0 Maxelbot itself

5   Experiments and Demonstrations

The following subsections illustrate different exemplar tasks that we can perform by using the trilateration framework. It is important to note that given the small number of Maxelbots currently built (three) most of these tasks are not swarm tasks per se. Also, most of our control algorithms are currently behavior-based, and are generally not novel. However, it is important to keep in mind that the point of the demonstrations is (1) to test and debug our hardware, and (2) to show the utility and functionality of the trilateration framework.

5.1   Accuracy Experiment

To test the accuracy of the trilateration module, we placed a robot on our lab floor, with transducer **B** at $(0'', 0'')$. Then we placed an emitter along 24 grid points from $(-24'', -24'')$ to $(24'', 24'')$. The results are shown in Figure 6. The average error over all grid points is very low – $0.6''$, with a minimum of $0.1''$ and a maximum of $1.2''$.

5.2   Linear Formations

We are currently investigating the utility of linear formations of robots in corridor-like environments, such as sewers, pipes, ducts, etc. As stated above, each robot has a unique ID. Robot 0 is the leader. Robot 1 follows the leader. Robot 2 follows robot 1. Initially, the three robots are positioned in a line in the following order: robot 0, robot 1, robot 2, with robot 0 being at the head of the line. The distance between the neighboring robots is $12''$.

The behavior is as follows. Robot 0 moves forward in a right curved trajectory (for the sake of making the demonstration more interesting). Robot 0 continually monitors how far behind robot 1 is. If the distance behind is greater than $14''$, then robot 0 will stop, waiting for robot 1 to catch up. Robot 1 adjusts its

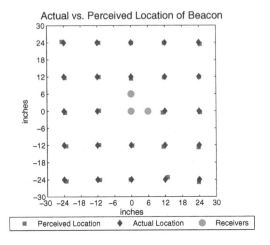

Fig. 6. The perceived location of the emitter, versus the actual location

own position to maintain robot 0 at coordinates $(0'', 12'')$ relative to its own coordinate system. Robot 2 acts the same way with respect to robot 1 (see Figure 7). The robots maintained the correct separation very well, while moving.

Fig. 7. Three Maxelbots in linear formation

5.3   Box/Baby Pulling

Another emphasis in our research is search and rescue. We have successfully used two robots to push (or pull) an unevenly weighted box across our lab. However, the friction of the box on the floor results in slippage of the robot tires. This produces random rotations of the box. Instead, Figure 8 shows a three robot approach, where one of the robots is not in physical contact with the box.

The behavior is as follows. Three robots are initialized in a triangular formation. Robot 0 is the leading robot while the remaining two robots stay behind the leader. Robot 1 positions itself such that the leader is at $(24'', 24'')$. Robot 2 positions itself such that the leader is at $(-18'', 24'')$. The asymmetric x values are used to compensate for the $6''$ baseline between transducers, yielding an isosceles triangle. Robot 0 moves forward along a left curved trajectory. Robot 0

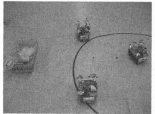

Fig. 8. Three Maxelbots pulling a "baby" to safety

continually monitors robot 1 and robot 2. If either of the two robots falls behind, robot 0 will stop and wait for both of the robots to be within the desired distance of 34″. Note that while robots 1 and 2 are tethered to the baby basket, robot 0 is not. Hence robot 0 (with the other two robots and the basket) follows a fairly well-controlled trajectory, subject to the limits of the accuracy of our shaft encoders and standard slippage.

5.4   Physicomimetics Formations for Chemical Plume Tracing

As a test of our hardware using a true swarm control algorithm, we implemented artificial physics (AP) on the robots[6]. Figure 9 shows three Maxelbots self-organizing into an equilateral triangle.

As has been shown in prior work[6,12] a goal force can be applied to AP formations, such that the formation moves towards the goal, without breaking the formation apart. We have used a light source for our goal, and have had success using the digital compass to drive the formation in a given direction. Since one of our research thrusts is chemical plume tracing (CPT)[13], we intend to use the CPT module (described above) as our goal force. The objective of CPT is to locate the source (e.g. a leaking pipe) of a hazardous airborne plume by measuring flow properties, such as toxin concentration and wind speed. Simulation studies in[13] suggested that faster and more accurate source localization is possible with collaborating plume-tracing vehicles. We constructed the CPT module to test this hypothesis on real ethanol plumes. In this section, we compare CPT performance of a single Maxelbot implementation against a distributed approach using three Maxelbots.

As the trace chemical we employ ethanol, a volatile organic compound (VOC), and measure the chemical concentration using Figaro TGS2620 metal-oxide VOC sensors. The single Maxelbot carries four of these sensors, mounted at each corner, while there are only three chemical sensors in the distributed implementation – one sensor per Maxelbot. In both versions, the HCS12 microprocessor performs analog-to-digital conversion of sensor output, and then navigates according to a CPT strategy. We employ one of the most widely-used CPT strategies called *chemotaxis*, which advances the vehicle in the direction of an increasing chemical gradient.

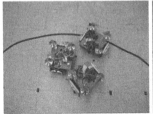

Fig. 9. Three Maxelbots using AP to self-organize into an equilateral triangle

For our first experiment, we performed 23 CPT evaluation experiments in a small $6' \times 11'$ room, using an ethanol-filled flask as the chemical source, with the single, more capable Maxelbot. The separation between the source and the starting location of the Maxelbot was $7.5'$ on average. Each run terminated when the Maxelbot came within $5''$ of the ethanol flask (a CPT *success*), or after 30 minutes of unsuccessful plume tracing. Of the 23 test runs, 17 were successful in locating the source (a 74% success rate), with the average localization time of 18 minutes ($\sigma_t = 6.2$ minutes). These results are consistent with those reported in the literature[14], although our definition of a CPT success is decidedly more stringent than the typical completion criterion used by others.

For our second experiment we used a much larger $25' \times 25'$ indoor environment. This environment is far more difficult – out of 9 trials, the single Maxelbot only succeeded twice, for a success rate of 22.2%. The variance in the time to success was very large; 3:30 and 17:30 minutes respectively ($\sigma_t = 9.9$ minutes). A typical movement trace is shown in Figure 10 (left). The Maxelbot's path indicates that it is having a very difficult time following the chemical gradient in this larger environment.

For our third experiment, we ran 10 experiments with the distributed Maxelbot implementation. As mentioned above, each of three Maxelbots carries only one chemical sensor. A triangular formation is maintained by the AP algorithm. Each Maxelbot shares the chemical sensor information with its neighbors, and then each Maxelbot independently computes the direction to move. Because the formation force is stronger than the goal force, the formation remains intact, and serves as a mechanism for moving the formation along a consensus route. Despite the fact that each Maxelbot senses far less chemical information than before (and the total number of chemical sensors has decreased from four to three), performance increased markedly! Out of 10 trials, the distributed implementation successfully found the chemical source six times, for a 60% success rate. Also, this implementation showed a far more consistent source emitter approach pattern, with an average search time of just seven minutes (and $\sigma_t = 5.8$ minutes). A typical path can be seen in Figure 10 (right). Snapshots of an actual run can be seen in Figure 11.

Performance statistics for each CPT implementation are given in Table 1. *Success rate* is simply the percentage of trials in which a Maxelbot drove within one foot of the emitter. *Search time* is a measure of how long it took for the

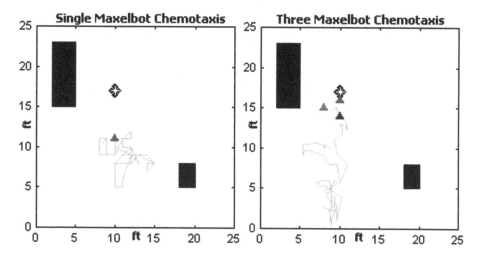

Fig. 10. Visualization of a sample CPT trace for each implementation. The large, dark rectangular blocks are obstacles (i.e., bulky laboratory equipment); the emitter is shown with the diamond shape, and each Maxelbot is depicted as a triangle. The Maxelbot path is drawn using a lightly-shaded line; for the multi-Maxelbot trace, the singular path is computed by averaging the locations of the three Maxelbots.

Maxelbots to find the emitter, computed for trials where the emitter was found. The *contact duration* is the total length of time that a Maxelbot was within one foot of the chemical emitter. To make the comparison fair for both implementations, the duration given for the Maxelbot swarm implementation includes at most one Maxelbot per time step. In practice, however, there is great value in having multiple Maxelbots near the emitter, for instance in order to identify a potential source and then extinguish it[13]. To place this in perspective, for the distributed implementation, when one Maxelbot is near the source, all three are near the source. However, if one is using the single Maxelbot implementation the success rate is 22.2%. Hence, the probability of having three of these independent non-collaborating robots near the source is approximately 1% (0.222^3), as opposed to a success rate of 60%.

Fig. 11. Three Maxelbot CPT test run; robots are moving from left to right

Table 1. CPT performance measures for both implementations: the swarm-based Maxelbot implementation outperforms the single Maxelbot version on each evaluation metric (standard deviation values are given in parenthesis)

Metric	Single Maxelbot	Three Maxelbots
Success Rate	22.2%	60.0%
Search Time	630.0 sec ($\sigma = 594.0$)	415.0 sec ($\sigma = 349.4$)
Contact Duration	532.5 sec ($\sigma = 668.2$)	677.5 sec ($\sigma = 361.2$)

6 Summary

This paper describes a novel 2D trilateration framework for the accurate localization of neighboring robots. The framework uses three acoustic transceivers and one RF transceiver. By also using the RF to exchange information between robots, we couple localization with data exchange. Our framework is designed to be modular, so that it can be used on different robotic platforms, and is not restricted to any particular class of control algorithms. Although we do not rely on GPS, stationary beacons, or environmental landmarks, their use is not precluded. Our framework is fully distributed, inexpensive, scalable, and robust.

There are several advantages to our framework. First, the basic trilateration equations are elegant and could be implemented purely in hardware. Second, the system is well-conditioned, indicating minimal sensitivity to measurement error. Third, it should provide greater localization accuracy than IR localization methods, especially in outdoor situations. The quality of the accuracy is confirmed via empirical tests.

To illustrate the general utility of our framework, we demonstrate the application of three of our robots on three different tasks: linear formations, box pulling, and geometric formation control for chemical plume tracing. The trilateration hardware performed well on all three tasks. The first two tasks utilize behavior-based control algorithms, while the latter uses artificial physics (AP). The latter is especially interesting, because it demonstrates the application of a true swarm-based control algorithm. One of our primary research interests is chemical plume tracing, using AP. In order to accomplish this task, a special chemical sensing module has also been built in-house. On the third task AP is combined with the chemical sensing module to perform chemical plume tracing. Experimental results indicate that a small swarm of less capable Maxelbots easily outperforms one more capable Maxelbot.

Open Source Project URL

http://www.cs.uwyo.edu/~wspears/maxelbot provides details on this project.

References

1. Borenstein, J., Everett, H., Feng, L.: Where am I? Sensors and methods for mobile robot positioning. Technical report, University of Michigan (1996)
2. Balch, T., Hybinette, M.: Social potentials for scalable multirobot formations. In: IEEE Transactions on Robotics and Automation. Volume 1. (2000) 73–80
3. Fax, J., Murray, R.: Information flow and cooperative control of vehicle formations. IEEE Transactions on Automatic Control **49** (2004) 1465–1476
4. Fierro, R., Song, P., Das, A., Kumar, V.: Cooperative control of robot formations. In Murphey, R., Pardalos, P., eds.: Cooperative Control and Optimization. Volume 66., Hingham, MA, Kluwer Academic Press (2002) 73–93
5. Brogan, D., Hodgins, J.: Group behaviors for systems with significant dynamics. Autonomous Robots **4** (1997) 137–153
6. Spears, W., Spears, D., Hamann, J., Heil, R.: Distributed, physics-based control of swarms of vehicles. Autonomous Robots **17** (2004) 137–162
7. L. Navarro-Serment, L., Paredis, C., Khosla, P.: A beacon system for the localization of distributed robotic teams. In: International Conference on Field and Service Robots, Pittsburgh, PA (1999) 232–237
8. MacArthur, D.: Design and implementation of an ultrasonic position system for multiple vehicle control. Master's thesis, University of Florida (2003)
9. Rothermich, J., Ecemis, I., Gaudiano, P.: Distributed localization and mapping with a robotic swarm. In Şahin, E., Spears, W., eds.: Swarm Robotics, Springer-Verlag (2004) 59–71
10. Payton, D., Estkowski, R., Howard, M.: Pheromone robotics and the logic of virtual pheromones. In Şahin, E., Spears, W., eds.: Swarm Robotics, Springer-Verlag (2004) 46–58
11. Heil, R.: A trilaterative localization system for small mobile robots in swarms. Master's thesis, University of Wyoming, Laramie, WY (2004)
12. Spears, W., Heil, R., Zarzhitsky, D.: Artificial physics for mobile robot formations. In: Proceedings IEEE International Conference on Systems, Man, and Cybernetics. (2005) 2287–2292
13. Zarzitsky, D., Spears, D., Spears, W.: Distributed robotics approach to chemical plume tracing. In: IEEE/RSJ International Conference on Intelligent Robots and Systems (IROS'05). (2005) 4034–4039
14. Lilienthal, A.: Gas Distribution Mapping and Gas Source Localisation with a Mobile Robot. PhD thesis, University of Tübingen (2004)

Collective Perception in a Robot Swarm

Thomas Schmickl[1], Christoph Möslinger[2], and Karl Crailsheim[1]

[1] Department for Zoology, University of Graz, 8010 Graz, Austria
`schmickl@nextra.at`
[2] FH St. Pölten, 3100 St. Pölten, Austria

Abstract. In swarm robotics, hundreds or thousands of robots have to reach a common goal autonomously. Usually, the robots are small and their abilities are very limited. The autonomy of the robots requires that the robots' behaviors are purely based on their local perceptions, which are usually rather limited. If the robot swarm is able to join multiple instances of individual perceptions to one big global picture (e.g. to collectively construct a sort of map), then the swarm can perform efficiently and such a swarm can target complex tasks. We here present two approaches to realize 'collective perception' in a robot swarm. Both require only limited abilities in communication and in calculation. We compare these strategies in different environments and evaluate the swarm's perform-ance in simulations of fluctuating environmental conditions and with varying parameter settings.

1 Introduction

In robot swarms, hundreds or thousands of small and simple robots have to perform in a well-organized and efficient way to pursue common goals. With increasing size of the swarms, external controllers that have a 'global view' of the swarm's environment get inefficient because the control of each single robot within the swarm gets intracta-ble even for strong computers. Also pre-calculated plans represent no solution with swarm sizes beyond a few hundred robots. Another problem is the inter-robot com-munication in such huge swarms, because if every robot has to communicate with every other robot, the required width of the communication channel increases non-linearly with the swarm size. In the I-SWARM project [1][2][3], we want to im-plement a swarm of very small robots (approx. 8mm³ size) that is able to perform col-lective perception. To us, the term "collective perception" describes a way that allows taking advantage at the global (swarm) level from a mass of complex data sensed in parallel on the individual level. The final swarm decision is made at the conceptual level by a group of collaborative agents. This ability can enhance the performance of a swarm (e.g. optimize patch selection for foraging tasks [4]) and expands its range of application. The I-SWARM robots have only limited sensorial abilities and can com-municate only at short distance by LED's and photodiodes. These restrictions create a demand for simple solutions of collective perception strategies.

Animal swarms demonstrate that a set of relatively primitive individual behaviors enhanced with local communication can produce a large set of complex swarm behav-iors. Such animal swarms show self-organization [5] and swarm-intelligence [6][7]:

E. Şahin et al. (Eds.): Swarm Robotics Ws, LNCS 4433, pp. 144–157, 2007.
© Springer-Verlag Berlin Heidelberg 2007

Bacteria, ants and bees are able to choose the optimal feeding site and to recruit an appropriate fraction of foragers to each food site. Ants use pheromones to manage this decision making collectively. Honeybees use a variety of dances performed near the hive entrance to choose their feeding sites and to recruit the appropriate number of forager bees and food-storage bees. In both cases, individual animals do not visit several feeding sites and do not compare them individually. In contrast, pheromones and dances generate a structured environment that is regulated by positive and by negative feedback loops. These specialized environments act like 'maps' that are built up collectively and that are 'read' by many individuals in parallel. The most fascinating examples of 'collective perception' are found in honeybees. Forager bees and storage bees evaluate simple cues like queuing delays [8][9][10], searching times for empty combs [11] and multiple nectar transfers [12] to assess the current global workload balancing, the global need for comb construction and the environmental nectar flow.

Our approach to a bio-inspired technique for collective perception in swarm robotics is inspired by one of these examples of 'collective perception' in honeybees: By evaluating trophallactic contacts[1] forager bees can indirectly assess the current ratio of brood demand to pollen supply in the colony without inspecting brood area and pollen stores individually [13][14][15]. Nurse bees eat and digest pollen to derive a proteinaceous food (jelly) from it [16]. This jelly is fed to larvae and is exchanged frequently among adult bees. In times with high pollen demand, when a lot of brood has to be fed, the larvae consume the main part of the proteins, so that forager bees do not receive high amounts of proteins through trophallaxis. It is assumed that foragers are therefore more "protein hungry" and are more likely to forage for pollen instead of nectar. This way, the colony responds to a high pollen demand by recruiting more foragers to pollen collecting. The collective of forager bees indirectly perceives the current ratio of brood to food. In addition to proteins, the brood also consumes large amounts of nectar and nectar is also passed from bee to bee via trophallaxis.

Our goal was to use mechanisms in our robot swarm that are as simple as the biological examples mentioned above. We tested two approaches, one is a rather technical solution and was already used in swarm robotics, and the other approach is inspired by the trophallactic interactions of honeybees. Both methods are compared in the same simulated environment. The bio-inspired strategy is evaluated in detail and the importance of its parameters is analyzed in detail. Finally, the bio-inspired approach had to demonstrate its advantages in a fluctuating environment.

2 The Scenario

In the experiments described here, we used our simulation platform LaRoSim (Large Robotswarm Simulator), which we already described in [17][18]. The simulator is a multi-agent simulation of approx. 1000 robots that move in an arena. These robots can communicate by LED's and photodiodes and can also sense walls and obstacles this way. In addition to that, special (color) marks on the floor can be sensed, but only if the robot is located directly above such a mark.

---

[1] Trophallaxis is the mouth-to-mouth transfer of fluid food between adult honeybees.

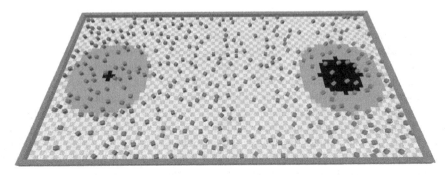

Fig. 1. A screen shot of our simulation platform LaRoSim. The two black areas (small left and huge right) represent target areas for aggregation. The gray circles indicate the zones in which we counted the robots for evaluating the aggregation success. Gray boxes represent robots.

Figure 1 shows a screen shot of the scenario the robot swarm has to perform in. Two black marks indicate aggregation areas (e.g., places to work). These areas can be of different sizes. The goal of the swarm is:

1. Explore the arena to detect these target sites.
2. Communicate the location of the targets to the other robots, so that they can aggregate there.
3. Recruit cohorts of robots to each target. The sizes of these cohorts should correspond to the size of the target areas.

In conclusion, the robot swarm has to manage to measure and to compare the sizes and the distances of the two target areas collectively. This goal can only be achieved collectively, because it goes far beyond the sensorial capabilities of a single robot. We chose a very simple example of work that has to be performed by the robot swarm (pure aggregation), because we wanted to concentrate on the problem of 'collective perception' in this study. More sophisticated work in LaRoSim, e.g. collective floor cleaning and optimal route finding, was already shown in [17][18]. To evaluate the

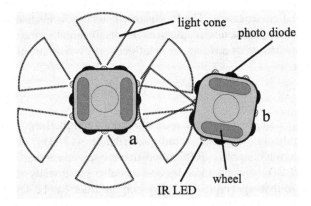

Fig. 2. Morphology of the robots in the simulation environment. In the picture, the two robots can establish a bi-directional communication, because one receptor of each robot is within the light cone of the other robot.

recruitment of robot cohorts to the two targets, we measured the number of aggregated robots in a radius of 10 robot-diameters (rd) around the center of each target area, as indicated by the gray circles around all black target areas in figure 1. Please note, that the robots have no ability for long-distance communication and no long-range sensing for target areas. The information about the location of the target areas has to be propagated through the swarm by using only nearest-neighbor communication, as depicted in figure 2. The communication radius is 3.5 rd.

2.1 The Hop-Count Strategy

The first strategy that we implemented in our robots is called 'hop-count' strategy. This strategy works as follows: The robots move randomly and try to avoid collisions and walls. Each robot i has an internal memory $hc(i,t)$ that is set to the maximum possible hop-count $hc(i,t)=hc_{max}$. If a robot encounters a target area, it sets $hc(i,t)=0$. During the run, all robots communicate with their nearest neighbors within their communication radius. The focal robot i compares its own hop-count with every neighbor j. If the neighbor has a lower hop-count ($hc(j,t)<hc(i,t)$), robot i copies the hop-count value of the neighbor and increases it by 1. Every t_f time steps, the robot i increases its hop-count value by 1 spontaneously ($hc(i,t)=hc(i,t-1)+1$). This process is called 'forgetting', because it forces wrong or out-dated information to leave the system over time. If $hc(i,t)$ exceeds hc_{max}, $hc(i,t)$ is set to hc_{max}. This way a gradient emerges within the robot swarm that points downhill to the target areas. A robot that experiences a neighbor with

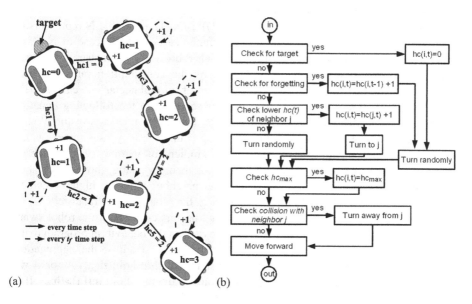

(a)   (b)

Fig. 3. (a) The gradient of hop-counts that emerges in the 'hop-count' strategy. The robot on the target sets its hop-count to 0. All robots copy the lowest hop-count from their neighbors and increase it by 1. After some (t_f) time steps, they increase the hop-count spontaneously ('forgetting'). (b) Behavioral program of a robot in the 'hop-count' strategy. This program is executed every time step.

a hop-count that is smaller than or equal its own hop-count navigates towards this neighbor. If more than one neighbor has the same low hop-count, the robot calculates its direction by averaging the vectors towards these neighbors. Figure 3a depicts the emergence of the gradient within the robot swarm. Figure 3b shows the behavioral program that is executed by each robot at every time step.

2.2 The 'Trophallaxis-inspired' Strategy

The 'trophallaxis-inspired' strategy is inspired by a behavior that is frequently found in social insects: The mouth-to-mouth transfer of liquid food between adult animals. In honeybees, beekeepers often install feeders in the hives to provide the bees with sugar-water. At these feeders, some bees fill their crops and then move away. On their way through the hive, they meet other bees and can share parts of their nectar load with them. It is assumed, that the more nectar the donor bee has and the less nectar the receiver bee has, the more nectar is transferred on average. On their way, the bees also consume a fraction of their nectar load to gain energy from it.

In the robot-swarm, the nectar crop of the bee is represented by a memory place inside of the robot. Basically each robot i starts with random movement and with a memory value $m(i,t)=0$. If the robot encounters a target, it adds a defined amount of 'virtual nectar' to its memory $a_a(i,t)=r_a$ (r_a: addition-rate, $a_a(i,t)$: amount of addition). Every time step, robot i communicates with its local neighbors j and exchanges an amount of 'virtual nectar' with them. The amount $a_t(i,t)$ of this exchange is proportional to the differences in the memory values among the robots and is determined by the transfer-rate r_t: $a_t(i,t)=0.5*(m(j,t-1)-m(i,t-1))*r_t/N$. The variable N represents the number of local neighbors the focal robot communicates with. In case of $N=0$, the value of $a_t(i,t)$ is set to 0. Every time-step, each robot i also decreases its memory value by an amount $a_c(i,t)$ which is defined by the consumption rate r_c. $a_c(i,t)=m(i,t-1)*r_c$. After all these in-flows and out-flows of 'virtual nectar' are calculated by each robot the memory-value can be updated according to the following equation: $m(i,t)=m(i,t-1)+a_a(i,t)+a_t(i,t)-a_c(i,t)$. Please note that the 'trophallaxis-inspired' strategy uses floating point numbers, while the 'hop-count' strategy uses integer values only. By the rules mentioned above, again a gradient of memory values emerges within the robot swarm. If a robot i reaches a memory value above a threshold ($m(i,t)>th_{agg}$), the robot turns towards its local neighbor with the highest memory value. If the memory value is below or equal th_{agg}, the robot i moves randomly.

Figure 4a depicts how the gradient of 'virtual nectar' emerges in the robot swarm in the 'trophallaxis-inspired' strategy. Figure 4b depicts the behavioral program that is executed by every robot in every time step. In order to adjust the aggregation-sensitivity of the swarm we implemented a behavioral threshold th_{agg}. A robot will only follow the gradient if its memory value is above the threshold $m(i,t)>th_{agg}$. If its memory value is below or equal th_{agg}, the robot will move randomly. Figure 4a depicts how the gradient of 'virtual nectar' emerges in the robot swarm in the 'trophallaxis-inspired' strategy. Figure 4b depicts the behavioral program that is executed by every robot in every time step.

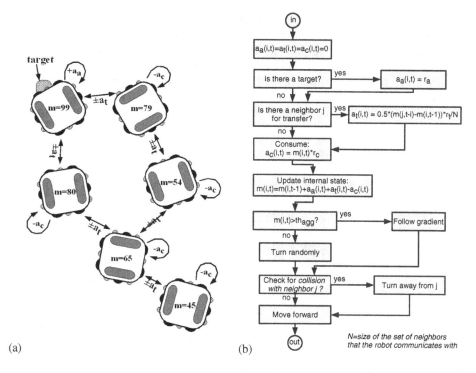

Fig. 4. (a) The gradient of 'virtual nectar' that emerges in the 'trophallaxis-inspired' strategy. The robot at the target adds 'virtual nectar' to its memory. All robots exchange fractions of the 'virtual nectar' proportionally to the inter-robot differences. All robots consume 'virtual nectar' over time, thus they decrease their memory values ('forgetting'). (b) Behavioral program of a robot in the 'trophallaxis-inspired' strategy. This program is executed every time step.

3 Results

In our simulation runs, both strategies were able to produce the desired aggregation behavior at the target areas. But this was not the main focus of this study. The main question was, whether or not the swarm will be able to collectively measure the sizes of the target areas and to proportionally recruit the appropriate number of robots to these targets.

3.1 Scaling the Sizes of the Target Areas

In this experiment, we tested both strategies in environments with varying differences in the size of the target areas. The sizes of the targets areas were defined by their radii. We tested the following ratios of radii: 1:5, 2:4, 3:3, 4:2, and 5:1. We started 375 robots that were (uniformly) randomly distributed within the arena. The results of these simulation runs are depicted in figure 5. The 'hop-count' strategy recruited more robots during the runtime of the experiments (=250 time steps) than the other strategy, but failed to recruit the robots according to the target sizes. The aggregation was measured by counting the number of robots within a radius of 10 robot-diameters around the center of each target (see figure 1). For the simulation runs, we used the following parameters: $r_a=50$, $r_c=0.01$, $r_t=1$, $hc_{max}=40$, $t_f=5$. The aggregation threshold th_{agg} was set to 100. For collision avoidance, the robots tried to stay away from each other half of their communication radius (coll-dist=0.5). Robot speed was 0.25 robot-diameters per step. The trophallaxis-inspired strategy recruited lower robot numbers but managed to recruit the robots accordingly to the

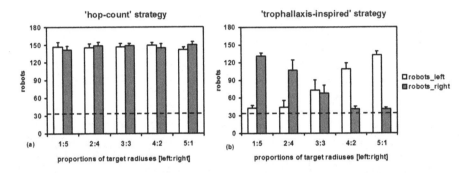

Fig. 5. Collective decisions made by the robot swarm in different environments. The dashed line shows the expected number of robots that would have been in the measurement area (radius=10 each) if there had been no aggregation behavior at all. N=10 per setting. Bars represent mean values and whiskers indicate standard deviations. Duration: 250 time steps.

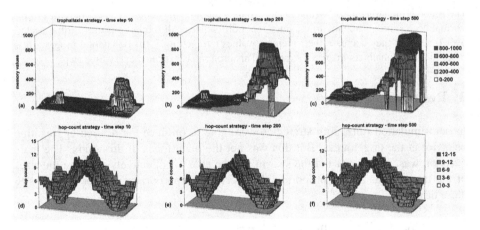

Fig. 6. The dynamics of the emerging gradients in our experiment. (a-c): The dynamics of the gradient in the trophallaxis inspired strategy. For generating the picture, we assigned the maximum memory value of all visible robots to each location in the arena. (d-f): The dynamics of the gradient in the hop-count strategy. Here we assigned the minimum hop-count of all visible robots to each position in the arena. Both simulation runs used extreme environmental conditions: The left target was very small (radius=1) and the right target was large (radius=5).

sizes of the target areas. An explanation for these results can be found in figure 6, which depicts two simulation runs with very extreme conditions: A small target on the left side (radius=1) and a huge target on the right side of the arena (radius=5). The hop-count strategy generates two bowl-shaped gradients that immediately reach the whole arena. The two bowls are of almost equal size and so the recruited cohorts of robots were also of almost equal size. In the trophallaxis-inspired strategy, the emergence of the gradient is much slower. But the bigger target on the right side allows more robots to add 'virtual nectar' to the system through their addition- and transfer-rates. This leads to a much higher 'mountain' that is able to recruit the majority of the robots to the right side. Obviously, the hop-count strategy is only able to report the distance of the target to other robots, while the trophallaxis-inspired strategy is able to report also the sizes of the targets.

3.2 The Importance of the Swarm Density

In swarm robotics, the swarm density is an important factor. To test how swarm densities affect the abilities of swarms to perform collective perception we further investigated the experiment with the biggest difference in target sizes (radii left:right = 1:5).

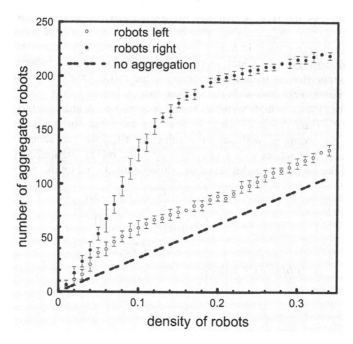

Fig. 7. Aggregation of robots to the small left target area (radius=1) and to the large right target area (radius=5) with varying swarm densities. The dashed line shows the expected number of robots that would have been in the measurement area (radius=10 each) if there had been no aggregation behavior at all. N=10 per setting. Duration: 250 time steps.

We only tested swarms using the trophallaxis-inspired strategy because swarms using the hop-count strategy couldn't differentiate between target sizes (see sub-section 3.1, figures 5,6). For the following analysis we used the same parameter settings as we used in sub-section 3.1. The only varied parameter was the density of the robots, which we scaled between **0.01** and **0.34**, which corresponds to swarm sizes of **30** robots and **1047** robots. Figure 7 shows the results of these experiments: Aggregation was performed on both target areas. With a swarm density of **0.17**, the maximum preferential aggregation was found at the large target. With higher densities (> **0.2**), no increase in aggregation is found anymore, the number of robots increases linearly as a product of pure random walk (dashed line). This analysis was made with a value of **th_{agg}=-50** to demonstrate that with the trophallaxis-strategy the swarm can also perceive small target areas (see section 3.3 for details). With **th_{agg}=0**, no aggregation on the small target size can be observed (data not shown), the number of robots around the small target is predictable by considering solely the random walk.

3.3   The Role of the Aggregation Threshold (th_{agg})

The results of the experiments in subsection 3.1 demonstrate that in the trophallaxis-inspired strategy, the huge gradient that emerges from the large target area increases over time and dominates over the gradient emerging at the location of the small target area. Nevertheless, the small target also recruited a few robots (see figure 5). By adjusting the threshold **th_{agg}** we were able to indirectly determine the minimum target size that lead to aggregation. In our strategy, the strength of aggregation was regulated by the variable **weight(i,t)**, which represents the ratio of directed movements to random movements. Robots with a low memory value **m(i,t)** have a low **weight(i,t)** and thus they perform a random walk most of the time, whereas robots with a high memory value **m(i,t)** have a high **weight(i,t)** and will move towards the target in a very directed way. Thus threshold **th_{agg}** is used as an offset in our computation of **weight(i,t)**. For example, with negative values of **th_{agg}** we can achieve a more directed movement of robots with a low memory value **m(i,t)**. Figure 8 depicts the dependency of the variable **weight(i,t)** on the variable **m(i,t)** and on the parameter **th_{agg}**.

$$weight(i,t) = \max\left\{\begin{array}{l} \min\left\{\begin{array}{l} \dfrac{m(i,t) - th_{agg}}{1000} \\[2mm] 0.75 \end{array}\right. \\[8mm] 0 \end{array}\right. \tag{1}$$

In the following experiment, we wanted to test, whether or not an adjustment of the threshold **th_{agg}** can modulate the sensitivity of the swarm for smaller target areas. Figure 9 shows the results of this experiment: Between **0 < th_{agg} <300**, the aggregation at the large target is negatively correlated with the value of **th_{agg}**, the small target is almost ignored by the swarm. With negative values of $\mathbf{th_{agg}}$, the aggregation at the small target increases significantly, without affecting the aggregation at the large target area. This shows that adjustment of $\mathbf{th_{agg}}$ leads to recruitment of previously non-recruited robots around the small target.

3.4   The Role of the Negative Feedback (r_c)

In swarm robotics, the decay of information is important as soon as the swarm of robots has to act in changing environments. It is needed to allow out-dated, thus not reinforced, information to leave the system. In the trophallaxis-inspired strategy, this is achieved by a constant consumption of 'virtual nectar'. If a target area disappears, there will be no local addition of 'virtual nectar' and the gradient will disappear. To investigate this, we performed an experiment with very extreme differences in target sizes (radii left:right = 1:5). After 500 time steps, we changed the sizes of the targets:

The big area got small and the small area got big (radii left:right 5:1). After the same time span, we investigated how the swarm responded to this fluctuation by counting the newly recruited robots at the left target and the robots that abandoned the right target after 1000 time-steps.

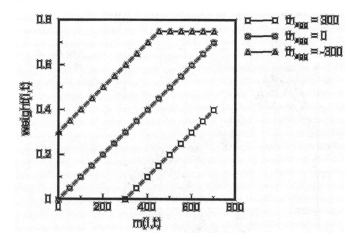

Fig. 8. Values of **weight(i,t)** as a measurement for directedness of a robot's movement depending on its memory value **m(i,t)** and the threshold th_{agg}. Shown for a positive threshold $\mathbf{th_{agg}}$=300, no threshold $\mathbf{th_{agg}}$=0, and a negative threshold $\mathbf{th_{agg}}$=-300.

We initially implemented the 'forgetting' also into the hop-count strategy (t_f), but this strategy failed to recruit proportional cohort to differently sized target areas in a stable environment (sub-section 3.1, figures 5,6). Without such a proportional response of the swarm, it is useless to perform such a test in a fluctuating environment, so we only analyzed the trophallaxis-inspired strategy here. We kept all parameter settings identical to the runs shown in subsection 3.1, but we varied the values of the

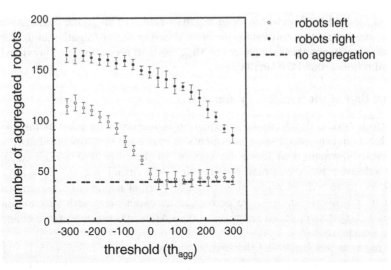

Fig. 9. Aggregation of robots to the small left target area (radius=1) and to the large right target area (radius=5) with varying threshold (th_{agg}). The dashed line shows the expected number of robots that would have been in the measurement area (radius=10 each) if there had been no aggregation behavior at all. N=10 per setting. Duration: 250 time steps.

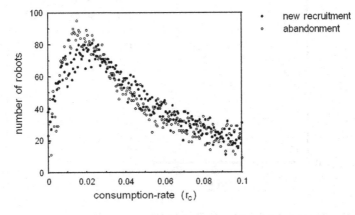

Fig. 10. New recruitment and abandonment of robots in a changing environment and with varying values of the consumption-rate (r_c). High values of new recruitment and of abandonment indicate a high flexibility of the collective decisions of the robots swarm. N=1 per setting. Measurements were made 500 time steps after the environmental fluctuation.

consumption rate r_c between 0 and 0.1. So we compared never-forgetting swarms, moderately fast forgetting swarms and quickly forgetting swarms. Figure 10 shows the results of this experiment: Never-forgetting swarms ($r_c < 0.01$) failed to adjust to the switch because the strong gradient that had emerged around the right target before the switch kept dominating throughout the arena. Quickly forgetting swarms ($r_c > 0.03$) on the other hand were not able to establish a gradient that reached robots that were far from the target and thus changes in the environment were not noticed by most robots. With a consumption-rate between 0.01 and 0.03, the swarm showed the highest flexibility in its decisions.

4 Discussion

Our simulation experiments focused purely on the questions of collective perception in a robot swarm. We showed that a system that exploits purely 'hop-counts' of messages is able to navigate robots to target areas but fails to perform a collective perception of target area sizes. Such 'hop-count'-based strategies were used (and published) several times in swarm robotics [19][20][21][22]. Some times these techniques are called 'virtual pheromones', a term that we (as biologists) do not think is appropriate. A pheromone is a chemical substance that is released by an animal in the environment and that causes a behavioral change or a physiological change in a receiving animal. For a swarm robot, it is very difficult to deposit something in the environment; therefore hop-counts that are communicated from robot to robot are often used to mimic pheromone gradients. But such a system has significant differences to real pheromones, because hop-count values do not remain in place in the environment, they move with the robot that carries it. We think that these hop-counts and also the memory-values used in our trophallaxis-inspired strategies have much more analogies to the crop loads of (social) animals. They are bound to their 'carrier'-animals and it is often found in nature, that crop volumes are transferred from one animal to another (ants, termites, bees, wasps, birds, vampire bats). In contrast to the hop-count strategy, the trophallaxis-inspired strategy [17] was able to perform collective perception successfully (figure 5,6). By using this method, the swarm was able to collectively measure the size of the target areas and to communicate these sizes throughout the swarm.

Please note that a single robot cannot measure the size of the target area, it can only determine whether or not it is located on a target area. The observed effect is caused by the fact that a larger target area can contain more robots and thus more 'addition' is made to the system. The three parameters 'addition-rate', 'transfer-rate', 'consumption-rate' can be used to regulate the system. A higher addition makes the gradients higher. The transfer rate allows the gradient to reach further, thus it can be used to regulate the range of the attraction of the targets. We showed that in changing environments, a moderate forgetting of collective perceptions plays an important role. With a consumption-rate that was too low, the robot swarm was not able to re-decide after the environmental fluctuation. With a consumption-rate that was too high, the swarm was not able to perform any collective decision at all. The threshold th_{agg} is an important factor to adjust the 'collective sensitivity' of the robot swarm. By adjusting this parameter, smaller target areas can be made invisible for the swarm, so that it focuses on the bigger target areas first. Our scenario (and the strategy) can be extended in several ways. In honeybees, the brood acts as a sink for food. In the case shown here, we used only target areas that led to an addition of 'virtual nectar'. If the scenario contains also areas that should be preferentially avoided (e.g., holes [23]), we could easily add such a sink to our system. Robots that encounter such areas reduce their memory values to 0. The threshold th_{agg} is currently a global parameter in our strategy. It will be interesting to introduce habituation and reinforcement to adjust this parameter individually, based on the prior work experience of a robot.

In conclusion, we demonstrated that collective perception of a robot swarm can be performed with simple nearest-neighbor communication, with rather narrow communication channels and with messages that include only little semantics. The system was shown to be robust, because our results were not significantly affected by random error (which we introduced in our simulation on motion, sensing and communication) or by initial conditions (robots were spread randomly in the arena). In addition, the collective decisions were flexible (see figure 10). Computational effort was low and the number of robots was rather high. All these features mentioned above indicate that the found collective perception was an emergent phenomenon of self-organization [5] and of swarm-intelligence [6][7].

Acknowledgement

This work is partially supported by: EU IST-FET-project 'I-Swarm', no. 507006.

References

1. Seyfried, J., Szymanski, M., Bender, N., Estana, R., Thiel, M., Wörn, H.: The I-SWARM Project: Intelligent Small World Autonomous Robots for Micro-Manipulation. In: Sahin, E., Spears, W.M. (eds.) Swarm Robotics. Springer LNCS 3342, (2005) 70 – 83
2. Kornienko, S., Kornienko, O. Constantinescu. C., Pradier, M., Levi, P.: Cognitive micro-agents: individual and collective perception in a microrobotic swarm. In: Proceedings of the IJCAI-05 Workshop on Agents in Real-Time and Dynamic Environment, Edinburgh, Scotland, (2005) 33 – 42
3. Kornienko, S., Kornienko, O., Levi, P.: Minimalistic approach towards communication and perception in microrobotic swarms. In: Proceedings of IEEE/RSJ International Conference on Intelligent Robots and Systems, Edmonton, Alberta, Canada (2005) 4005 – 4011
4. Liu, Y., Passino, K.M.: Biomimicry of Social Foraging Behavior for Distributed Optimization: Models, Principles, and Emergent Behaviors. Journal of Optimization Theory and Applications, V 115, N 3, (2002) 603 – 628
5. Camazine, S., Deneubourg, J.L., Franks, N., Sneyd, J., Theraulaz, G., Bonabeau, E.: Self-organization in biological systems. Princeton University Press, NJ, USA (2001)
6. Bonabeau, E., Dorigo, M., Theraulaz, G.: Swarm intelligence: From natural to artificial systems. Oxford University Press, New York, NY, USA (1999)
7. Kennedy, J., Eberhart, R.C.: Swarm Intelligence. Morgan Kaufmann Publishers, Academic Press, USA. (2001)
8. Anderson, C, Ratnieks, F.L.W.: Task partitioning in insect societies. I. Effect of colony size on queueing delay and colony ergonomic efficiency, Am. Naturalist 154, (1999) 521 – 535
9. Ratnieks, F.L.W., Anderson, C.: Task partitioning in insect societies. II. Use of queueing delay information in recruitment, Am. Naturalist 154, (1999) 536 – 548
10. Seeley, T., Towey, C.: Why search time to find a food-storer bee accurately indicates the relative rates of nectar collecting and nectar processing in honey bee colonies. Animal Behaviour, 47, (1994), 311 – 316

11. Pratt, S.C.: Optimal timing of comb construction by honeybee (*Apis mellifera*) colonies: a dynamic programming model and experimental tests. Behavioral Ecology and Sociobiology 46, (1999) 30 – 42
12. Huang, M., Seeley, T.: Multiple unloadings by nectar foragers in honey bees: a matter of information improvement or crop fullness? Insectes Sociaux 50, (2003), 1 – 10
13. Camazine, S.: The regulation of pollen foraging by honey bees: How foragers assess the colony's need for pollen, Behavioral Ecology and Sociobiology 32, (1993) 265 – 273
14. Camazine, S., Crailsheim, K., Hrassnigg, N., Robinson, G.E., Leonhard, B., Kropiunigg, H.: Protein trophallaxis and the regulation of pollen foraging by honey bees (*Apis mellifera* L.), Apidologie 29, (1998) 113 – 126
15. Schmickl, T., Crailsheim, K.: Inner nest homeostasis in a changing environment with special emphasis on honeybee brood nursing and pollen supply. Apidologie 35, (2004) 249-263
16. Crailsheim, K.: The flow of jelly within a honeybee colony, Journal of Comparative Physiology B 162, (1992) 681 – 689
17. Schmickl, T., Crailsheim, K.: Trophallaxis among swarm-robots: A biological inspired strategy for swarm robotics. In: Proceedings of BioRob 2006, Biomedical Robotics and Biomechatronics, Pisa, Italy. (2006) ISBN 1-4244-0040-6
18. Valdastri, P., Corradi, P., Menciassi, A., Schmickl, T., Crailsheim, K., Seyfried, J., Dario, P.: Micromanipulation, communication and swarm intelligence issues in a microrobotic platform. Robotics and Automation Systems (in press).
19. Payton, D., Daily, M., Estowski, R., Howard, M., Lee, C.: Pheromone Robotics. Autonomous Robots 11 (2001) 319 – 324
20. Payton, D., Estkowski, R., Howard, M.: Compound behaviors in pheromone robotics. Robotics and Autonomous Systems 44 (2003) 229 – 240
21. Stoy, K., How do construct dense objects with self-reconfigurable robots. In: Christensen, H.I. (eds.) European Robotics Symposium 2006, STAR 22 (2006) 27 – 37
22. McLurkin, J.D.: Stupid robot tricks: a behavior-based distributed algorithm library for programming swarms of robots. Master thesis at the MIT (2004)
23. Trianni, V., Nolfi, S., Dorigo, M.: Hole Avoidance: Experiments in Coordinated Motion on Rough Terrain. In: Groen, F, Amato, N., Bonarini, A., Yoshida, E., Krose, B., (eds.), Intelligent Autonomous Systems 8, (2004) 29-36

Distributed Task Selection in Multi-agent Based Swarms Using Heuristic Strategies

David Miller[1], Prithviraj Dasgupta[2], and Timothy Judkins[3]

[1] Department of Mechanical Engineering, University of Nebraska-Lincoln
[2] Computer Science Department, University of Nebraska-Omaha
[3] HPER Biomechanics Laboratory, University of Nebraska-Omaha
pdasgupta@mail.unomaha.edu

Abstract. Swarm-based systems have emerged as an attractive paradigm for implementing distributed autonomous systems for various applications in commercial, military and business domains. One of the major operations in a swarm-based system is to ensure that the individual swarm units process the tasks in the environment in an efficient manner. This can be achieved using a suitable task selection mechanism that allocates the desired number of swarm units to each task while reducing inter-task latencies and communication overhead, and, ensuring adequate commitment of resources to tasks. In this paper, we describe a multi-agent based distributed task selection mechanism for swarm-based systems. We show that the distributed task selection problem is NP-complete and propose polynomial-time heuristic-based algorithms. Our simulation results show that heuristics in which each swarm unit considers both the effects of other swarm units on tasks and its own relative position to other swarm units achieve better task processing efficiency and improved distribution of swarm units over tasks.

Keywords: multi-agent swarming, task allocation, heuristics, Webots.

1 Introduction

Over the past few years, emergent computation based techniques such as swarming have been used extensively to model and develop algorithms for distributed systems for diverse applications including telecommunication networks[8], data mining [1], and robotics[20]. Swarming enables a system to manifest the desired global objectives by embedding simple behavior patterns, possibly inspired from nature, at the level of the individual units in the system. This makes swarming an attractive mechanism for designing complex, large-scale distributed systems using numerous behaviorally simple, possibly inexpensive units without worrying about problems such as designing centralized algorithms for load balancing, congestion control and scalability. However, in the absence of centralized control mechanisms, monitoring the operations of a distributed swarm-based system to ensure efficient performance becomes a challenging problem. In this paper, we focus on the task selection mechanism used by the individual swarm units to process the tasks in the environment. Previous researchers[10,17] have addressed this

E. Şahin et al. (Eds.): Swarm Robotics Ws, LNCS 4433, pp. 158–172, 2007.

problem using centralized task allocation algorithms where information about tasks are shared between the swarm units using shared memory-based techniques. In contrast, ensuring efficient task selection by the swarm units becomes a challenging problem in a distributed setting because of the dynamic nature of the environment, differences in characteristics of the swarm units and possible inconsistencies in information between the different swarm units. In this paper, we model swarming within a multi-agent setting where each swarm unit is modeled as an agent. We formulate the distributed task selection problem in a swarm as a dynamic traveling salesman problem(TSP) and provide heuristic-based algorithms to solve it. Our simulation results for a distributed automatic target recognition(ATR) application using our heuristic-based task selection strategies in a swarm show that the performance of the system improves when each swarm unit considers the effects of other swarm units on tasks as well as its own relative position to other swarm units.

2 Multi-agent Swarming

The technique of swarming involves movement of entities (for e.g. insects, humans or combat vehicles) individually or in small-sized units to search and act upon objects of interest such as food, prey, or enemy within a search space. The problem space consists of objects of interest that are distributed randomly in a 2-dimensional environment. Individual units lack the necessary power to perform the complete set of actions required on an object of interest. When an individual or unit discovers an object of interest, it communicates the information to other units. The other units then converge on the object to perform the required actions on the object(for e.g., consuming food, subsuming prey, etc.) using the combined power of the congregated units amassed together. After completing the task on an object, each unit reverts to individual searching.

A computational system using swarming consists of multiple computation units that are capable of moving within an unknown environment. Because of the dynamic nature of the environment, each unit must also be capable of continuously searching, communicating and executing tasks corresponding to objects of interest as long as it is active in the environment. Agents provide a suitable paradigm to implement the computation units for swarming. Agents are software entities that are capable of executing the actions programmed within them autonomously without continuous supervision by humans. Agents are also characterized by a small footprint and are suitable for embedding on mobile platforms such as ground vehicles and aircrafts for encapsulating the functionalities of individual units in a swarm. Following are the features of a distributed swarmed system:

1. The boundaries of the area (environment) in which the agents are deployed is known *a priori* by the agents.
2. A task corresponds to a set of actions that need to be taken by agents on objects of interest. The spatial and temporal distribution of tasks is not known *a priori* and must be discovered by the agents in real-time.

3. A single agent is only capable of discovering and partially executing tasks, but lacks the computational resources required to completely execute a task.
4. A task can be completed only if multiple agents share their computational resources towards executing the task.
5. To enlist the cooperation of other agents required to complete a task, an agent that discovers a task communicates the task's information to other agents. In contrast to some recent swarm-based systems[10,17], this communication has to be done in a distributed manner without using a central location or shared memory to facilitate information exchange among agents.
6. An agent requires to move to the vicinity of a task discovered by another agent to execute it. Each agent executes the tasks independently and on completing its portion of execution on the task, communicates the progress of its execution (fraction of task still incomplete) to other agents within its communication range.

To realize the swarming behavior in our system, we use the *stigmergetic* activity of social insects such as ants [5]. Stigmergy is an interaction mechanism that enables insects to coordinate actions with each other through direct contact or indirect communication via the environment. For example, ants searching searching for food deposit trails of a chemical substance called pheromone. Pheromone provides positive reinforcement to future ants, and, ants searching for the food later on get attracted to the pheromone to locate and possibly consume the food. In our system, when an agent encounters a task, it deposits a certain amount of synthetic pheromone to mark the location and priority of the task. Pheromone decays over time. The set of tasks and the corresponding pheromones that each agent is aware of is stored in a local data structure called the *pheromone landscape* within the agent and corresponds to the agent's task list. An agent communicates its task list to other agents within its communication range to disseminate task information across the swarm. The operations performed by an agent to manifest swarming can be divided into the following phases:

- **Deployment.** Agents are deployed by a central manager into the environment. Once the agents are deployed, the manager does not supervise the agents. The agents revert to the manager only when their lifetime expires. For better overall coverage, the manager might choose to divide the environment into smaller sub-areas and deploy a subset of agent into each sub-area[6].
- **Search and Discovery.** In this phase, individual agents perform a blind or uninformed search within the search space to discover objects of interest. We assume that each agent is provided with appropriate sensors, algorithms and information to enable it to identify objects of interest. When an agent discovers an object of interest, it associates a certain amount of pheromone with the object to indicate the urgency with which other agents should arrive at the object to complete the task associated with that object.
- **Communication.** After an agent discovers a task, it has to inform other agents about the parameters of the task including the task's location and

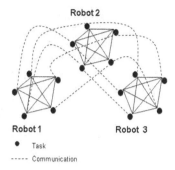

Fig. 1. Task allocation between 5 tasks and 3 robots, assuming all robots are aware of all tasks

pheromone. To achieve this in a distributed manner, an agent uses a point-to-point communication model to disseminate information about tasks it is aware of to other agents within its communication range.

- **Task Selection.** An agent stores information about incomplete tasks in the search space that it receives from other agents in a task list. An agent must select a subset of tasks from its task list it wants to execute partially and the order in which it to visit the selected tasks to plan its path.
- **Task Execution.** On arriving at the location corresponding to a task/object, an agent performs the actions required on the object to complete its share of task. After completing its portion of execution for all the tasks on its task list, an agent reverts to searching.

In the rest of the paper, we focus on the task selection problem in swarming. Algorithms for deployment, search and discovery, communication and task execution for swarming are implemented in our system using the algorithms described in [6]. Functionally, each computational unit in our swarmed system is a mobile robot that contains a processor executing the algorithms implemented by an agent. Therefore, in the rest of the paper we use the terms robot and agent interchangeably.

3   Task Selection in Swarming

Task selection is one of the most crucial phases of the swarming mechanism as it determines the efficiency with which tasks are completed in the system. A suitable task selection algorithm ensures controlled swarming towards task to ensure appropriate commitment of resources to tasks, ability of the swarm to separate adaptively into sub-swarms and reduction in communication overhead.

3.1   Distributed Task Selection Model

Our model for the task selection problem comprises a set of R robots that need to execute a set of T tasks in the environment as described in Section 2. Each robot

$r \in R$ is aware of a subset of tasks $T_r \subseteq T$. T_r changes dynamically as tasks get executed by r and removed from T_r and new tasks arrive via communication from other robots and get added to T_r. Each task $t \in T_r$ involves two components: a) a non-zero wait-time $w_{t,r}$ corresponding to the time required by robot r to reach the task from the robot's current location, and b) an execution time $x_{t,r}$ required to execute robot r's portion of the task. $x_{t,r}$ is inversely proportional to the amount of instantaneous pheromone associated with task t. Both $w_{t,r}$ and $x_{t,r}$ change dynamically as robots move in the environment and deposit pheromone at tasks. Robot r orders the tasks in T_r to solve the following dynamic optimization problem: $min \sum_{t \in T_r} w_{t,r} + x_{t,r}$. From the viewpoint of a single robot, the task selection problem can be modeled as an instance of the dynamic TSP, where the cost for robot r to reach and execute a task t corresponds to $(w_{t,r} + x_{t,r})$. Figure 1 shows a scenario consisting of $\mid T \mid = 5$ tasks, each task requiring $\mid R \mid = 3$ robots to be completed. Each fully connected subgraph in Figure 1 represents robot r's view of the tasks. For simplifying the analysis, we assume that all robots are aware of all the tasks in the environment and are within communication range of each other. However, different robots execute the tasks in different order depending on various factors including the robots' initial locations, speed and obstacles along their path. As soon as a robot finishes executing its portion of a task on its task graph, it updates the status of that task (deposits pheromone) and communicates the updated status to the other robots. We assume that the communication latency (shown by broken lines in Figure 1) is much less than the task wait-time $w_{t,r}$. When a robot updates the status of a task, the costs of edges connected to the vertex t changes for each robot r that still has $t \in T_r$. Let $G_r(\tau) = (V_r(\tau), E_r(\tau)) \mid V_r(\tau) = T_r(\tau)$ represent the task graph of robot r at time τ, where $V_r(\tau)$ and $E_r(\tau)$ are, respectively, the vertices and edges comprising $G_r(\tau)$. Let $c_r(i, j, \tau)$ represent the cost to robot r to reach vertex(task) j from vertex i in $G_r(\tau)$. The dynamic TSP problem can then be written as:

$$DTSP = \{<G(\tau), c_r, k> : G(\tau) = \{G_r(\tau)\} \mid r \in R, \tau = \{0, 1, 2...\}$$
$$G_r(\tau) = (V_r(\tau), E_r(\tau)) \text{ is the task-graph of } r \in R,$$
$$c_r : i \times j \times \tau \to \mathcal{Z} \mid i, j \in V_r(\tau)$$
$$k \in \mathcal{Z}, \text{and}$$
$$\forall r, G_r(\tau) \text{has a traveling-salesman tour with cost at most } k\}.$$
$$(1)$$

Proposition: *The dynamic TSP is NP-complete.*

Proof. (by reduction to TSP) In Figure 1, consider a scenario where $r = 2, 3$ have completed visiting the all vertices in G_2 and G_3, while $r = 1$ has yet to visit any vertex in G_1. Let the time at which such a scenario occurs be $\tau = \tau_f$. Let $G_1(\tau_f) = (V_1(\tau_f), E_1(\tau_f))$ be an instance of TSP. We construct an instance of DTSP as follows. We form the complete graph $G'_1(\tau_f) = (V_1(\tau_f), E'_1(\tau_f))$ where $E'_1(\tau_f) = \{(i, j) : i, j \in V_1(\tau_f) \text{and} i \neq j\}$, and we define the cost function $c_1(\tau_f)$ by:

$$c_1(i, j, \tau_f) = \begin{cases} 0 \text{ if } (i, j) \in E_1(\tau_f), \\ 1 \text{ otherwise.} \end{cases} \tag{2}$$

The instance of DTSP is then $(G'_1(\tau_f), c_1(\tau_f), 0)$. We now show that graph $G_1(\tau_f)$ has a TSP-tour iff graph $G'_1(\tau_f)$ has a TSP-tour of cost at most 0. Suppose that graph $G_1(\tau_f)$ has a traveling salesman tour θ. Each edge in θ being to $E_1(\tau_f)$ and thus has cost 0 in $G'_1(\tau_f)$. Thus, θ is a traveling salesman tour in $G'_1(\tau_f)$ with cost 0. Conversely, suppose that graph $G'_1(\tau_f)$ has a traveling-salesman tour θ' of cost at most 0. Since the costs of the edges in $E'_1(\tau_f)$ are 0 and 1, the cost of tour θ' is exactly 0 and each edge of the tour must have cost 0. Therefore, θ' contains only edges in $E_1(\tau_f)$. We conclude that θ' is a traveling-salesman tour in graph $G_1(\tau_f)$. □

The cost of the edges in the DTSP are determined by the time required by robot $r \in R$ to reach and execute a task $t \in T$. However, the time to execute a task is proportional to the amount of pheromone already associated with the task by other robots and is determined by the robots' pheromone update mechanism. Therefore, vertices in the DTSP do not necessarily follow the triangle inequality and consequently, cannot be solved using a polynomial time approximation algorithm. In the next section, we describe polynomial time heuristic-based solutions to the DTSP.

4   Heuristic-Based Task Selection Strategies

The parameters used by the heuristic-based strategies are the following:

R Set of robots
N_r Number of robots required to complete a task
r_i i-th robot, $r_i \in R$
P_i *OtherRobots* list of robot r_i comprising set of robots it is aware of
$p_{j,i}$ j-th robot $\in P_i$, $p_{j,i} = \{id, conf, loc, time, t_{id}\}$, where id is the Id of robot $p_{j,i}$, $conf \in [0, 1]$ is the confidence in the current location of $p_{j,i}$, loc is the last known location of $p_{j,i}$, $time$ is the time of last update of location of $p_{j,i}$ and t_{id} is the id of the last task executed by $p_{j,i}$.
Ψ_i Task list of robot r_i comprising set of tasks it is aware of.
$\psi_{j,i}$ j-th task in task list Ψ_i of robot r_i, $\psi_{j,i} = \{pher, loc, hops, time, id, visits\}$, where, $pher$ is the amount of pheromone associated with $\psi_{j,i}$, loc is the location(2-d coordinates)of $\psi_{j,i}$, $hops$ is the number of hops made by the message containing information about $\psi_{j,i}$ before reaching robot r_i, $time$ is the time at which $\psi_{j,i}$ was last updated by another robot, id is the id of the robot that last updated $\psi_{j,i}$, and, $visits$ is the number of robots that have already visited $\psi_{j,i}$.

In the heuristic-based algorithms, each robot r_i inspects its task list Ψ_i and robot list P_i and selects the task $\psi_{j,i} \in \Psi_i$ that returns the best value of the heuristic being used. A robot runs the heuristic based algorithm every time its task list and robot list is updated. The different heuristic strategies that can be used by a robot are the following:

- **Distance-based heuristic**: In the distance based heuristic, each robot r_i selects the task $\psi_{j,i} \in \Psi_i$ that is closest to it and has the highest amount of pheromone using Equation 3 below. Distances between r_i and each task $\psi_{j,i}$ are normalized over the sum of distances to enable comparison between the distances.

$$\arg\max_j \left(\psi_{j,i}.pher \times (1 - \frac{dist(\psi_{j,i}.loc, r_i.loc)}{\sum_j dist(\psi_{j,i}.loc, r_i.loc)}) \right). \qquad (3)$$

- **Robot Density-based heuristic**: This heuristic is based on the premise that incomplete tasks that have the least number of robots in their vicinity are likely to be requiring more robots for completing them. Therefore, the robot density-based heuristic directs a robot towards the task in its task list that has the least density of robots in its vicinity. To calculate the relative location of other robots, robot r_i uses the location attribute $p_{j,i}.loc$ of each robot $p_{j,i} \in P_i$. However, $p_{j,i}.loc$ changes dynamically as robot $p_{j,i}$ moves continuously in the environment. Therefore, robot r_i uses a probabilistic weight $p_{j,i}.conf$ to reflect its confidence of the location $p_{j,i}.loc$. $p_{j,i}.conf$ is inversely proportional to the time elapsed since the location of $p_{j,i}$ was last received by robot r_i. Robot r_i then selects the task that has the lowest robot density in its vicinity using Equation 4:

$$\arg\min_j \sum_k \left(p_{k,i}.conf \times \psi_{j,i}.pher \times (1 - \frac{dist(\psi_{j,i}.loc, p_{k,i}.loc)}{\sum_k dist(\psi_{j,i}.loc, p_{k,i}.loc)}) \right).$$
$$(4)$$

- **Robot Preference-based heuristic**: This heuristic extends the robot density-based heuristic by considering the number of robots still required to complete a task. In addition to preferring tasks with lower robot densities in their vicinity, robot r_i, using the preference-base heuristic selects tasks that are nearing completion and therefore, require fewer robots for completion, as shown in Equation 5:

$$\arg\min_j \sum_k \left(p_{k,i}.conf \times \frac{N_r - \psi_{j,i}.visits}{N_r} \times \psi_{j,i}.pher \right.$$
$$\left. \times (1 - \frac{dist(\psi_{j,i}.loc, p_{k,i}.loc)}{\sum_k dist(\psi_{j,i}.loc, p_{k,i}.loc)}) \right). \qquad (5)$$

- **Robot Proximity-based heuristic**: In the robot density and preference-based heuristics, each robot considers the effect of other robots on tasks in its task list, but does not consider its own relative position to those robots. In contrast, in the robot proximity heuristic, robot r_i first determines how many other robots are closer to task $\psi_{j,i} \in \Psi_i$ than itself. It then selects the task that has the least number of robots closer to the task than itself and the least number of robots required for completion as shown in Equation 6:

$$\arg\min_{j} \left(\sum_{k} \psi_{j,i,k}.n \times \frac{N_r - \psi_{j,i}.visits}{N_r} \right) , \text{ where}$$

$$\psi_{j,i,k}.n = \begin{cases} 1, \text{ if } p_{k,i}.conf \times \psi_{j,i}.pher \times \\ \quad (1 - \frac{dist(\psi_{j,i}.loc, p_{k,i}.loc)}{\sum_{k} dist(\psi_{j,i}.loc, p_{k,i}.loc)}) > (1 - \frac{dist(\psi_{j,i}.loc, r_i.loc)}{\sum_{j} dist(\psi_{j,i}.loc, r_i.loc)}) \\ 0, \quad \text{otherwise} \end{cases}$$

$$(6)$$

Proposition: *The processing time required by robots using the heuristic-based algorithms to complete all the tasks in the environment has a polynomial upper-bound.*

Proof: In each of the heuristic-based strategies described above, every time robot r_i's task list is updated, it has to process all the tasks in its task list Ψ_i to find the 'best' task. In addition, all the strategies, except the distance-based strategy, requires robot r_i to process each member of its *OtherRobots* list P_i. Therefore, for each update in its task list, a robot has to process $| \Psi_i | \times | P_i |$ elements. To determine the upper-bounds on the computation done in the swarm using the heuristic strategies, let us assume that in the worst case, each robots task list contains all the tasks in the environment, i.e., $| \Psi_i | = O(| T |)$. Also, in the worst case, each robots *OtherRobots* list would contain every other robot in the environment, i.e. $| P_i | = O(| R |)$. Substituting these worst case values for the cardinalities of the task and *OtherRobots* list, we see that each update of the task list at a robot requires $O(| T || R |)$ steps. How many task list updates are possible at each robot to complete all the tasks? Assuming that in the worst case scenario, each task must be processed by every robot, the task list of a robot gets updated every time another robot visits and executes a task. Since the environment has $| R |$ robots, each with a task list of size $O(| T |)$, the total number of times robots visit and execute tasks to generate updates to other robots' tasks lists is $O(| T || R |)$. Each such update takes $O(| T || R |)$ steps as discussed above. Therefore, the total processing time required to complete all the tasks in the system is bounded by $O((| T || R |)^2)$.

5   Simulation Results

We have implemented our swarming algorithms for a distributed automatic target recognition(ATR) application using unmanned aerial robots[6]. The scenario consists of targets distributed randomly in an environment. The objective of the robots is to identify all the targets. However, each robot has limited computational resources, and, although a robot can independently discover a target, it requires the cooperation of at least 3 other robots to confirm a discovered object as a target. In this scenario, a task corresponds to the actions performed by a robot on a target. For example, in distributed ATR the task of a single robot

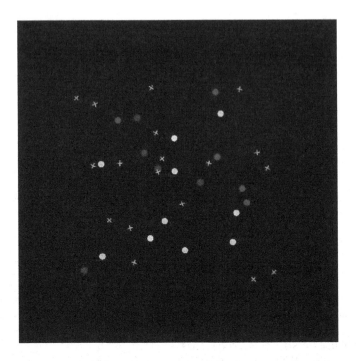

Fig. 2. Screenshot from the Webots simulator showing 20 targets(circles) and 18 robots (airplane icons) in a 50 × 50 environment

could be to execute an image identification algorithm when it encounters a possible target. To confirm a possible target definitively, 4 different robots need to successfully execute their image identification algorithm on the target.

5.1   Experimental Setup

All our experiments were run with 18 robots and 20 targets placed randomly inside a 50 × 50 environment on the Webots robotic simulation platform, as shown in Figure 2. Each robot is simulated as a generic *DifferentialWheels* model whose speed and direction are controlled by changing the relative rotation speed between the two wheels. The maximum speed of each wheel was set to 40. Each robot has the following sensors: (1) GPS: x, z location and heading, (2)Downward looking IR sensor for target detection with a measurement range between 0 and 2048, (3) Short-range radio transmitter and receiver for sending and receiving ping messages over channel 1 with a range of 1.5 units, and, (4) Long-range radio transmitter and receiver for sending and receiving gossip messages over channel 0 with a range of 7.5 units.

Target Detection: The floor of the environment is black and corresponds to a zero intensity value on a robot's downward-looking IR sensor. Targets are given 4 different colors (red, grey, green, purple) to simulate different target types that require different amounts of computation. 20 targets, 5 of each color are placed at random coordinates within the environment. When the IR sensor on a robot encounters a target, it returns a non-zero intensity value determined by the color of the target. The robot then associates a particular amount of pheromone with the target using the following values: Red= 0.8, Grey=0.6, Green= 0.4, Purple=0.2. Pheromone decays at a rate of 0.01 per simulator tick. Each target needs to be visited by $N_r = 4$ robots to be completely identified.

Robot Communication: When a target is found by a robot, it sends a gossip message to other robots within communication range of its long-range transmitter. Gossip messages are forwarded by robots using the probabilistic flooding algorithm described in [6] to disseminate information about a recently discovered target across the swarm. The format of the gossip message is given by: $< id, x, z, ttl, v, found_{id}, t_x, t_z, t_{pher} >$, where

id	id of robot sending the message
x, z	2-d coordinates of the robot sending the message
ttl	Number of hops (time-to-live)from its source after which the gossip message ceases to be forwarded by robots
v	Number of visits by robots to the target contained in the message
$found_{id}$	Id of the robot that discovered the target in the message
t_x, t_z	2-d coordinates of the target contained in the message
t_{pher}	Pheromone value associated with target in the message

On receiving a gossip message, a robot decrements its ttl and if $ttl > 0$, it forwards the message over its long-range transmitter after updating the values of the first three parameters of the message with its own id and location.

Obstacle and Collision Avoidance: To prevent collision between robots, each robot uses a potential field based object avoidance technique described in [6]. Collision avoidance takes precedence over all other actions.

5.2   Experimental Results

In the experiments performed we measure the efficiency of the swarmed system using our task selection heuristics along three metrics: (i) time required to complete all tasks, (ii) distribution of tasks over robots, and (iii) distribution of robots over tasks. Figure 3 compares the time required to complete all tasks in the environment with different heuristic strategies used by the robots. We observe that when robots use the robot preference-based and robot proximity-based heuristics, all tasks get completed more rapidly than the other heuristics. These two heuristics include information about the amount of computation remaining to complete a task when a robot selects a task. Therefore, we can infer that information about the progress of the task plays a positive role in improving the efficiency of task completion. Moreover, the robot proximity based heuristic performs slightly better than the robot preference based heuristic without using any extra information. This implies that considering the effect of other robots on tasks as well as a robot's own position relative to other robots while

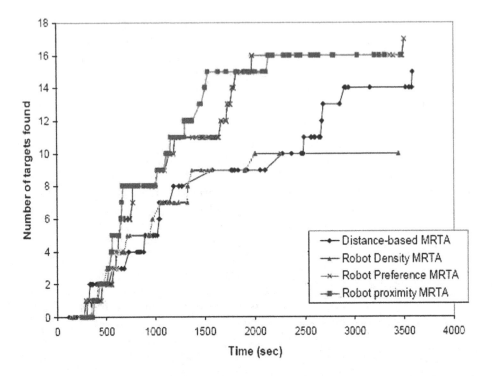

Fig. 3. Time taken by robots to identify all targets in the environment using different strategies

selecting a task enables rapid task processing. The distance-based and density-based heuristics are unable to complete all tasks (identify all the targets) in the environment. This behavior can be attributed to inadequate dispersion of robots across the environment in these two strategies. In these strategies, as soon as a robot receives gossiped information about a task, it starts heading to the task without considering the effect of other robots on the task such as their proximity to the task, their possibility of acting on the task before the current robot, and the progress of the task due to other robots' actions. Consequently, most robots end up moving towards the same task. This triggers the collision avoidance mechanism as soon as robots reach within close range of each other before reaching the task. In such a scenario, most robots start exhibiting an oscillatory behavior moving back and forth around the task unable to reach it.

Figure 4 compares the number of times each task is visited by different robots for the different heuristics. We observe that for all heuristics except the robot proximity-based, each task was visited by approximately 4 robots (number of robots required to complete a task for our setting) in most cases. Figure 4 further shows that the robot preference-based heuristic outperforms all the other heuristics in maintaining an average of 4 visits/task. The robot proximity-based heuristic allows more than 4 robots to visit a task because the robots stay more dispersed across the environment than in the other heuristics. This delays some

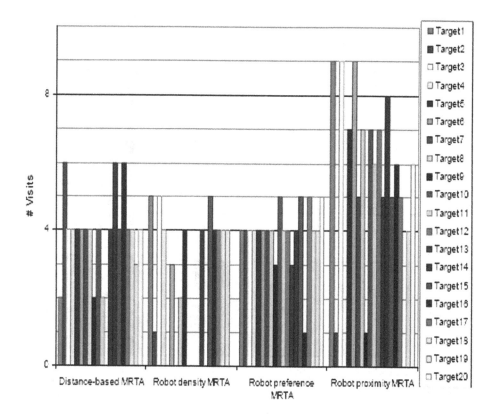

Fig. 4. Number of times each target is visited by a robot using different strategies

robots from receiving information about a task until the task's gossip message gets flooded across all the robots. Figure 5 shows the performance of each robot across different tasks. For our setting of 20 tasks(targets), 18 robots and 4 robots required to complete a task, the average number of tasks that each robot should visit is given by $\lceil \frac{20 \times 4}{18} \rceil = 5$. However, we observe that, except in the robot preference-based heuristic, some robots visited more than the average number of tasks while other robots visited far less than average. The robot distance-based and density-based heuristics perform poorly due to the oscillatory movements of robots unable to reach tasks due to mutual collision avoidance discussed earlier. The proximity-based heuristic has more than the required number of robot visits/task due to its communication related inefficiencies discussed earlier.

In summary, we can infer that the preference-based and proximity-based heuristics improve the efficiency in the system as compared to the other heuristics. The former achieves better task and robot distribution across the environment while with the latter robots are able to complete tasks more rapidly. Both heuristics require the same amount of communication while the preference-based heuristic requires less computation than the proximity-based heuristic.

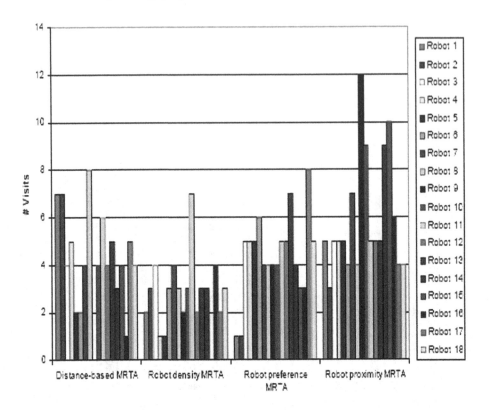

Fig. 5. Number of targets visited by each robot using different strategies

Therefore, if overall task completion time is a constraint, robots should use the proximity-based heuristic. On the other hand, if the efficiency of individual robots is more important then robots should use the preference-based heuristic.

6   Related Work

Swarming-based systems have been abundant in nature and human history[9]. In the recent past, several computational systems using swarming have been developed for different applications including self-repairing formation control for mobile agents [20], adaptive control in overlay networks[4], and for military applications[6,17,19]. Most of these approaches do not address the task selection problem in swarming as a independent issue and use straight-forward approaches such as greedy algorithms within a centralized shared memory setting [10,17] that facilitates rapid information exchange between the swarm units. In contrast, in this paper we describe different heuristic-based strategies in a distributed task selection model for swarming. In [2], distributed heuristic based strategies for capturing the collective aggregation dynamics in multi-agent swarms for gathering and clustering tasks are described. [13] describes heuristic-based strategies for task constraints and signal reinforcement to analyze the effects of diversity and specialization on multi-agent swarms. These studies are complementary to the work described in this paper.

Independent of swarming, the problem of multi-robot task allocation(MRTA) has been investigated using different techniques such as physical modeling[16], distributed planning[15] and market-based techniques[7,11]. Task allocation in a multi-robot distributed system using a contract-net based protocol for the COMETS-UAV system has been described in [12]. The mechanism relies on one robot being elected as a leader(auctioneer) using a token-ring technique. In addition, the task allocation mechanism requires the leader to have knowledge about all the tasks it allocates to other robots(contractors). In contrast, the task selection strategies used in this paper do not require leader election and the information about tasks is maintained locally on each UAV in a distributed manner. Other approaches to multi-agent cooperation algorithms include the Martha system[3] that focuses on planning and distributed cooperation schemes, coordination between agent teams using distributed constraint optimization techniques[14], and neogitation based mutli-agent task allocation[18]. Most of these approaches are complementary to our work and consider scenarios where an agent has to allocate shared resources across multiple tasks.

7   Conclusion and Future Work

In this paper we have described and compared different heuristic-based strategies for addressing task-selection in a distributed swarmed system in a multi-agent setting. Experimental results within a simulated environment show that although robots are able to complete the tasks in the system within reasonable time, the performance of the system, especially in the distribution of tasks and robots is sub-optimal. Although this is not very surprising in a nature-inspired, engineered system, there is scope for addressing these issues using sophisticated techniques that reduce communication overhead between robots without significant loss of information. In our previous work[6], we have experimented with different number of agents(4 − 20) and targets/tasks(1 − 27) in the environment and demonstrated that our agent-based swarm system scales efficiently both in the number of agents and number of tasks for a distributed automatic target recognition application using unmanned aerial vehicles. Communication overhead also plays an important role in the performance of the system[6]. With more communication, the information processing time at each agents increases but the overall performance of the system improves. Currently, we are investigating social network based communication models and probabilistic inference based techniques to reduce the communication overhead between agents without compromising the performance of the system. We envisage that with accurately engineered systems and appropriate mechanisms underlying the operations, distributed swarm-based systems can be used to solve many challenging problems in the near future.

References

1. A. Abraham, C. Grosan, V. Ramos (eds.), "Swarm Intelligence in Data Mining," Studies in Computational Intelligence , vol. 34, Springer, 2006.
2. W. Agassounon, A. Martinoli, K. Easton, "Macroscopic Modeling of Aggregation Experiments using Embodied Agents in Teams of Constant and Time-Varying Sizes," Autonomous Robots, vol. 17, no. 2-3, 2004, pp. 163-192.
3. R. Alami, S. Fleury, M. Herrb, F. Ingrand, and F. Robert, "Multi-robot cooperation in the MARTHA project," IEEE Robotics and Automation, vol. 5, no. 1, 1998, pp. 36-47.
4. O. Babaoglu, H. Meling, A. Montresor, "Anthill: A Framework for the Development of Agent-Based Peer-to-Peer Systems," Proc. of the 22nd Intl. Conf. on Distributed Computing Systems, Vienna, Austria, July 2002, pp. 15-22.
5. E. Bonabeau, M. Dorigo and G. Theraulaz, "Swarm Intelligence: From Natural to Artificial Systems," Oxford University Press, 1999.
6. P. Dasgupta, S. O'Hara, P. Petrov, "A Multi-agent UAV Swarm for Automatic Target Recognition," Springer LNCS, vol. 3890, 2005, pp. 80-91.
7. M.B. Dias, R.M. Zlot, N. Kalra, and A. Stentz, "Market-Based Multirobot Coordination: A Survey and Analysis," Tech. report CMU-RI-TR-05-13, Robotics Institute, Carnegie Mellon University, 2005.
8. G. Di Caro, F. Ducatelle, L. Gambardella, "AntHocNet: An Ant-Based Hybrid Routing Algorithm for Mobile Ad Hoc Networks," PPSN 2004, pp. 461-470.
9. S. Edwards, "Swarming on the Battlefield: Past, present and future," RAND National Security Research Division Report, 2000.
10. F. Gaudiano, E. Bonabeau, B. Shargel, "Evolving behaviors for a swarm of unmanned air vehicles," Proc. IEEE Swarm Intelligence Symposium, Pasadena, CA, 2005.
11. B. Gerkey, "On multi-robot task allocation," Ph.D Thesis, Univ. of Southern California, 2003.
12. T. Lemaire, R. Alami, and S. Lacroix, "A distributed tasks allocation scheme in multi-uav context," Proc. ICRA'04, New Orleans, LA (USA), April 2004.
13. L. Li, A. Martinoli, Y. Abu-Mostafa, "Learning and Measuring Specialization in Collaborative Swarm Systems," Adaptive Behavior, Adaptive Behavior, Vol. 12, No. 3-4, 2004, pp. 199-212.
14. R. Mailler, V. Lesser, "A cooperative mediation based protocol for dynamic, distributed resource allocation," IEEE Trans. on System, Man, Cybernetics, Part C.
15. C. Oritz, R. Vincent and B. Morriset, " Task Inference and Distributed Task Management in the Centibots Robotic System," Proc. of AAMAS'05, Utrecht, The Netherlands, 2005, pp. 870-877.
16. L. Parker, Distributed Algorithms for Multi-Robot Observation of Multiple Moving Targets, Autonomous Robots, vol. 12, no. 3, 2002, pp. 231-255.
17. J. Sauter, R. Matthews, H. Parunak, and S. Brueckner, "Performance of Digital Pheromones for Swarming Vehicle Control," Proc. AAMAS'05, Utrecht, The Netherlands, 2005, pp. 903-910.
18. O. Shehory, S. Kraus, "Methods for task allocation via agent coalition formation," Artif. Intell., vol. 101 no. 1-2, 1998, pp. 165-200.
19. H. Parunak, S. Brueckner, J. Odell, "Swarming coordination of multiple UAVs for collaborative sensing," AIAA Unmanned Unlimited, 2002.
20. J. Werfel, Y. Bar-Yam and R. Nagpal, "Building Patterned Structures with Robot Swarms," Intl. Joint Conference on Artificial Intelligence (IJCAI '05), Edinburgh, Scotland, UK, August 2005, pp. 1495-1504.

Evolution of Signalling in a Group of Robots Controlled by Dynamic Neural Networks

Christos Ampatzis[1], Elio Tuci[1], Vito Trianni[2], and Marco Dorigo[1]

[1] IRIDIA, CoDE, Université Libre de Bruxelles
{campatzi,etuci,mdorigo}@ulb.ac.be
http://iridia.ulb.ac.be/
[2] ISTC-CNR, Rome, Italy
vito.trianni@istc.cnr.it

Abstract. Communication is a point of central importance in swarms of robots. This paper describes a set of simulations in which artificial evolution is used as a means to engineer robot neuro-controllers capable of guiding groups of robots in a categorisation task by producing appropriate actions. Communicative behaviour emerges, notwithstanding the absence of explicit selective pressure (coded into the fitness function) to favour signalling over non-signalling groups. Post-evaluation analyses illustrate the adaptive function of the evolved signals and show that they are tightly linked to the behavioural repertoire of the agents. Finally, our approach for developing controllers is validated by successfully porting one evolved controller on real robots.

1 Introduction

Recently, there has been a growing interest in multi-robot systems since, with respect to a single robot system, they provide increased robustness by taking advantage of inherent parallelism and redundancy. Moreover, the versatility of a multi-robot system can provide the heterogeneity of structures and functions required to undertake different missions in unknown environmental conditions. Among the possible theoretical perspectives which currently guide the design of multi-robot systems, the swarm robotics approach is characterised by its emphasis on aspects such as decentralisation of the control, limited communication abilities among robots, use of local information, emergence of global behaviour and robustness [1].

Given a multi-robot system with such properties, a global distributed knowledge of, for example, the status of the environment, can be achieved by exploiting the local knowledge of each single robot and by propagating the latter through various forms of communication. For this reason, research in swarm robotics dedicates particular attention to the study of how local information can be efficiently communicated among the robots, so to improve the adaptiveness of the group (see [2]). In this paper, we describe a simulation work in which we provide a group of two robots with a sound signalling system (i.e., "ears" and "mouth")

E. Şahin et al. (Eds.): Swarm Robotics Ws, LNCS 4433, pp. 173–188, 2007.

and we investigate the conditions which favour the emergence of a communication protocol. In particular, our work studies the evolution of signalling in a group of autonomous robots within the context of *decision making* and *action selection*, where robots have to make decisions by categorising their environment and perform different actions. The categorisation of the environment results from how the robots' sensory inputs unfold in time (see [3,4] for similar examples). The decision making is performed at the individual level, and a collective action should be the observed response to the individual decision.

In order to perform our study, we make use of the research method referred to as Evolutionary Robotics (ER, see [5]). Roughly speaking, ER is a methodological tool to automate the design of robots' controllers. Based on artificial evolution, ER finds sets of parameters for artificial neural networks (ANN's) that guide the robots to the accomplishment of their objective. ER can be employed to look at the effects that the physical interactions among embodied agents and their world have on the evolution of individual behaviour and social skills (see [6]). ER also permits the co-evolution of communicative and non-communicative behaviour, since it lets different characteristics co-adapt, only requiring an overall evaluation of the group (see [7]). Note that one of the main features of this work is that we do not explicitly reward the group for displaying signalling behaviour. That is, the adaptive pressure coded into the fitness function does not explicitly favour signalling over non-signalling groups. Therefore, if the evolved robot controllers display any kind of signalling behaviour, the adaptive significance of this feature has to be investigated. The reason to entirely leave the development of communicative behaviour to artificial evolution resides in the fact that in this way the co-adaptation of all mechanisms can produce more effective ways to categorise sensory-motor information. Evolution can produce solutions better adapted to the problem than hand-coded signalling behaviour (see [2]).

Our aim is to examine the evolution of communication in a group of homogeneous robots, in close relation to the mechanisms that govern the robots' behaviour with respect to the task. We will show that communication is beneficial for the group and that its adaptive function is tightly connected to *action selection* and *decision making*. Finally, we will download the evolved controllers on real robots, which is the only way to prove the validity of the chosen design methodology (i.e., artificial evolution). Even though multiple works treat the issue of porting a non-reactive controller to reality, the literature lacks works addressing tasks where the integration over time of sensory input is required. In these cases, the decision making relies on how the inputs unfold in time and possible errors will accumulate through time and could severely disrupt the performance. In what follows, we describe the task (Section 2), the simulation model (Section 3), the controller and the evolutionary algorithm (Section 4), and the fitness function employed (Section 5). Results in simulation are presented in Section 6, results on real hardware are discussed in Section 7 and conclusions are drawn in Section 8.

2   Description of the Task

At the start of each trial, two simulated robots are placed in a circular arena with a radius of 120 cm (see Fig. 1), at the centre of which a light bulb is always turned on. The robots are positioned randomly at a distance between 75 and 95 cm from the light, with a random orientation between $-120°$ and $+120°$ with respect to it. The robots perceive the light through their ambient light sensors. The colour of the arena floor is white except for a circular band, centred around the lamp covering an area between 40 and 60 cm from it. The band is divided in three sub-zones of equal width but coloured differently—i.e., light grey, dark grey, and black. Each robot perceives the colour of the floor through its floor sensors, positioned under its chassis. Robots are not allowed to cross the black edge of the band close to the light. There are two types of environment. In one type—referred to as *Env A*—the band presents a discontinuity, called the *way in* zone, where the floor is white (see Fig. 1a). In the other type, referred to as *Env B*, the band completely surrounds the light (see Fig. 1b). The *way in* zone represents the path along which the robots are allowed to safely reach the *target area* in *Env A*—an area of 25 cm around the light. On the contrary, they cannot reach the proximity of the light in *Env B*, and in this situation their goal is to leave the band and reach a certain distance from the light source. Robots have to explore the arena, in order to get as close as possible to the light. If they encounter the circular band they have to start looking for the *way in* zone in order to continue approaching the light, and once they find it, they should get closer to the light and remain both in its proximity for 30 sec. After this time interval, the trial is successfully terminated. If there is no *way in* zone (i.e., the current environment is an *Env B*), the robots should be capable of "recognising" the absence of the *way in* zone and leave the band by performing antiphototaxis. Artificial evolution is used to design controllers capable of providing the robots with the mechanisms required to solve the task.

Each robot is required to use a temporal cue in order to discriminate between *Env A* and *Env B*, as in [4]. This discrimination is based on the persistence of the perception of a particular sensorial state (the floor, the light or both) for the

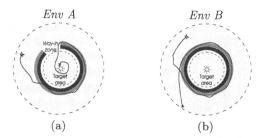

Fig. 1. The task. (a) *Env A* is characterised by the *way in* zone. The *target area* is indicated by the dashed circle. (b) In *Env B* the *target area* cannot be reached. The continuous arrows are an example of a good navigational strategy for one robot.

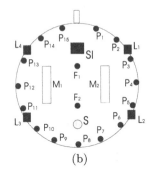

(a)   (b)

Fig. 2. (a) A picture of an *s-bot*. (b) Plan of the simulated robot, showing sensors and motors. The robot is equipped with four ambient light sensors (L_1 to L_4), two floor sensors F_1 and F_2, 15 proximity sensors (P_1 to P_{15}) and a binary sound sensor, called SI (see text for details). The wheel motors are indicated by M_1 and M_2. S is the sound signalling system (loud speaker).

amount of time that, given the trajectory and speed of the robot, corresponds to the time required to make a loop around the light. The integration over time of the robots' sensorial inputs is used to trigger antiphototaxis in *Env B*.

Communication is not required to solve the task described above. However, robots are provided with a sound signalling system that can be used for communication. Given that we provide the agents with "mouth" and "ears", whenever a robot produces a signal ("talker"), this signal is "heard" by itself and the other agent. The fitness function we use does not explicitly reward the use of signalling. We investigate whether or not the latter evolves and in case it does, what its adaptive function is. Finally, we use a homogeneous group of robots, that is the same neural controller is cloned on both robots.

3   The Simulation Model

The controllers are evolved in a simulation environment which models some of the hardware characteristics of the *s-bots* (see Fig. 2a). The *s-bots* are small wheeled cylindrical robots, 5.8 cm of radius, equipped with a variety of sensors, and whose mobility is ensured by a differential drive system [8]. In this work, we make use of four ambient light sensors, placed at $-112.5°$ (L_1), $-67.5°$ (L_2), $67.5°$ (L_3), and $112.5°$ (L_4) with respect to its heading, fifteen infra-red proximity sensors placed around its turret (P_1 to P_{15}), two floor sensors F_1 and F_2 positioned facing down on the underside of the robot with a distance of 4.5 cm between them, an omni-directional sound sensor (SI), and a loud speaker S (see Fig. 2b). The motion of the robot implemented by the two wheel actuators (M_1 and M_2) is simulated by the differential drive kinematics equations, as presented in [9]. Light and proximity sensor values are simulated through a sampling technique. The robot floor sensors output the following values: 0 if the robot is positioned over white floor; $\frac{1}{3}$ if the robot is positioned over light grey floor; $\frac{2}{3}$ if the robot is

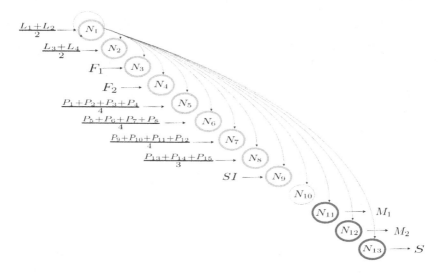

Fig. 3. The fully connected CTRNN architecture. Only the efferent connections for N_1 are drawn and all neurons behave in the same way. Neurons are represented as circles. Circles with the light grey outline represent the input neurons, while circles with the heavy grey outline represent the output neurons. We show for all input neurons the combination of sensors that serve as inputs, and for all output neurons the corresponding actuator. N_{10} is not connected to any sensor or actuator.

positioned over dark grey floor; 1 if the robot is positioned over black floor. The loud speaker is simulated as producing a binary output (on/off); the sound sensor has no directionality and intensity features. During evolution, 10% uniform noise was added to the light and proximity sensor readings, the motor outputs and the position of the robot. We also added noise of 5% on the reading of the two floor sensors, by randomly flipping between the four aforementioned values.

4   The Controller and the Evolutionary Algorithm

Given that the task we want to study requires the use of time-dependent structures, we use fully connected, thirteen neuron Continuous Time Recurrent Neural Networks (CTRNN's see [10])—see Fig. 3 for a depiction of the network. All neurons are governed by the following state equation:

$$\frac{dy_i}{dt} = \frac{1}{\tau_i}\left(-y_i + \sum_{j=1}^{13}\omega_{ji}\sigma(y_j + \beta_j) + gI_i\right), \qquad \sigma(x) = \frac{1}{1 + e^{-x}} \qquad (1)$$

where, using terms derived from an analogy with real neurons, τ_i is the decay constant, y_i represents the cell potential, ω_{ji} the strength of the synaptic connection from neuron j to neuron i, $\sigma(y_j + \beta_j)$ the firing rate, β_j the bias term,

g the gain and I_i the intensity of the sensory perturbation on sensory neuron i. The connections of all neurons to sensors and actuators is shown in Fig. 3. Neurons N_1 to N_8 receive as input a real value in the range $[0,1]$. Neuron N_1 takes as input $\frac{L_1+L_2}{2}$, $N_2 \leftarrow \frac{L_3+L_4}{2}$, $N_3 \leftarrow F_1$, $N_4 \leftarrow F_2$, $N_5 \leftarrow \frac{P_1+P_2+P_3+P_4}{4}$, $N_6 \leftarrow \frac{P_5+P_6+P_7+P_8}{4}$, $N_7 \leftarrow \frac{P_9+P_{10}+P_{11}+P_{12}}{4}$ and $N_8 \leftarrow \frac{P_{13}+P_{14}+P_{15}}{3}$.

N_9 receives a binary input (i.e., 1 if a tone is emitted by either agent, 0 otherwise) from the microphone SI, while N_{10} does not receive input from any sensor. The cell potentials (y_i) of N_{11} and N_{12}, mapped into $[0,1]$ by a sigmoid function (σ) and then linearly scaled into $[-4.0,4.0]$, set the robot motors output. The cell potential of N_{13}, mapped into $[0,1]$ by a sigmoid function (σ) is used by the robot to control the sound signalling system (the robot emits a sound if $y_{13} \geq 0.5$). The parameters ω_{ji}, τ_i, β_j and g are genetically encoded. Cell potentials are set to 0 when the network is initialised or reset, and circuits are integrated using the forward Euler method with an integration step-size of 0.1.

A simple generational genetic algorithm is employed to set the parameters of the networks [11]. The population contains 100 genotypes. Generations after the first are produced by a combination of selection with elitism, recombination and mutation. More details on the evolutionary algorithm employed and on the genotypes' component values can be found in [12].

5   The Fitness Function

During evolution, each genotype is coded into a robot controller, and is evaluated for 10 trials, 5 in each environment. The sequence order of environments within the ten trials has no bearing on the overall performance of the group since each robot controller is reset at the beginning of each trial. Each trial differs from the others in the initialisation of the random number generator, which influences the robots' starting position and orientation, the position and amplitude of the *way in* zone (between $45°$ to $81°$), and the noise added to motors and sensors. Within a trial, the robot life-span is 100 s (1000 simulation cycles). The final fitness attributed to each genotype is the average fitness score of the 10 trials. In each trial, the fitness function E is given by the formula $E = \frac{E_1+E_2}{2*(n_c+1)}$, where: n_c is the number of (virtual) collisions in a trial, that is the number of times the robots get closer than 2.5 cm to each other (if $n_c > 3$, the trial is terminated) and E_i, $i = 1, 2$, is the fitness score of robot i, calculated as follows:

- If the trial is in *Env A*, or the robot in either environment has not yet touched the band in shades of grey or crossed the black edge of the band, then its fitness score is given by $E_i = \frac{d_i-d_f}{d_i}$.
- Otherwise, that is if the band is reached in *Env B*, $E_i = 1 + \frac{d_f-40}{d_{max}-40}$.

d_i is the initial distance of the robot to the light, d_f is the distance of the robot to the light at the end of the trial and $d_{max} = 120$ cm is the maximum possible distance of a robot from the light. In case $robot_i$ ends up in the *target area* in *Env A*, we set $E_i = 2$. From the above equations we can see that this is also

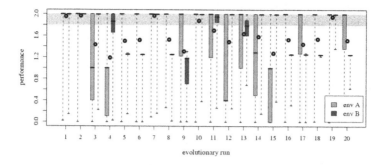

Fig. 4. Box-and-whisker plot visualising the post-evaluated fitness of groups a1-a20 in both environments. The box comprises observations ranging from the first to the third quartile. The median is indicated by a horizontal bar. When the observations are too close the box degenerates to the median. The whiskers extend to the most extreme data point which is no more than 1.5 times the interquartile range. The gray area denotes the area into which the average fitness value for both environments (black circles) must be, in order for the group to be called successful.

the maximum value E_i can obtain for a robot in *Env B*, and this corresponds to the robot ending up at 120 cm from the light ($d_f = 120$). So if both robots are successful, the trial gets the maximum score of 2. An important feature of this fitness function is that it rewards agents that develop successful discrimination strategies and end up doing the correct action in each environment, regardless of any use of sound signalling. That is, a genotype that controls a group that solves the task without any signalling/communication gets the same fitness as one that makes use of communication.

6 Results

Twenty evolutionary simulations, each using a different random initialisation, were run for 12000 generations. It is important to note that the fitness of the best evolved controllers during evolution may have been an overestimation of their ability to guide the robots in the task. In general, the best fitness scores take advantage of favourable conditions, which are determined by the existence of between-generation variation in starting position and orientation and other simulation parameters. In order to have a better estimate of the behavioural capabilities of the evolved controllers, we post-evaluate, for each run, groups controlled by the best genotype of the last generation. Groups controlled by neural networks built by those genotypes will be from now on referred to as a1-a20. The entire set of post-evaluations (500 trials in *Env A* and 500 trials in *Env B*) should establish whether (i) a group of robots can solve the task (ii) a sound signalling mechanism has been evolved and what its functionality is. The results of the post-evaluation phase are shown in Fig. 4. We define as successful a genotype that after this phase has an average fitness value above 1.8.

This roughly corresponds to both robots reaching the *target area* in *Env A* and leaving the band performing antiphototaxis in *Env B*. The results suggest that five of the groups produced satisfying solutions to the task (a1, a2, a7, a10, a19). Table 1 shows that four of the successful groups (a1, a2, a7, a19) make large use of signalling in *Env B*, while in *Env A* signalling is negligible—see columns 6 and 8, which refer to the average percentage of time either robot emits a signal during a trial. Among the successful groups only a10 did not use signalling. To unveil the relationship between the emission of sound signals and the completion of the task, we perform a behavioural analysis of the successful evolutionary runs. Thus, we evaluate the five successful groups in a different setup in which the robots are not able to perceive any sound from the environment: their sound input is set to 0 all the time. We refer to this condition as the *deaf* setup. The results of this analysis are shown in Table 1, together with the results for the *normal* setup—i.e., without applying any disruption. The first observation that we make is that, for group a10, the average fitness in the *deaf* setup (see Table 1 columns 10, 12) is exactly the same as the one in the *normal* setup (see Table 1 columns 2, 4). For the other groups, the average fitness for *Env B* drops considerably in the *deaf* setup, while for *Env A* it remains approximately the same. This suggests that group a10 does not rely on the activation of the sound input in order to solve the task in *Env B* while the other groups do. Furthermore, for the latter groups, the fitness value in the *deaf* setup in *Env B* corresponds to both robots not performing antiphototaxis; that is, the robots stay on the band and keep circling around the light. In order to understand the function of these signals, we looked more carefully at the behaviour of groups a2 and a10 during a successful trial in each environment. In particular, our analysis focused on the relationship between the robot-light distances and the firing rate of neuron N_{13} of each controller of a group, since this neuron triggers

Table 1. Further results of post-evaluation tests with *normal* and *deaf* setups for the five successful groups. For the *normal* setup, the table shows: (i) the average and standard deviation of the fitness over 500 trials in *Env A* (see columns 2, and 3) and in *Env B* (see columns 4, and 5); (ii) the average and standard deviation of the percentage of time-steps the sound was on by either robot over 500 trials in *Env A* (see columns 6, and 7) and in *Env B* (see columns 8, and 9). For the *deaf* setup the table shows the average and standard deviation of the fitness over 500 trials in *Env A* (see columns 10, and 11) and in *Env B* (see columns 12, and 13).

group	normal								deaf			
	fitness				signalling (%)				fitness			
	Env A		Env B		Env A		Env B		Env A		Env B	
	mean	sd	mean	sd	mean	sd	mean	sd	mean	sd	mean	sd
a1	1.927	0.310	1.982	0.134	0.03	0.57	21.62	3.82	1.937	0.292	1.0526	0.239
a2	1.937	0.277	1.995	0.002	0.77	4.49	18.48	1.17	1.969	0.156	1.256	0.094
a7	1.988	0.113	1.950	0.198	0	0	17.19	2.54	1.988	0.113	1.266	0.250
a10	1.789	0.467	1.968	0.183	0	0	0	0	1.789	0.467	1.968	0.183
a19	1.914	0.236	1.984	0.059	0.08	0.72	13.88	1.03	1.923	0.214	1.137	0.016

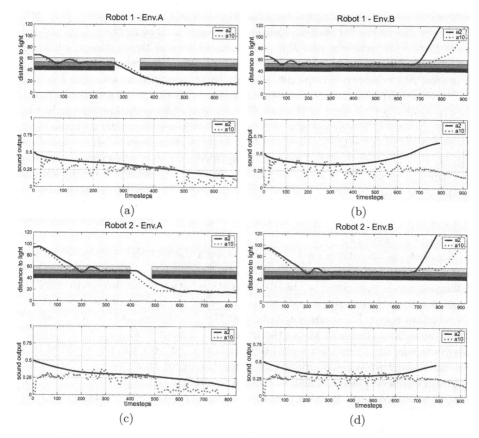

Fig. 5. The graphs show some features of the behaviour of robots of groups a2 (continuous lines) and a10 (dashed lines), during a successful trial in *Env A* and in *Env B*. Top graphs a, b, c, and d show the distance to the light in cm. Bottom graphs a, b, c, and d show the firing rate of neuron N_{13} (i.e., the sound output) of each robot controller.

the emission of sound. Fig. 5a, b, c, d (top) show the distances of each robot to the light at every timestep. The areas in shades of grey in these graphs represent the circular band. Fig. 5a, b, c, d (bottom) show the firing rate of N_{13} (i.e., the sound output) of both robots of a group. In all graphs, continuous lines refer to robots of group a2, dashed lines refer to robots of group a10.

As shown in Fig. 5a, b, c, d (top), the behaviour of the robots can be divided in three phases. In the first two phases the robots of both groups (a2 and a10) behave in the same way in both environments. The robot-light distance initially decreases up to the point where the robots touch the band (phototaxis phase) and then stays quite constant as the robots circle around the band trying to find the *way in* zone (integration over time phase). In the third phase the groups behave differently according to the characteristics of the environment. For both groups, in *Env A* the robot-light distance decreases further as the robots end up in the *target area*, while in *Env B* it increases and reaches the maximum distance as the robots leave the band (antiphototaxis phase). Concerning the firing rate of neuron N_{13}, the two groups differentiate in both environments (see Fig. 5a, b, c, d (bottom)). In *Env B*, the firing rate for both robots of group a10 never goes beyond the threshold of 0.5 (see Fig. 5b, d (bottom) dashed lines). In the case of a2 though, the firing rate of N_{13} of Robot 1 is rising until it passes over the threshold of 0.5 just before the robot starts performing antiphototaxis (see Fig. 5b, d, continuous lines). This behaviour of N_{13} for a2 reflects the integration over time process, which leads to passing over the threshold of 0.5 in *Env B* (decision making), while it is interrupted in *Env A*, when the *way in* zone is found (see Fig. 5a, c, continuous lines). Differently, for a10 this neuron does not perform the integration process, so the latter should be taking place in another neuron of the network.

The observations above for a2, combined with the fact that this group in the *deaf* setup does not display antiphototaxis in *Env B*, suggest that the sound signalling system is connected to the discrimination between the two environments. In other words, the antiphototaxis is a result of the perception of the sound emitted by either robot. Furthermore, looking at Fig. 5d we observe that for group a2 (continuous line), Robot 2 leaves the band the moment Robot 1 emits a signal, despite the fact that its own sound output is not yet over the threshold of 0.5. We can summarise what happens as follows: the agent that "realises" first that its group has been placed in *Env B*, emits a sound signal, the perception of which triggers antiphototaxis in both robots of the group. We refer to this process as *external action selection*, since the selection of the appropriated action (i.e., the switch from phototaxis to antiphototaxis) is driven by the perception of an environmental cue (i.e., the sound signal) produced by either robot of the group. On the contrary, looking at the behaviour of group a10, we observe a process that we refer to as *internal action selection*, since the antiphototaxis is not triggered by a distinctive perceptual cue but solely by the internal dynamics of the neural network controller. While the *internal action selection* does not involve any form of communication, the *external action selection* determines the emergence of a simple form of communication between the robots of a group, since the robot that does not emit the signal initiates antiphototaxis by reacting to the other robot's signal.

The results of a pairwise Wilcoxon test among the fitness values of successful groups as recorded during 1000 evaluations in the *normal* setup, show that groups relying on an *external action selection* process to discriminate between *Env A* and *Env B* (i.e., groups a1, a2, a7, a19) outperform with a confidence level of 99% the only successful group which relies on an *internal action selection* process (a10). We also compared the fitness scores achieved by the former groups in the *normal* setup, with fitness scores achieved if the communication channel between the robots is disabled, that is the robots are only capable of perceiving their own signals. The results show that these genotypes perform worse with a

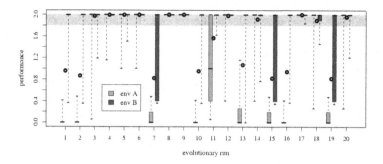

Fig. 6. Box-and-whisker plot visualising the post-evaluated fitness of groups n1-n20 in both environments. The box comprises observations ranging from the first to the third quartile. The median is indicated by a horizontal bar. When the observations are too close the box degenerates to the median. The whiskers extend to the most extreme data point which is no more than 1.5 times the interquartile range. The gray area denotes the area into which the average fitness value for both environments (black circles) must be, in order for the group to be called successful.

confidence level of 99% with the communication channel disabled with respect to the *normal* setup. These analyses seem to suggest that, once evolved through random mutations, mechanisms involved in the process of *external action selection* give to a group a selective advantage over those groups which do not possess these mechanisms.

This advantage might be related to the communication that results from the exploitation of an *external action selection* process. That is, by communicating the outcome of their decision about the state of the environment, robots may counterbalance the disruptive effect of the sensors and actuators' noise on the decision making mechanisms. In other words, the effectiveness of the mechanisms that integrate sensory information over time in order to disambiguate *Env A* from *Env B* may be sensibly disrupted by the noise inherent in the sensors' reading and in the outcome of any "planned" action. Equally, by communicating their decision, robots can eradicate decision delay between them: due to initialisation noise, one robot will on average perform the discrimination first. If the antiphototaxis is triggered by the perception of sound (*external action selection*) rather than by an internal state of the controller (*internal action selection*), then a robot which by itself is not capable or not yet ready to make a decision concerning the nature of the environment can rely on the decision taken by the other robot of the group. The former simply reacts to the sound signal emitted by the latter by initiating an antiphototactic behaviour (as happens for Robot 2 in Fig. 5d).

In order to test the "communication-noise hypothesis" (introduced above) as the main factor which determines the selective advantage of signalling over non-signalling groups, we run another set of twenty evolutionary runs. In this additional series of simulations we removed any source of environmental noise which may interfere with the mechanisms for integration over time—i.e., no noise in sensors/actuators—and initialised the robots at exactly the anti-diametrical positions. Due to these choices, both robot controllers are at identical states during their lifetime and thus the potential advantage related to the communication that results from the exploitation of an *external action selection* process is removed. The results of the post-evaluation phase are shown in Fig. 6. Groups controlled by the best genotypes of the last generation of runs 1 to 20 are called n1-n20, respectively. The results show that eleven of the groups effectively solved the task (n3, n4, n5, n6, n8, n9, n12, n14, n17, n18, n20). Table 2 shows results of the post-evaluation tests for two of the successful groups (n8, n17)[1]. These groups use signalling in *Env B* (see column 8), and given their failure to produce antiphototaxis in the *deaf* setup in *Env B* (see column 12), we can conclude that they employ an *external action selection* process to discriminate between *Env A* and *Env B* (exactly as a2). This suggests that there may be other factor(s) which cause the evolution of groups that exploit the *external action selection*. Genetic drift might be a possible explanation. Alternatively, we may speculate that sound evolves simply because, if emitted at the end of a complete tour around the light, it is a perceptual cue which an emitter robot can employ to initiate antiphototaxis. Robots that do not emit sound may find it more difficult to switch from phototaxis to antiphototaxis in the absence of a clear perceptual cue which triggers the latter response. Obviously, the latter hypothesis does not rule out the possibility that sound could acquire a communicative function in a subsequent time because of its potential beneficial effect against environmental noise and decision delay on behalf of one robot, as explained above.

Table 2. Further results of post-evaluation tests with *normal* and *deaf* setups for two of the successful groups among n1-n20. For the *normal* setup, the table shows: (i) the average and standard deviation of the fitness over 500 trials in *Env A* (see columns 2, and 3) and in *Env B* (see columns 4, and 5); (ii) the average and standard deviation of the percentage of timesteps the sound was on by either robot over 500 trials in *Env A* (see columns 6, and 7) and in *Env B* (see columns 8, and 9). For the *deaf* setup the table shows the average and standard deviation of the fitness over 500 trials in *Env A* (see columns 10, and 11) and in *Env B* (see columns 12, and 13).

group	normal								deaf			
	fitness				signalling (%)				fitness			
	Env A		Env B		Env A		Env B		Env A		Env B	
	mean	sd	mean	sd	mean	sd	mean	sd	mean	sd	mean	sd
n8	2	0	1.999	0.000	0	0	26.40	0.64	2	0	1.169	0.007
n17	2	0	1.998	0.007	0	0	26.70	1.14	2	0	1.084	0.002

---

[1] Other groups employ an *external action selection* process but use different signalling conventions, and others employ an *internal action selection* process. The analysis of these controllers is beyond the scope of this paper.

7   Porting on Real Robots

The task described in this paper is characterised by the fact that not only the change but also the persistence of particular sensorial states are directly linked to the effectiveness of the evolved strategies (see previous section). However, the evolved strategies are generated by robot controllers developed in a simulated world, which is responsible for modelling the sensory states of *s-bots* acting in *Env A* or *Env B*. If the physics of our simulated world are insufficiently and/or incorrectly defined, the evolved behavioural strategies may exploit loop-holes which would strongly limit their effectiveness to an unrealistic scenario. Porting the controllers evolved in simulation onto a real robot is the best way to rule out the above mentioned problem (see [13]). However, as already pointed out in Section 1, this practice has not been taken into account in previous research work in which CTRNN's have been evolved to deal with tasks that required integration over time of sensory states. In this paper, we provide evidence of the "portability" of the evolved controllers by showing the results of tests in which real robots of group a2 are repeatedly evaluated in *Env A* and *Env B*.

In [14], the author claims that the robot does not have to move identically in simulation and reality in order for the porting to be called successful, but its behaviour has to satisfy some criteria defined by the experimenter. Following this principle, real robots are considered successful if they carry out the main requirements of our task. That is, the robots have to reach the band in shades of grey regardless of the type of environment and subsequently (i) end up in the *target area* in *Env A*, without crossing the inner black edge of the circular band; (ii) end up as far as possible from the light in *Env B*. The robots should also avoid collisions.

Two *s-bots* (*s-bot₁* and *s-bot₂*) were randomly positioned at a distance of 85 cm from the light with a random orientation. In *Env A*, we randomly varied the position of the *way in* zone but we fixed its width to 45°, which is the smallest value encountered during evolution and the most difficult case for a possible misinterpretation of an *Env A* for an *Env B*. We performed 40 trials, 20 in each environment. The results were 100% successful: there were no wrong discriminations, collisions or crossings of the black edge of the band[2]. As it was the case for the simulated robots of group a2, the *s-bots* accomplished the task through an *external action selection* process. That is, it is the sound emitted by one *s-bot* that triggers antiphototaxis in both robots. The results of our tests show that in *Env B* it is always *s-bot₁* that emits a signal. Since the discrimination of *Env B* from *Env A*—that is, the emission of a sound signal and the following antiphototactic response—is based on the persistence of a particular sensory state, we can attribute the fact that *s-bot₁* always signals earlier than *s-bot₂* to mechanical and/or sensor differences between the two *s-bots*. However, the fact that we did not have any wrong discrimination proves that the simulation used to develop our controllers is sufficiently and correctly defined.

---

[2] The movies that correspond to all experiments can be found at
http://iridia.ulb.ac.be/supp/IridiaSupp2006-004

In order to understand to what extent real world noise influences the accomplishment of the task, we performed further analyses. We compute the offset between the entrance position in the circular band of the robot that first emits a signal and the position at which this robot starts to signal. This measure, called offset Δ, takes value $0°$ if the robot signals exactly after covering a complete loop around the circular band. Negative values of the offset Δ suggest that the robot signals before having performed a complete loop, while positive values correspond to the situation in which the robot emits a tone after having performed a loop around the light (see [4] for details on how to calculate Δ).

Table 3. Average and standard deviation of the offset Δ over: (i) 20 trials in *Env B* performed by the *s-bots*; (ii) 500 trials in *Env B* performed by the simulated robots

Offset Δ	avg	sd
s-bots	-30.6	11.75
simulated robots	+31.6	16.05

As shown in Table 3, we see that the *s-bot* that first emits a signal—which, as mentioned above, is always *s-bot*$_1$—does so on average before completing a loop. However, being the magnitude of the offset Δ smaller than the width of the *way in* zone the group does not run into the risk of misinterpreting an *Env A* for an *Env B*. Further tests have proved that, if left to act alone in an *Env B*, *s-bot*$_2$ always signals after completing a loop (i.e., positive offset Δ, data not shown). This result can be accounted for by calling upon the inter *s-bot* differences, that can hardly be captured by the simulated world.

In Table 3 we compare the average offset Δ of a group of *s-bots* with the one recorded by the simulated robots of group a2 (with the same initialisation conditions). Contrary to the *s-bots*, the simulated robots signal on average after completing the loop. This result is due to the differences between simulated and real world. Still, these differences did not produce any errors when dealing with the real hardware. The reason for this is that simulated robots of group a2 are rather "conservative". That is, robots emit signals rather late, on average $31.6°$ after completing a loop. Adding to this number the minimum width of the *way in* zone ($45°$), we can see that the margin of fault tolerance is very wide.

8   Conclusions

In this work, we used artificial evolution as a means to engineer the emergence of communication in a group of robots but also to design robot controllers that can successfully cross the simulation-reality gap. Signals serve as "cues" that trigger behavioural switches in the group. Obviously, the evolved signalling system is simple, mainly because we only allow agents to emit binary signals. In order to move to more complex signalling behaviours, we need to consider a sound system with more degrees of freedom, always in close relation to the task under consideration. Still, we observed that when agents are provided with "mouth" and "ears", communication can emerge, even without explicit fitness reward, providing groups that use it with a selective advantage over those that do not. Given this result, the question that arises is whether we should aim at evolving communication in any swarm robotics task. Obviously this work does not provide enough evidence to answer positively. Any communication system that escapes from the local and simple interactions (e.g., communication through infra-red sensors—see [6]) might present disadvantages as well as advantages. In fact, when we move from a robot-to-robot to a robot-to-many interaction, not only the benefit of the knowledge of the environment acquired, but also possible errors spread faster. For example, in the task we studied, if a robot emits a signal, both robots can exploit it. However, if the signal is the product of a wrong decision (misinterpretation of environments) then both robots fail and the whole system collapses. The importance and the effect of such an event on the group performance is amplified as the swarm size increases, and therefore the reliability of signals assumes a very important role. This in turn might require more complex controllers. To summarise, the experimenter has to balance the costs and benefits of communication before considering it as a path that might lead to the solution of a given task.

Acknowledgements

E. Tuci and M. Dorigo acknowledge European Commission support via the *ECAgents* project, funded by the Future and Emerging Technologies programme (grant IST-1940). The authors thank their colleagues at IRIDIA for stimulating discussions and feedback during the preparation of this paper, and the three anonymous reviewers for their helpful comments. M. Dorigo acknowledges support from the Belgian FNRS, of which he is a Research Director. M. Dorigo and C. Ampatzis acknowledge support from the "ANTS" project, an "Action de Recherche Concertée" funded by the Scientific Research Directorate of the French Community of Belgium. The information provided is the sole responsibility of the authors and does not reflect the Community's opinion. The Community is not responsible for any use that might be made of data appearing in this publication.

References

1. Bonabeau, E., Dorigo, M., Theraulaz, G.: Swarm Intelligence: From Natural to Artificial Systems. Oxford University Press, New York, NY (1999)
2. Trianni, V., Dorigo, M.: Self-organisation and communication in groups of simulated and physical robots. Biological Cybernetics (2006) In press.
3. Nolfi, S., Marocco, D.: Evolving robots able to integrate sensory-motor information over time. Theory in Biosciences **120** (2001) 287–310
4. Tuci, E., Trianni, V., Dorigo, M.: 'Feeling' the flow of time through sensory/motor coordination. Connection Science **16** (2004) 1–24

5. Nolfi, S., Floreano, D.: Evolutionary Robotics: The Biology, Intelligence, and Technology of Self-Organizing Machines. MIT Press, Cambridge, MA (2000)
6. Quinn, M., Smith, L., Mayley, G., Husbands, P.: Evolving controllers for a homogeneous system of physical robots: Structured cooperation with minimal sensors. Philosophical Transactions of the Royal Society of London, Series A: Mathematical, Physical and Engineering Sciences **361** (2003) 2321–2344
7. Nolfi, S.: Emergence of communication in embodied agents: Co-adapting communicative and non-communicative behaviours. Connection Science **17** (2005) 231–248
8. Mondada, F., Pettinaro, G.C., Guignard, A., Kwee, I.V., Floreano, D., Deneubourg, J.L., Nolfi, S., Gambardella, L.M., Dorigo, M.: SWARM-BOT: A new distributed robotic concept. Autonomous Robots **17** (2004) 193–221
9. Dudek, G., Jenkin, M.: Computational Principles of Mobile Robotics. Cambridge University Press, Cambridge, UK (2000)
10. Beer, R., Gallagher, J.: Evolving dynamical neural networks for adaptive behavior. Adaptive Behavior **1** (1992) 91–122
11. Goldberg, D.E.: Genetic Algorithms in Search, Optimization and Machine Learning. Addison-Wesley, Reading, MA (1989)
12. Ampatzis, C., Tuci, E., Trianni, V., Dorigo, M.: Evolving communicating agents that integrate information over time: a real robot experiment. Technical Report TR/IRIDIA/2005-012, IRIDIA, Université Libre de Bruxelles (2005) This paper is available at `http://iridia.ulb.ac.be/IridiaTrSeries`.
13. Brooks, R.: Artificial life and real robots. In Varela, F., Bourgine, P., eds.: Towards a Practice of Autonomous Systems: Proceedings of the First European Conference on Artificial Life, MIT Press, Cambridge, MA (1992) 3–10
14. Jakobi, N.: Evolutionary robotics and the radical envelope of noise hypothesis. Adaptive Behavior **6** (1997) 325–368

Collective Specialization for Evolutionary Design of a Multi-robot System

Agoston E. Eiben, Geoff S. Nitschke, and Martijn C. Schut

Computational Intelligence Group, Vrije Universiteit Amsterdam, De Boelelaan 1081a, 1081 HV Amsterdam, The Netherlands
gusz@cs.vu.nl, nitschke@cs.vu.nl, schut@cs.vu.nl

Abstract. This research is positioned in the context of controller design for (simulated) multi-robot applications. Inspired by research in survey and exploration of unknown environments where a multi-robot system is to discover features of interest given strict time and energy constraints, we defined an abstract task domain with adaptable features of interest. Additionally, we parameterized the behavioral features of the robots, so that we could classify behavioral specialization in the space of these parameters. This allowed systematic experimentation over a range of task instances and types of specialization in order to investigate the advantage of specialization. These experiments also delivered a novel neuro-evolution approach to controller design, called the collective specialization method. Results elucidated that this method derived multi-robot system controllers that outperformed a high performance heuristic and conventional neuro-evolution method.

1 Introduction

Biological social systems have long been a source of inspiration to engineers. In particular, research in multi-robot and artificial life collective behavior systems, has often attempted to replicate the success of social insect societies at decomposing the labor of a group into composite specialized and complementary roles so as to accomplish collectively, global goals that could not otherwise be accomplished by individual insects. Mechanisms and design principles that facilitate emergent behavioral specialization have been studied in biological [7], artificial life [1], and multi-robot systems [10] research. However, collective behavior design methods for harnessing and utilizing emergent specialization for the benefit for problem solving are lacking in current swarm engineering approaches.

This paper describes a comparative study testing *Neuro-Evolution* (NE) and heuristic methods with respect to the role of specialization in solving a collective behavior task[1]. NE is an approach that combines techniques native to both neural networks and evolutionary computation research. Both of these techniques

---

[1] Terms used herein are defined as follows: *task*: what has to be done, *activity*: what is being done, *role*: the task assigned to a specific individual within a set of responsibilities given to a group of individuals, *caste*: a group of individuals specialized in the same role [10].

E. Şahin et al. (Eds.): Swarm Robotics Ws, LNCS 4433, pp. 189–205, 2007.

have historically been successful in addressing single agent control problems [6] and have recently had some success for controller design in collective behavior research [2]. The advantages of applying NE to collective behavior research have been illustrated in a variety of applications including multi-agent computer games [2], RoboCup [17], and robot controller design [1]. Such applications have highlighted that NE is most appropriately applied to complex problems that are neither effectively addressed via pure evolutionary computation methods or neural processing approaches.

It has been suggested that autonomous robotic explorers whose behavioral or morphological design (or both) is biologically inspired could be feasible and cost-effective in future planetary exploration [16], as well as providing an alternative to traditional, labor-intensive, tele-robotic operations [18]. The challenge addressed in this paper concerned developing controllers for a group of simulated Unmanned Autonomous Vehicles (UAV's) given a *search and find task* constrained by limited resources.

Environmental factors such as resource distribution greatly influence social organization in biological [7], and artificial social systems [10], given specific types of tasks such as collective foraging. In this paper, heuristic methods highlighted that specialization was beneficial in a search and find task, given specific types of resource distribution in the environment. For this task, we defined what we termed the *Collective NE* (CONE) method that was successful in deriving a *caste*[1] that outperformed a heuristic and conventional NE method.

1.1   Research Goal

The research goal was to demonstrate a NE method capable of deriving specialization for increasing task performance in environments where specialization was beneficial.

1.2   Specialization

Specialization was defined at the *agent* level (1 aerial explorer) and the *group* level (*n* aerial explorers). An agent was specialized if *more than 50%* of its lifetime was dedicated to one role. We defined a caste where *more than 50%* of the group members assumed one role for *more than 50%* of their respective lifetimes.

1.3   First Hypothesis

There exist particular types of task environments where specialization increases task performance.

To support our first hypothesis, the value of specialization in particular types of task environments was demonstrated using a heuristic method that tested the task performance of pre-defined *castes*.

1.4   Second Hypothesis

That the collective specialization NE method is appropriate for deriving special-ized groups (that is: *castes*) with high task performance.

To support our second hypothesis of specialization being a requisite for in-creased task performance, the performance of the collective specialization method (where we supposed that emergent specialization would be observed to benefit performance), was compared to that of a conventional NE method.

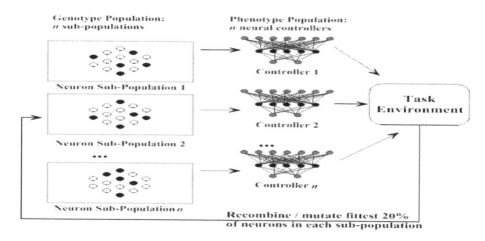

Fig. 1. CONE: Collective Neuro-Evolution. See section 2 for details.

2   CONE: Collective Neuro-Evolution

As illustrated in figure 1, after each of the n sub-populations, were randomly initial-ized with m genotypes the process of the CONE method was as executed follows.

1. n agents (neural controllers) were constructed via selecting p genotypes (neu-rons) from each sub-population of genotypes. These p neurons then became the hidden layer of each of the n controllers, which were subsequently placed in the task environment. The group of controllers was thus heterogeneous, given that each was constructed via selecting a set of p hidden layer neurons from each of the n sub-populations. Evolutionary operators were not applied between the n sub-populations.
2. The n controllers were tested together in the task environment for a *life-time* of q epochs, where an epoch was a test scenario lasting for w iterations of simulation time. Each epoch tested different task dependent agent and environment conditions, such as agent starting positions and locations of re-sources in the environment. For each of the q epochs (where $q \geq m$ genotypes in a sub-population), each genotype in a given sub-population was selected and tested in combination with p-1 other neurons (thus forming a controller) randomly selected from the same sub-population.

3. Thus p neurons from each of the n sub-populations would concurrently be evaluated in the task environments and assigned a fitness. Testing of neurons within each sub-population would continue until all neurons had been tested at least once.
4. At the end of an agents lifetime (q epochs) a fitness value was assigned to each set of p neurons that participated in each of the controllers. The assigned fitness of each set of p neurons was calculated as the average of fitness values attained over all epochs of an agents lifetime.
5. For each sub-population, recombination and mutation of the fittest 20% of genotypes then occurred, where the fittest 20% were arranged into pairs of genotypes, and each pair produced 5 child genotypes, so as to propagate the next generation of each sub-population.
6. A single genotype was randomly selected from the fittest 20% of the newly recombined genotypes within each of the n sub-populations. These n selected genotypes were then decoded into controllers, placed in the task environment, and executed as the next generation. This process was then repeated for r (table 1) generations.

2.1   Online Versus Offline Adaptation in the CONE Method

Most NE methods were originally designed to run offline, meaning that all genotypes in a population were successively tested and evaluated, and after the whole population had been tested, evolutionary operators were applied in order to create the next population. The fittest genotypes of any given population could then be selected as those best suited to solving the given task. Recently there has been some success in applying NE methods for online adaptation in certain collective behavior tasks such as multi-agent computer games [14].

As with the other NE methods applied to collective behavior tasks, such as NEAT [15] and rtNEAT [14], the evolutionary cycle of selection and replacement operated continually as controllers interacted with their task environment, effectuating the emergence of new controllers in response to dynamic challenges in the task environment. Dissimilar to other online NE methods, the CONE method derived a new controller (phenotype) from each of n sub-populations of genotypes at the turn of each generation of artificial evolution, where a separate evolutionary process of selection and replacement operated within each of the n sub-populations. Hence, as the n controllers worked to accomplish their task, each sub-population was progressively (and not necessarily synchronously) updated, such that the ith controller, where $i \, \varepsilon \, n$, was in turn updated (decoded) from the *fittest* genotype from the ith sub-population.

3   Conventional Neuro-Evolution

The conventional NE method was adapted from that used for previous evolutionary robotics experiments [12], and as illustrated in figure 2 used only a

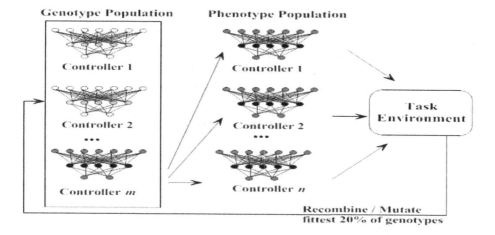

Fig. 2. Conventional neuro-evolution. See section 3 for details.

single population of genotypes. After, randomly initializing a population of m genotypes, the conventional NE process operated as follows.

1. Initially, n genotypes were randomly selected from the population of m genotypes, and decoded into n agents (neural controllers).
2. These n controllers were then placed in the task environment, to be tested and evaluated.
3. Each controller was tested for a *lifetime* of q epochs, where each epoch constituted a test scenario (section 2) that lasted for w iterations of simulation time.
4. At the end of each controllers lifetime (q epochs), a fitness value was assigned to the genotype corresponding to each controller. The fitness assigned to a genotype was calculated as the average of all fitness values attained for all epochs of its lifetime.
5. Each of the m genotypes was systematically decoded into a neural controller and tested, together with n-1 other (randomly) selected genotypes, in the task environment. The testing of all m genotypes in the population constituted one generation of the NE process.
6. The fittest 20% of genotypes were then arranged into randomly selected pairs, and each pair recombined to produce 5 child genotypes each, so as to replace the current genotype population.
7. n genotypes were then randomly selected from the fittest 20% of the next generation of genotypes. Each selected genotype was decoded into its corresponding controller and placed in the task environment.
8. This process was repeated for the r generations that the conventional NE method was executed for (table 1).

4   Genotypes

For both the CONE (figure 1) and conventional NE (figure 2) methods, the populations of genotypes were encoded as a string of floating point values (table 1), which represented neural network weights connecting all sensory input neurons and all motor output neurons to a given hidden layer neuron.

4.1   Recombination of Genotypes: Crossover and Mutation

Each child genotype was produced using single point crossover [4], and *Burst* mutation with a *Cauchy* distribution [8]. As illustrated in table 1 mutation of a random value in the range [-1.0, +1.0] was applied to each gene (connection weight) with a 0.05 degree of probability, and weights of each genotype were kept within the range [-10.0, +10.0]. Burst mutation was used to ensure that most weight changes were small whilst allowing for larger changes to some weights.

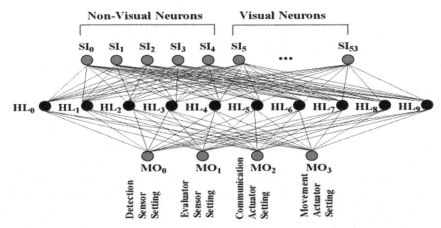

Fig. 3. Adaptive topology neural controller. See section 7.2 for explanation.

4.2   Fitness Calculation

At the end of each generation (section 2) a fitness value was assigned to each of the n controllers, where each of the neurons participating in each controller was assigned an equal portion of the fitness value. These individual neuron fitness values were then assigned back to the sub-population corresponding to each of the controllers. Although this fitness estimation method, known as *fitness sharing* [3] was convenient for deriving the contribution of each neuron to a controller, it was problematic in that it potentially prevented the selection of the best neurons across successive generations. However, this was offset by the advantage that there was no disparity between controller fitness and the fitness of individual neurons.

5   Phenotypes: Constructing Controllers from Neurons

An agent phenotype (feed-forward neural controller) was constructed from a set of 10 genotypes (hidden layer neurons). Given that the CONE method operated at the neuron (not the controller [11]) level, a controller was constructed via selecting p neurons from one sub-population of neurons. The setting of specific neurons in specific hidden layer locations has the well investigated consequence that different neurons become specialized for different controller sub-tasks [15], over the course of a NE process. Hence, each neuron in each sub-population was assigned to a fixed position in the hidden layer of any given controller. The position that the ith neuron (g_i) would take in a hidden layer of p neurons, where g_i was selected from any sub-population of m neurons, was calculated as follows.

Each of the m neurons in a sub-population were initially assigned a random and unique ranking in the range $[0, m\text{-}1]$. A sub-population was divided into approximately equal portions $(m\ /\ p)$, where if g_i was within the kth portion (where: $k = [1, p]$) then g_i would adopt the kth position in the hidden layer.

Table 1. Neuro-evolution parameter settings

Neuro-Evolution Parameter Settings	
Runs per NE method	20
Generations	500
Epochs	50
Iterations / Epoch	1000
Mutation probability	0.05
Mutation range	[-1.0, +1.0]
Weight range	[-10.0, +10.0]
Initial Weights	Random
Crossover	single point
Hidden neurons	10
Phenotypes	100 Controllers
Genotype length	18 (14 + 4) weights
Genotypes	100 (Conventional NE) / 10000 (CONE)

5.1   Dynamic Topologies

Many NE methods have used a process known as *complexification* which changes the topology of a neural controller, and thus its corresponding genotype length, as part of an evolutionary process [9]. However, only a few of such methods have been successfully applied to collective behavior tasks [14].

The CONE method also uses complexification to dynamically change genotype lengths as part of the evolutionary process. Where as, [14] used *synapsis* to recombine genotypes of different lengths, this was not necessary in CONE, as all genotypes within a given sub-population were kept the same length, and recombination of genotypes from different sub-populations did not occur. Also, the CONE method only changed the number of sensory input neurons, and the number of hidden layer and motor output neurons were kept static.

6   Collective Survey Task

Inspired by UAV survey and exploration missions of unknown environments [16], a group of 101 simulated UAV's (100 *explorer* agents and 1 *lander* agent) were given the task of maximizing the number of features of interest (herein termed: *red rocks*) discovered within a *survey area* of an environment given limited sensor and actuator capabilities, battery power and mission time. Red rock locations and distributions were initially unknown to the agents. The lander had no active role in the discovery of red rocks. Its role was to act as a base station that received red rock data (locations and value of features of interest) communicated to it, and to recharge explorer agents that successfully accomplished their task.

6.1   Environment

The simulation environment[2] was represented as a discrete three dimensional environment of 200 x 200 x 200 voxels.

Table 2. Adaptive controller topology. MOV: Motor Output Value 1 (MO_0 in figure 3). FOV: Field of View. PODS: Probability Of Detection Success. See section 7.2 for explanation.

Adaptive Input Layer Topology of Neural Controller			
Detection Sensor Setting	Genotype Length	Visual Neurons	Total Input Neurons
3 ($0.75 < MOV1 \leq 1.0$)	**58**	**49** (FOV=49); PODS=0.99	**54**
2 ($0.5 < MOV1 \leq 0.75$)	**34**	**25** (FOV=25); PODS=0.89	**30**
1 ($0.25 < MOV1 \leq 0.5$)	**18**	**9** (FOV=9); PODS=0.79	**14**
0 ($0.0 < MOV1 \leq 0.25$)	**10**	**1** (FOV=1); PODS=0.69	**6**

6.2   Red Rocks (Features of Interest)

As described by the red rock discovery algorithm (section 8.2), when an agent had discovered a red rock using its *detection sensor* the red rock location was moved to, using the *movement actuator*, red rock value (evaluation data) was then ascertained, using the *evaluation sensor*. Evaluation data was communicated from the agent to the lander, using the *communication actuator* and the red rock value communicated back to the agent from the lander. Red rocks either had a value (1) or not (0). A red rock with value was marked as *evaluated*, so it

---

[2] Demo's, source code and documentation of the simulation environment is available at: www.cs.vu.nl/ nitschke/MarsScape/

would not again be subject to evaluation. Thus the number of resources in the environment diminished with successful task accomplishment. Agents that had evaluated red rocks with value would be marked as being eligible for an energy reward, and also immediately receive a fitness reward (section 4.2) equal to the value of the last red rock evaluated.

Red rock value served two purposes. First, it provided a performance measure for the agent group. Second, it was translated into energy and fitness rewards. When an agents energy depleted to below 500 units, it would return to the lander and the total red rock value that the agent had gathered thus far would be translated directly into an energy reward.

6.3   Red Rock Distribution

A simulation consisted of 40000 red rocks distributed over the base of the environment. That is, a red rock could be placed at each possible x_i, y_i, z_j, where $0 \leq i < 200$, j=0. We described red rock distribution (degree of structure) in the environment using a two dimensional *Gaussian mixture model* [13]. The mixture model was specified with 4 centroids, where the radius of each determined the spatial distribution of red rock around each. 10 radii were tested, such that red rock distributions generated ranged from a uniform (such an environment was termed as having a *low degree of structure*) through to a clustered distribution (such an environment was termed as having a *high degree of structure*). We labeled these environment types from *0* (low degree of structure) through to *9* (high degree of structure). All 10 environment types were tested using the heuristic (section 8), CONE (section 2) and conventional neuro-evolution methods (section 3).

Table 3. Heuristic Method: Specialized agent types and their probabilistic preferences for action selection

Agent Type	Detect	Evaluate	Move	Communicate
Detector	0.6	0.1	0.2	0.1
Evaluator	0.1	0.6	0.2	0.1
Communicator	0.1	0.1	0.2	0.6

7   Agents

At simulation initialization, each aerial explorer was placed in a random voxel (x_i, y_i, z_i, where, $0 \leq i < 200$). A maximum of 4 aerial explorers could occupy a given voxel.

7.1   Morphology: Sensors and Actuators

Agent morphology was defined in terms of 1 *detection sensor*, 1 *evaluation sensor*, 1 *movement actuator*, and 1 *communication actuator*. This selection of sensors and actuators was based upon design proposals for rotorcraft that are to operate as autonomous aerial explorers [18]. Rotorcraft are considered advantageous given their vertical lift capabilities, allowing them to *detect* red rocks in flight using a directional visual sensor, perform some preliminary categorization of red rocks, *move* in order to *evaluate* selected red rocks using a physical contact sensor, and then *communicate* red rock data. Rotorcraft are also able to land to recharge at a base station.

7.2   Controllers: Adaptive Topology Neural Network

Figure 3 illustrates the feed forward neural controller used by the explorer agents. The controller connected all sensory input nodes to 10 hidden layer nodes, (HL_0..HL_9) to 4 motor output nodes (MO_0..MO_3). The number of non-visual, hidden-layer and output nodes remained static at 5, 10, and 4 respectively.

Sensory inputs: Non-visual. Non-visual input nodes (SI_0..SI_4) took as input the 4 motor output (MO_0-MO_3) values, and the red rock evaluation value from the previous simulation iteration, respectively. These previous values were teaching inputs [12] which influenced the next motor outputs.

Sensory inputs: Visual. Figure 3 also illustrates that the number of visual neurons in the sensory input layer was dynamic within the range SI_5 (one voxel viewable) and SI_{53} (49 voxels viewable). All values taken by sensory input nodes were normalized.

The number of sensory input neurons determined the accuracy of sensor readings for detecting (table 2) features of interest (red rocks) in the environment. In this case, more sensory input neurons indicated that more discrete locations in the environment (voxels) could be observed with the directional red rock detection sensor (table 6).

Motor outputs. Motor outputs (MO_0..MO_3) corresponded to the 4 actions an agent could select. MO_0 and MO_1 activated the detection and evaluation sensors, respectively. MO_2 and MO_3 activated the movement and communications actuators, respectively. The motor output node that generated the highest value was the action selected. All values generated by motor output nodes were normalized.

Genotype Representation. A single genotype was encoded as a string in the interval of [10, 58] connection weights. The genotype to phenotype (hidden layer neuron) mapping scheme was a direct one-to-one mapping, where each connection weight corresponded to a floating-point number in the interval [-10, +10]. A controller was constructed from a set of 10 genotypes (encoded hidden layer neurons). So as to simplify assembly of a neural controller, all genotypes within a sub-population (CONE method), or population (conventional NE method) of genotypes were kept the same length. Also, the given NE method was applied separately to the part of a genotype encoding input-hidden weights versus the part encoding hidden-output weights, so as not to recombine parts of a genotype responsible for distinctly different neural functions.

The genotype length was determined by the detection sensor (field of vision) setting (given by motor output MO_0). That is, the NE method also determined (indirectly via evolution of hidden-output connection weights) the field of vision most appropriate for a given controller (agent). As the value of MO_0 changed (given that it was the highest of all motor-output values at a given simulation time step), so to would the number of visual neurons in the sensory input layer, and the number of weights connecting visual neurons to hidden layer neurons.

As presented in table 2, the minimum genotype length was 10, and the maximum was 58. That is, 5 input-hidden weights connected the 5 non-visual neurons ($SI_0..SI_4$), between 1 and 49 input-hidden weights connected the same number of visual neurons ($SI_5..SI_{53}$), and 4 output-hidden weights connected the 4 motor output neurons ($MO_0..MO_3$) to the a given hidden layer neuron ($HL_0..HL_9$).

Action selection. Action selection depended on whether the agent was using a heuristic or a NE method (comparative experiments were executed). In the case of a heuristic method, selection was according to a probabilistic preference, where as in the case of NE, selection was determined by the motor output node yielding the highest output value.

8 Heuristic Methods

For the heuristic method, we *hand-coded* specialization at the agent (table 3) and group (table 4) level, according to our definition of specialization (section 1.2). An agent was considered to be specialized if it dedicated more than 50% of its lifetime to one activity. A group was considered to be specialized if more than 50% of its agents were dedicated to one activity over the course of the groups lifetime.

The heuristic method used probabilistic preferences to determine which action to execute at each simulation iteration. The degree of agent specialization was thus defined and labeled, via setting a probabilistic bias to one of the four possible actions.

Table 4. Heuristic Method: Specialized group types. The portion of Communicators is calculated as 1 minus portion of Detectors (DP) minus the portion of Evaluators (EP).

		Portion of Evaluators in Group (EP)					
		0	1/5	2/5	3/5	4/5	1
Portion	0	A	B	C	D	E	F
of	1/5	G	H	I	J	K	
Detectors	2/5	L	M	N	O		
in	3/5	P	Q	R			
Group	4/5	S	T				
(DP)	1	U					

Table 3 presents the specialized agent types tested in experiments using the heuristic method. The composition of specialized (caste) versus non-specialized

Table 5. Heuristic method: Non-specialized group types. The portion of Communicators is calculated as 1 minus portion of Detectors (DP) minus the portion of Evaluators (EP).

		Portion of Evaluators in Group (EP)		
		0	1/3	1/2
Portion of	0			W
Detectors in	1/3		V	X
Group (DP)	1/2	Y	Z	ZA

groups is specified in tables 4 and 5 respectively. For these specifications, CP denotes the portion of communicators, EP denotes the portion of evaluators, and DP denotes the portion of detectors. CP = 1 - DP - EP. The letters (V-ZA) denote the non-specialized group types. A blank space denotes a non applicable combination of detectors, evaluators, and communicators.

8.1   Specialized and Non-specialized Group Types

Specialized group types were defined by setting more than 50% of a group to be of one specialized agent type (table 3). Table 4 presents the specialized group types tested using the heuristic method. Note that not all the group types presented in table 4 are specialized according to this definition. Group types M and N do not have a greater than 50% majority of any one agent type in their group composition. Non-specialized group types were defined when no single agent type had a greater than 50% majority in the groups composition. Table 5 presents the non-specialized group types tested using the heuristic method.

8.2   Red Rock Discovery Algorithm

The red rock discovery algorithm described the activity of aerial explorers with respect to discovering and evaluating red rocks, regardless of the controller type.

```
Red Rock Discovery Algorithm()
{ Simulate for N iterations (agent lifetime)
  {
   IF red rock evaluation data in memory (not communicated) THEN
   {
    Communicate red rock evaluation data to lander;
    Get fitness reward = r, and energy reward = e;
    IF lander not within communication range
    THEN communicate red rock data to agents in communication range;
   }
   Select action:[Detect, Evaluate, Move, Communicate];
   IF red rock detected THEN
   {
    Move to closest red rock with value
    Evaluate red rock (store in memory as red rock evaluation data);
    Communicate red rock evaluation data to lander;
    Get fitness reward = r, and energy reward = e;
    IF lander not within communication range
    THEN communicate red rock data to agents in communication range;
   }
   IF current energy < minimum energy threshold Move back to lander
   to recharge e units;
  } }
```

Table 6. Agent and environment simulation parameters

Experimental Parameters	
Communication Range	100 voxels
Communication Type	broadcast
Initial Aerial Explorer / Lander Battery	1000 / 100000 units
Detection / Evaluation Sensor Cost	0.5
Movement / Communication Actuator Cost	0.5
Maximum Move / Iteration	3 voxels
Simulation Length	2500
Initial Agent Positions	Random
Reproduce (Apply NE operators)	After evaluation
Energy / Fitness reward per red rock	100 / 1
Number of red rocks per simulation	40000
Simulation runs per experiment	20

Table 7. Highest performing group types and the environment type (0-9) they performed best in

Environment Types									
0	1	2	3	4	5	6	7	8	9
P	U	R	R	O	R	P	Q	R	Q

9 Experiments and Results

We designed two sets of experiments. The first experiment set applied and measured the performance of the heuristic method using specialized and non-specialized agent groups. The second experiment set applied a conventional NE and the CONE method and tested their task performance comparatively with the 27 configurations 19 *specialized* group types and 8 *non-specialized* group types) of the heuristic method. Each experiment set was tested for 10 degrees of structure in 10 test environments (section 6.3). For all experiments, the performance measure used was the Red Rock Value Gathered (RRVG). Averages and standard deviations were calculated over 20 runs, where a single run consisted of 2500 iterations and a given method. The method used was either heuristic, or NE. The experimental agent and environment simulation parameters are presented in table 6.

9.1 Heuristic Method Comparison: Specialized Versus Non-specialized Groups

Table 8 presents the performance results from the heuristic method applied with specialized and non-specialized groups. The values in parentheses are the corresponding standard deviations. Highlighted values are the highest values attained for both specialized and non-specialized groups. Table 7 illustrates the highest

Table 8. Average RRVG for specialized (A-L; O-U) versus non-specialized group types (M, N, V-ZA)

			Specialized versus Non-Specialized Group Types	
			Group Types: Specialized	Group Types: Non-Specialized
		0	2846 (855)	2124 (388)
D	S	1	2923 (931)	2103 (669)
E O	T	2	3178 (345)	**2723 (628)**
G F	R	3	3197 (285)	2501 (744)
R	U	4	3313 (421)	2414 (594)
E	C	5	3218 (977)	2115 (597)
E	T	6	3507 (818)	2470 (644)
	U	7	**3636 (322)**	2538 (776)
	R	8	3412 (847)	2475 (647)
	E	9	3313 (618)	2397 (713)

performing groups for each of the 10 test environments (each degree of structure). Only group types in the range are (H-U) are displayed, since these were the highest performing group types.

9.2   Neuro-Evolution Method Comparison

Table 9 presents the performance results for the conventional NE method (A) versus the CONE method (B) when applied to the 10 test environments. The highlighted values are the RRVG attained for each method. The value in parentheses are the corresponding standard deviations. For the NE methods, we determined if a given agent in a given group assumed a particular role via measuring what portion of its lifetime was spent on each of the detection, evaluation, and communication activities. An agent that spent the majority (more than 50%) of its lifetime on the detection activity was termed a detector. Similarly, the terms evaluator and communicator were applied for agents that spent a majority of their lifetimes on evaluation and communication. Likewise, convergence to a caste, via measuring the portion of detectors, evaluators and communicators that comprised a group, for the majority of the groups lifetime.

10   Analysis and Discussion

In order to draw conclusions from this comparative study, we performed a set of statistic tests in order to gauge respective differences between heuristic and NE method results. First, we determined results from the specialized and non-specialized heuristic (table 8), CONE and conventional NE (table 9) methods to be normal distributions via applying the Kolmogorov-Smirnov test [5]. P values were P=0.72, P=0.99, P=1.0, and P=0.98, respectively. To determine the statistical significance of difference between each of these data sets we applied an independent t-test [5]. For each t-test we selected 0.05 as the threshold for statistical significance, and stated the null hypothesis as two data sets not significantly differing. The t-test was first applied to the comparative specialized and

Table 9. Average RRVG for the conventional NE (A) versus the CONE (B) method

			Neuro-Evolution Method Comparison	
			Method A: Conventional NE	Method B: CONE
		0	2874 (365)	4290 (265)
D	S	1	3338 (341)	4229 (350)
E O	T	2	3218 (417)	4189 (421)
G F	R	3	3040 (430)	4394(304)
R	U	4	**3988 (451)**	4511 (321)
E	C	5	3956 (338)	4898 (444)
E	T	6	3633 (314)	4658 (321)
	U	7	3466 (384)	**4907 (481)**
	R	8	3525 (253)	4602 (406)
	E	9	2971 (441)	4638 (375)

Table 10. Comparative group compositions of best performing groups using conventional NE and the CONE methods. DoS denotes Degree of Structure.

Group Composition of Conventional Neuro-Evolution Method					
Detectors	Evaluators	Communicators	No Specialization	DoS	Average RRVG
0.37	0.36	0.15	0.12	4	3988
Group Composition of Collective Neuro-Evolution Method					
Detectors	Evaluators	Communicators	No Specialization	DoS	Average RRVG
0.52	0.25	0.22	0.01	7	4907

non-specialized heuristic method data sets. P=0.00003 was calculated, meaning the null hypothesis was rejected. This served to support our first hypothesis of specialization being advantageous in terms of increasing task performance in particular environment types. Second, we applied the t-test to the comparative NE method results. A P=0.00007 was calculated, meaning the null hypothesis was rejected. This partially supported our second hypothesis that the CONE method would yield a high task performance.

Finally, we applied the t-test to the specialized heuristic method (table 8) and the conventional NE method (table 9) results. A P=0.32 was calculated, meaning the null hypothesis was accepted and there was no significant difference between task performance results. This served to partially support our second hypothesis that specialization was beneficial for task performance, via illustrating that an adaptive method with no specialization (table 10) yielded no significant advantage in performance. In terms of supporting our second hypothesis, that the CONE method derived specialized groups yielding high task performance, it is necessary to compare table 7 and table 10. The heuristic method showed that the best performing specialized group type (*caste Q*) was operating within *environment type 7*. As presented in table 4 the group composition of *caste Q* was such that a (60%) majority was the agent type *detector*. The remainder of the group composition was split between *evaluators* and *communicators*. Table 10 presents the group composition derived by the CONE method in *environment type 7* consisted of a majority of *detector* agents (0.52) and minor portions of *evaluator*

(0.25) and *communicator* (0.22) agent types. This group composition resembled the *caste* Q in terms of consisting of a majority of detectors and two minorities of evaluators and communicators. This was not the case for the conventional NE method. This method yielded on average a comparable performance to the heuristic method using specialized group types for all test environments. Additionally, the conventional NE method was unable to out-perform the CONE method for all test environments (table 9). Table 10 illustrates that the best performing conventional NE run (test environment 4) as not converging to a caste. In table 10 only the group composition for environment type 4 is presented, however, this held true for all environment types. It is theorized that the inferior performance of the conventional NE (comparative to the CONE) method was a lack of derived specialization.

11   Conclusions

This paper described a comparative study of neuro-evolution and heuristic methods designed to test the efficacy and benefits of utilizing specialization as a means of increasing performance in a search and find task given a range of test environments. Performance comparisons were made according to the total value of features of interest (termed *red rocks*) discovered by a simulated multi-robot system. In support of our first hypothesis, a heuristic method using pre-defined specialized multi-robot groups elucidated that specialization was beneficial in a range of test environments (defined by different resource distributions. In support of our second hypothesis, our neuro-evolution method yielded a higher performance in all test environments, comparative to a conventional neuro-evolution method. The best performing group using the collective neuro-evolution method converged to a specialized group composition (such that the majority of the agents assumed one role) that resembled the group composition of the highest performing specialized group tested with the heuristic method. The comparatively low performance of the conventional method was deemed to be consequent of the lack of specialization exhibited in group compositions derived.

References

1. G. Baldassarre, S. Nolfi, and D. Parisi. Evolving mobile robots able to display collective behavior. *Artificial Life*, 9(1):255–267, 2003.
2. B. Bryant and R. Miikkulainen. Neuro-evolution for adaptive teams. In *Proceedings of the 2003 Congress on Evolutionary Computation*, pages 2194–2201. IEEE Press, Canberra, Australia, 2003.
3. L. Bull and J. Holland. Evolutionary computing in multi-agent environments: Eusociality. In *Proceedings of the Second Annual Conference on Genetic Programming*, pages 347–352. IEEE Press, San Francisco, USA., 1997.
4. A. Eiben and J. Smith. *Introduction to Evolutionary Computing*. Springer-Verlag, Berlin, Germany, 2003.
5. B. Flannery, S. Teukolsky, and W. Vetterling. *Numerical Recipes*. Cambridge University Press, Cambridge, 1986.

6. D. Floreano and J. Urzelai. Evolutionary robots with on-line self-organization and behavioral fitness. *Neural Networks*, 13(1):431–443, 2000.
7. J. Gautrais, G. Theraulaz, J. Deneubourg, and C. Anderson. Emergent polyethism as a consequence of increased colony size in insect societies. *Journal of Theoretical Biology*, 215(1):363–373, 2002.
8. F. Gomez and R. Miikkulainen. Incremental evolution of complex general behavior. *Adaptive Behavior*, 5(1):317–342, 1997.
9. N. Jakobi, P. Husbands, and I. Harvey. Noise and the reality gap: The use of simulation in evolutionary robotics. In *Proceedings of Third European Conference on Artificial Life (ECAL-95)*, pages 704–720. Springer-Verlag, Granada, Spain, 1995.
10. M. Kreiger and J. Billeter. The call of duty: Self-organized task allocation in a population of up to twelve mobile robots. *Robotics and Autonomous Systems*, 30: 65–84, 2000.
11. S. Nolfi and D. Floreano. Learning and evolution. *Autonomous Robots*, 7(1):89–113, 1999.
12. S. Nolfi and D. Parisi. Learning to adapt to changing environments in evolving neural networks. *Adaptive Behavior*, 1(5):75–98, 1997.
13. P. Paalanen, J. Kamarainen, J. Ilonen, and H. Kälviäinen. Feature representation and discrimination based on gaussian mixture model probability densities - practices and algorithms. *Pattern Recognition*, 39(7):1346–1358, 2006.
14. K. Stanley, B. Bryant, and R. Miikkulainen. Real-time neuro-evolution in the nero video game. *IEEE Transactions Evolutionary Computation*, 9(6):653–668, 2005.
15. K. Stanley and R. Miikkulainen. Competitive coevolution through evolutionary complexification. *Journal of Artificial Intelligence Research*, 21(1):63–100, 2004.
16. S. Thakoor. Bio-inspired engineering of exploration systems. *Journal of Space Mission Architecture*, 2(1):49–79, 2000.
17. S. Whiteson, N. Kohl, R. Miikkulainen, and P. Stone. Evolving keep-away soccer players through task decomposition. In *Proceeding of the Genetic and Evolutionary Computation Conference*, pages 356–368. AAAI Press, Chicago, 2003.
18. L. Young, E. Aiken, G. Briggs, V. Gulick, and R. Mancinelli. Rotorcraft as mars scouts. In *Proceeding of the IEEE Aerospace Conference*, pages 4–12. IEEE Press, Big Sky, USA, 2002.

Scalability in Evolved Neurocontrollers That Guide a Swarm of Robots in a Navigation Task

Federico Vicentini[1] and Elio Tuci[2]

[1] Robotics Lab, Mechanics Dept., Politecnico di Milano
federico.vicentini@polimi.it
[2] IRIDIA, CoDE, Université Libre de Bruxelles
etuci@ulb.ac.be

Abstract. Generally speaking, the behavioural strategies of a multi-robot system can be defined as scalable if the performance of the system does not drop by increasing the cardinality of the group. The research work presented in this paper studies the issue of scalability in artificial neural network controllers designed by evolutionary algorithms. The networks are evolved to control homogeneous group of autonomous robots required to solve a navigation task in an open arena. This work shows that, the controllers designed to solve the task, generate navigation strategies which are potentially scalable. However, through an analysis of the dynamics of the single robot controller we identify elements that significantly hinder the scalability of the system. The analysis we present in this paper helps to understand the principles underlying the concepts of scalability in this kind of multi-robot systems and to design more scalable solutions.

1 Introduction

The research work presented in this paper studies the issue of scalability in artificial neural network controllers designed by evolutionary algorithms. The networks are evolved to control a homogeneous group of autonomous robots required to solve a navigation task in an open arena.

The task, originally presented in [1], requires a group of three robots to move in any arbitrary direction by remaining close to each other while avoiding collisions. A homogeneous group is one in which the robots share the same controller, which is cloned in each member of the group. The difficulty of the task resides in the fact that each robot has a very limited perception of the world, based on the readings of the infrared sensors which surround the body of the agent. Therefore, the emergence of navigational strategies is based on a self-organisation process by which the robots coordinate their actions in order to: (i) choose a common direction of motion starting from random initial positions; (ii) dynamically assign roles, such as leader-follower, that may facilitates the accomplishment of the task.

In [1], the results of the research work show that dynamic neural networks can be designed by evolutionary computation techniques to control a group of autonomous robots capable of successfully carrying out the group navigation task. The analysis of the group behaviour shows that, during a successful trial

E. Şahin et al. (Eds.): Swarm Robotics Ws, LNCS 4433, pp. 206–220, 2007.

the behaviour of the group can be divided in two phases. During the first phase the robots display themselves in chain formation starting from any randomly chosen initial position. During the formation of chain there is also the emergence of roles, since one of the two robots at the end of the chain orients itself in the opposite way with respect to the other two. This robot can be considered to be the leader, since it chooses the direction of motion of the entire group. In the second phase, the chain starts moving in an arbitrary direction of motion, with the first robot (the leader) travelling forward. The others follow the leader by keeping the geometrical centre aligned and travelling backward.

The work presented in this paper firstly replicates the results discussed in [1]. Subsequently, it shows an analysis of the scalability of the evolved solutions. Note that, our work differentiates from the original one because we use a different robotic platform and a different type of dynamic neural network as robot controller. The issue of scalability is particularly relevant within the methodological framework employed in [1] and referred to as Evolutionary Robotics (ER, see [2]). Roughly speaking, ER is a methodological tool to automate the design of robots' controllers. ER is based on the use of artificial evolution to find sets of parameters for artificial neural networks that guide the robots to the accomplishment of their objective, avoiding dangers. Owing to its properties, ER can be employed to look at the effects that the physical interactions among embodied agents and their world have on the *evolution* of individual behaviour and social skills (see [3,4,1]).

One the most relevant features of ER is to allow the design of artificial neural network controllers for robots capable of facing circumstances never experienced during the training phase. This property is generally referred to as (i) "robustness" when the unexperienced circumstances are determined by changes in the characteristics of the environment; (ii) "scalability" when the unexperienced circumstances concern the cardinality of the group of robots. In this work we prove that, the controllers designed to solve the task originally described in [1] generate a navigation strategy which is potentially scalable. That is, the increment of the number of robots in the group should not cause any disruptive effect on the performance of the system. However, through an analysis of the dynamics of the single robot controller we identify elements that significantly hinder the scalability of the system. Although our analysis is limited to a single "case study", those elements which hinder the scalability of the solutions might be identified in other multi-robot systems in which the robots are controlled by dynamic neural networks designed by artificial evolution. We hope that the analysis we present in this paper helps (i) to understand the principles underlying the concepts of scalability in this kind of multi-robot systems (ii) to design more scalable solutions.

2   The Simulated Agents

The controllers are evolved in a simulation environment which models some of the hardware characteristics of the real *s-bots*. The *s-bots* (see Fig. 1a) are small wheeled cylindrical robots, 5.8 cm of radius, equipped with a variety of sensors, and whose mobility is ensured by a differential drive system (see [5] for details). The signal of the infrared sensors is a function of the distance between the robot and any perceived obstacle. Concerning the function that updates the position of the robots within the environment, we employed the Differential Drive Kinematics equations, as presented in [6]. 10% uniform noise is added to all sensor readings, the motor outputs and the position of the robot. The characteristics of the agent-environment model are explained in detail in [7].

3   The Controller and the Evolutionary Algorithm

The agent controller is made up of a feed-forward multilayer network (see Fig. 1c). The sensory neurons (from N_1 to N_5) receive input from the agent's infrared sensors. The inter-neuron network (from N_6 to N_8) is fully recurrently connected. Additionally, each inter-neuron receives one incoming synapse from each sensory neuron. Each output neuron (N_9 and N_{10}) receives one incoming synapse from each hidden layer neuron. There are no direct connections between sensory and output neurons. The network neurons are ruled by the following state equation:

$$\tau_i \dot{x}_i = \begin{cases} -x_i + g_i I_i & i = 1, ...5 \\ -x_i + \sum_{j=1}^{N} \omega_{ij} \sigma(x_j, \beta_j, g_j) & i = 6, ...10; \ \sigma(x, \beta, g) = \frac{1}{1+e^{-g(x+\beta)}} \end{cases} \quad (1)$$

where N is the number of neurons. This formulation is a sub-class of Hopfield networks [8] and, using terms derived from an analogy with real neurons, τ_i is the decay constant, x_i represents the cell potential, I_i is the intensity of the sensory perturbation on sensory neuron i amplified by a gain g_i, ω_{ij} the strength of the synaptic connection from neuron j to neuron i, β_j is the bias term, and $\sigma(x_j, \beta_j, g_j)$ represents the firing rate. The cell potentials (x_i) of the 9th and the 10th neuron, mapped into [0,1] by the sigmoid function (σ), are then linearly scaled into $[-6.5, 6.5]$ in order to set the robot motors output. The following

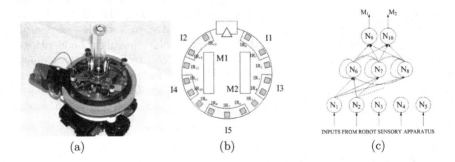

Fig. 1. (a) A picture of a real *s-bot*. (b) Plan of the simulated robot; (c) the network architecture. Only some of the connections are drawn. The input layer takes readings as follows: neuron N_1 takes input from $\frac{Ir_0+Ir_1}{2}$, N_2 from $\frac{Ir_{13}+Ir_{14}}{2}$, N_3 from $\frac{Ir_3+Ir_4}{2}$, N_4 from $\frac{Ir_{10}+Ir_{11}}{2}$, N_5 from $\frac{Ir_6+Ir_7+Ir_8}{3}$. All input values are scaled in the range of IR sensors readings. M_1 and M_2 are respectively the left and right motor.

parameters are genetically encoded: (i) the strength of synaptic connections ω_{ij}; (ii) the decay constant τ_i of the inter-neurons N_6, N_7 and N_8; (iii) the bias term β_j and (iv) the gain term g_j for the neurons in the input and hidden layers. All the neurons of each layer share the same bias term and gain term for the firing rate function. The neurons N_9 and N_{10} have not-evolved $\beta_{9,10} = 0.0$ and $g_{9,10} = 1.0$. The decay constant τ_i of the sensory neurons and of the output neurons are set equal to dt (see below). Cell potentials are set to 0 any time the network is initialised or reset, and circuits are integrated using the forward Euler method with an integration step-size of $dt = 0.1s$.

A simple generational genetic algorithm is employed to set the parameters of the networks [9]. The population contains 50 genotypes. Generations following the first one are produced by a combination of selection with elitism, recombination and mutation. Each genotype is a vector of 37 real values (i.e., 30 connection weights, 3 decay constants, 2 bias terms, and 2 gain factors).

4   The Fitness Function

During evolution, each genotype is translated into a robot controller, and cloned in each agent of a group. The evaluation of a group lasts E trials, where E is given by systematically varying the initial orientation of each robot according to the following criteria: we defined four possible initial orientations $\theta_{start} \in [0, \frac{\pi}{2}, \pi, \frac{3}{2}\pi]$ and we initialised the agents according to the all possible combinations of the four orientations for a group of three robots - i.e., $E = 4^3 = 64$ starting positions. Each trial differs from the others also in the initialisation of the random number generator, which influences the robots' starting position and the noise added to motors and sensors. The robot-robot initial distance is randomly chosen in the interval $[3.0, 13]cm$. In each trial, the group is rewarded by an evaluation function f_e which seeks to assess the ability of the team to move as far as possible in any arbitrarily chosen direction while avoiding collisions and staying within the range of the robots' infrared sensors. Taking inspiration from the work of Quinn et al. [1], the fitness score is computed as follows: $f_e = P\left\{ \sum_{t=i}^{T} (d_t - D_{t-1})[1 - tanh(S_t/R)] \right\}$, where time steps are indexed by t and T is the final time step of the trial, and

- $(d_t - D_{t-1})$ rewards the team for advancing in navigation. Distances are computed through the centroid of the group, in such way that d_t is the Euclidean distance between the group location at time step t and its location at time step $t = 0$, and D_{t-1} is the largest value that d_t has attained prior to time step t. This first component measures any gain that the team has made on its previous best distance from its initial location.
- $[1 - tanh(S_t/R)]$ reduces the fitness increment when one or more robots are outside of the infrared sensor range. S_t is a measure of the team's dispersal beyond the infra red sensor range R ($R = 24.6cm$) at time step t. If each robot is within the range R of at least another robot, then $S_t = 0$. The term related to the scattered position of the team is generalised from the original term in [1] considering the gap among clusters of agents instead of single agents. This is computed as the shortest distance d_{ij} among the

agents belonging to different clusters. All the computed distances are in the set $D_c = \{d_{ij} : d_{ij} = \min \|a_i, a_j\|, \forall a_i \in C_i, \forall a_j \in C_j\}$, where C_i, C_j are pairs of detected clusters C. If K clusters are detected, the computed gap is

$$S_t = \sum_{k=1}^{K-1} (d_k), \quad d_k \in D_c \tag{2}$$

where the considered distances d_k are the shortest $(K - 1)$ ones. $tanh()$ assures that, as the robots begin to disperse, the team's score increment falls sharply.

– $P = 1 - (\sum_{i=1}^{n} c_i/c_{max})$ reduces the score proportionally to the number of collisions which have occurred during the trial, where c_i is the number of collisions of the robot i and $c_{max} = 20$ is the maximum number of collisions allowed. c_i is computed for all the n agents at the end of the trial, so that the term P is multiplied once at a trial. Note that if the team exceeds the maximum number of allowed collisions $(\sum_{i=1}^{n} c_i > c_{max})$ the trial is terminated beforehand and $P = 0$.

5   Results

Two different experiments were set up in order to test the scalability of the evolved controllers: an environment *Env. 3* populated with 3 agents (like in [1]) and an augmented environment of 4 agents (*Env. 4*). In both the experiments, ten evolutionary simulations, each using a different random initialisation, ran for 3000 generations of the evolutionary algorithm. In each generation, every individual was evaluated 64 times. The termination criterion for each evaluation was set to a time equal to 200 seconds of simulated time or to the attainment of the maximum allowed distance covered during the team navigation $(D_{max} = 200cm)$. Three batches of these simulations were set up for developing 3 types of genotypes over the two experiments. The genotype types are: *geno33* evolved in *Env. 3* experiment, *geno44* evolved in *Env. 4* and *geno34* evolved in a mixed environment, i.e. in an environment corresponding to *Env. 3* half the evaluations and to *Env. 4* the remaining ones in each generation. In this way we evolved a genotype (*geno34*) fit for both the experiments for comparison purpose. Then, in order to have a better estimate of the behavioural capabilities of the evolved controllers, we post-evaluated the genotypes with the highest fitness in each of the 10 evolutionary runs. The post-evaluations were run for 10 trials each porting the evolved controller on the real *s-bot*. In the experimental results we reproduce the behaviour shown in [1]. The number of genotypes out of the 10 runs that successfully performs the task is not relevant to the interest of this paper and shall not be discussed any further. In fact, in order to study the scalability of the evolved controllers, we finally selected only the absolute best performing genotypes, one for each type *geno33*, *geno44* and *geno34*. They are re-evaluated for 20 runs in both *Env. 3* and *Env. 4*. Each re-evaluation run is made of 100 trials. A trial is successfully terminated after 200 seconds regardless the distance covered. In this way we have 2 genomes (*geno33* and *geno44*) available for the re-evaluation also in an extended (*geno33* in *Env. 4*) or reduced environment (*geno44* in *Env. 3*), and a comparison genome (*geno34*) to check the scaled solution since it experimented both environments. For both evolution and re-evaluation runs, the performances are measured through the fitness score. Any re-evaluation trial is considered successful if the team covers a distance greater than the 95% of D_{max} allowed during the evolution. The results of all the 20 re-evaluation runs are averaged and shown in Fig. 2. The results show that, regarding the same environments experienced during the evolution, the *geno33* is completely fit for its original *Env. 3*, whereas the *geno44* gets a lower success percentage in *Env. 4*. This is due to the fact that the *Env. 4* experiment implies a longer and more complex self-organising phase. In addition, the *geno34* scores as well as the non hybrid genotypes (*geno33* and *geno44*) in their own original environments. As predictable, the success of *geno34* is due to the experience of both environments during evolution, so this genotype is used to check whether a solution can be suitably extended over the 2 environments. However, the scalability property is strictly defined only for genotypes tested in different environment from where they were evolved. Therefore, in this work the following analysis is focused only on the behaviour of *geno33* in both *Env. 3* and *Env. 4* in order to study how the genotype reacts to the scaled experiment, i.e. increasing the number of agents. This single case (low number of agents, increasing the cardinality of the team by only one element) is devoted to the analysis of the local dynamics of the agents and of the behavioural mechanisms. It is so intended to be a first step towards a further complementary research on the increase of the agents number to a larger amount in both simulation and reality with the same approach, as well as on the decrease of the agents number, especially removed from a large swarm.

5.1 Scalability Results

In this session we discuss the scalability property from a task point of view. We observe the capability of the *geno33* in adapting to the new condition when it is cloned into each of the 4 agents of *Env. 4*. However, the solution to this latter experiment cannot be considered scalable because the same genotype has not the same performances in both *Env. 3* and *Env. 4*. An evident cause of failure in *Env. 4* occurs when only 3 agents out of 4 gather together and start moving forward as soon as they build a chain. The fourth agent is often left behind circling and searching for a chain to join. In other words, whenever the solution originally developed in *Env. 3* is available, the team starts to accomplish the task regardless the number of agents left behind. Another frequent failure mode is associated with the team splitting into two couples moving independently in different directions with one leader and only one follower. In the successful cases, on the contrary, the team is tightly bound in a chain of 4 agent and the task is accomplished without loss of formation. Likely, the self-organising mechanism could be intrinsically stable and successful, but it is heavily affected by the transient during the self-organisation phase before starting the movement in chain formation. Although the solution cannot generally be defined as scalable because of the failure during the transient, the analysis of the neuro-controller

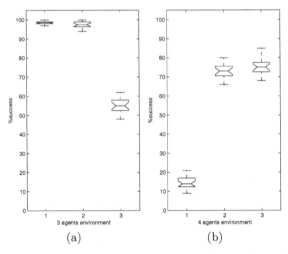

Fig. 2. Percentage of success during the re-evaluation test of genotype *geno33* (see box 1), genotype *geno34* (see box 2), and genotype *geno44* (see box 3) in environment *Env. 3* (see graphs a) and in environment *Env. 4* (see graphs b). The box plot shows the distribution of the success percentage over the 20 re-evaluation runs. Each box quotes the mean, the quartiles, the 5th and 95th percentiles of the number of successful trials among the 100 trials of each run.

suggests the presence of a scalable mechanism in the assignment of roles among the agents. However, this mechanism is not robust enough to reach a reliable solution. In the following discussion, every neural network is first evaluated in the state space of the neurons in order to analyse the network status during the task. Then, the team is considered as a global dynamical system since every action during the team performance is based on the interconnections of the state values of all the neurons. Hence, the agent dynamics and the team dynamics are discussed in order to investigate the causes of the loss of robustness in the accomplishment of the task.

5.2 Analysis of Controller Dynamics for a Single Agent

In this session we analyse the mechanism of role assignment in the team navigation. We give evidence of the scalability of a single role inside the team and of the absence of new roles in the scaled *Env. 4*. This provides the necessary condition to perform the scaled task. In next session, we discuss the reasons of the unsuccessful application in the task of this necessary but not sufficient condition. The analysis of role assignment takes evidence from the qualitative analysis of the dynamical system coded in each neural network acting as a controller. All the neurons in the Continuous Time Recurrent Neural Network of Equation 1 define a stable (see below) ODE (Ordinary Differential Equation) set. The flow $\Phi(\mathbf{x}, t)$ of solutions of Equations 1 is definitely converging to some stable solutions $\varphi(\mathbf{x}^*, t)$ inside the related domains of attraction $B(\varphi(\mathbf{x}^*, t), r)$, $\forall \varphi \in \mathbf{\Phi}$, of size r in which the state domain is split. Any trajectory $\varphi(\mathbf{x}, \mathbf{x}_0, t)$, starting

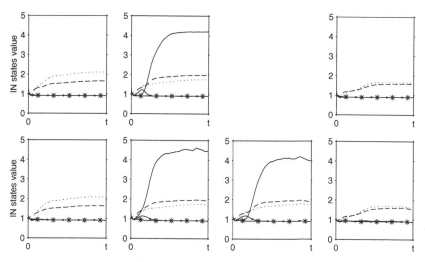

Fig. 3. State values $(x_1(t), ..., x_5(t))$ of the 5 neurons input layer for each team role averaged over the successful trials of *geno33* in *Env. 3*(above) and in *Env. 4* (below). In *Env. 4* the centre role is doubled and the related pattern similar for both central agents. (Legend: x_1 continuous line, x_2 dot markers, x_3 star markers, x_4 dot line, x_5 dashed line)

from the initial conditions $\mathbf{x}_0$ common for all controllers, is definitely caught in a different domain of attraction according to the states of the input neurons. For each agent, the I_i values provide different state patterns for input neurons and let the network to follow the resulting φ_{agent}. In this way the reached limit set makes all the neurons states become constant. Each controller assumes exactly the behaviour corresponding to a different set of constant states. The mechanism is clearly unpredictable and emerges as a result of the evolutionary process when performing the task. Moreover, the assignment of roles is not associated to any predefined feature of the agents but is only due to the self-organising phase. The state space values used in this analysis are provided by single step Euler integration of Equation 1 during the re-evaluation simulations. Then, the records of input states for each agent are analysed to recognise the role-related patterns (see Fig. 3). In both *Env. 3* and *Env. 4*, the activation values of the proximity sensors I_i, $i = 1, ..., 5$ in Equation 1 are correlated to the positions of the leader, the centre(s) and the follower inside the chain formation. Comparing the same re-evaluated genotype *geno33*, the regime sets are similar for both environments. In particular the central agents have the same patterns. In addition to role recognition, the analysis of the state space provides information about the behaviour of each agent. Unlike the external layers that have the same time constant as the clock update of the neuro-controller, the hidden (fully recurrently connected) layer evolved different time constants. As a result, the controller processes the input states and updates the output states according to the dynamics of $N6$, $N7$ and $N8$. The mechanism of role assignment is shown by the graph depicted in Fig. 4 that represents a 3D plot of the trajectory

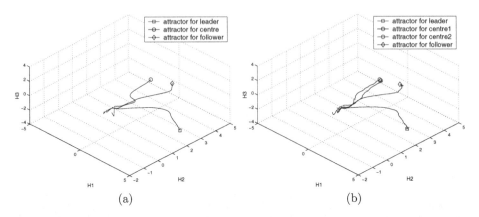

Fig. 4. Portrait in $H_1 \times H_2 \times H_3 \subseteq \mathbb{R}^3$, of the state values $x_6(t), x_7(t), x_8(t)$ of the 3 neurons in hidden layer for each role in the team coded with *geno33* in *Env. 3* (a) and in *Env. 4* (b). In (b) the centre role is doubled and the related trajectory is similar for both central agents.

of each agent, considering a $\mathbb{R}^3$ projection of the domain $\mathbb{R}^N$ where N is the number of neurons, i.e. the trajectories are those made only of the states of the hidden neurons. As an empirical result, the limit sets of $\varphi_n(\mathbf{x}, \mathbf{x}_0, t)$, for each $n = 1, ..., 3(4)$ agent, are equilibrium points, such as $\mathbf{x}^* : \varphi_n(\mathbf{x}^*, \mathbf{x}_0) = \mathbf{x}^*$. Each equilibrium point corresponds to a role in the team. To this end, the scalability of the solution is related to the local behaviour of the agent added in the team for testing the scale effect. The scaled solution can therefore be considered stable if the added agent does not affect the strategy and leaves unchanged the leading and ending positions. Thus, a scalable solution does not imply the emergence of other new role, but inserts the added agent into one of the existing roles. In this particular strategy it happens to be the central role (see Fig. 4b). As a consequence, the expected patterns in states dynamics of the added agent fall into the same domain of attraction of the corresponding shared role. In this way, the added neuro-controller manages the scaled condition in *Env. 4* according to the same behaviour evolved in the original conditions (*Env. 3*). This result may be confirmed by the analysis of the behaviour of the hybrid genotype *geno34*. It shows the same kind of dynamics, splitting the domain into role-related domains of attraction (see Fig. 5). Since this genotype is evolved in both *Env. 3* and *Env. 4*, the solution is fit for both the scaled and not scaled environment. Unlike the evaluation of *geno33* in *Env. 4* (see Fig. 2) the percentage of success of *geno34* is statistically equal to that belonging to *geno44*. So, whenever the mechanism is adulterated by the evolution in a mixed environment, the solution is much more robust than that previously analysed, but the mechanism of assignment of roles is the same. This is probably an evidence that the successful solution of the task for *geno33* is potentially scalable to higher number of agents with the same mechanism and strategy, but it is not accomplished enough reliably to reach every time the stable regime like in *Env. 3*.

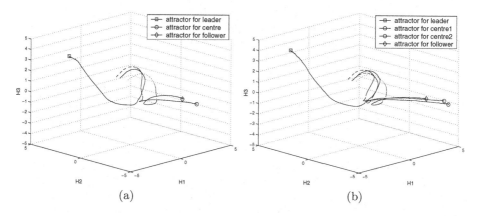

Fig. 5. Portrait in $H_1 \times H_2 \times H_3 \subseteq \mathbb{R}^3$, of the state values $x_6(t), x_7(t), x_8(t)$ of the 3 neurons in hidden layer for each role in the team coded with *geno34* in *Env. 3* (a) and in *Env. 4* (b). The trajectories of centres robots are statistically overlapping.

5.3   Analysis of Controller Dynamics for the Entire Team

In this session we use some results in the analysis of neural networks to discuss the phenomena that probably affect as sufficient conditions the reliability of the solution, given the necessary condition in the assignment of roles. The global behaviour of the team is ruled by dynamics similar to those studied for a single controller but extended to the complete system given by all the neural controllers concurrently interacting in a M-dimensional state space, where $M = nN$, N is the number of neurons of each of the n controllers playing in the experiment. In this way, each stable solution corresponds to a specific behaviour/strategy of the team as a whole. Therefore, the successful solution is likely to be defined by a stable limit set in the dynamics of the global system, and the robustness of the success is related to the type of convergence to that limit set. The coupled system is given by M equations rewritten in matrix form from Equations 1 and scaled in order to have $g_i I_i = 0$ for all $i = 1, ..., M$ (see [10] for details).

$$\dot{\mathbf{y}}(t) = -\mathbf{B}\mathbf{y}(t) + \mathbf{A}\sigma(\mathbf{y}(t)) \qquad (3)$$

where $\mathbf{y} = [y_1, ... y_M]^T$, $y_i = x_i - g_i I_i$, $\mathbf{B} = diag[1/\tau_i, ..., 1/\tau_M]$, $\mathbf{A} = [a_{ij}]$, $a_{ij} = \omega_{ij}/\tau_i$, $\sigma(\mathbf{y}) = [\sigma_1, ..., \sigma_M]^T$, $\sigma_i = \sigma(y_i + g_i I_i, \beta_i, g_i)$. In this notation $i = [1, 10]$ are derived from the first agent neurons, $i = [11, 20]$ from the second one and so on. Equation 3 is a Hopfield-class network for an autonomous system whose parameters are not time dependent and the neurons activation are not influenced by external inputs (see [11] for networks global analysis). The terms I_i, in fact, are an implicit expression of the output neurons states through the sensors activation related to the position of the agents. The system 3 is therefore in the form $\dot{\mathbf{y}} = \mathbf{F}(\mathbf{y}, \mathbf{y}_0)$ from $\dot{\mathbf{x}}(t) = \mathbf{F}(\mathbf{x}, \mathbf{x}_0, \mathbf{I}, t)$. Hopfield networks are often employed as associative memories and the equilibrium points represent the stored patterns. When used as controllers for autonomous agents, the stored patterns hold specific sets of states corresponding to stable behaviours. Although many equilibrium points are suitably storable by a network of Equation 3, only a few are fit for setting the neurons states during the accomplishment of an ER desired task. In particular, among the behaviours shown by the team in the present work, only one equilibrium point $\mathbf{y}^* = [y_1^*, ..., y_M^*]^T$ corresponds to the successful behaviour. The other previously described cases of failure correspond to equilibrium points characterised by a specific stored behaviour but unacceptable from a task point of view. As a consequence, the robustness in the scalability of the performed task is associated with the size and topology of the domain of attraction for the equilibrium point corresponding to the desired solution. According to the results proposed by [12], it is immediate to infer that the system of Equation 3 is not globally convergent but only locally on several $\mathbf{y}^*$. Hence, for the analysis of the performance of *geno33* in the scaled *Env. 4*, we consider the undesired equilibrium point $\tilde{\mathbf{y}}^*$, corresponding to the navigation of two couples of independent agents, in addition to $\mathbf{y}^*$, corresponding to the successful behaviour. Our hypothesis for the loss of robustness of the scalable solution is that $\mathbf{y}^*$ yields a domain of attraction smaller than $\tilde{\mathbf{y}}^*$. Formally, we let $\mathbf{v}$ be a generic vector and define a neighborhood $B_\delta(\mathbf{v}^*, \mathbf{v}_0, \delta) = \{\varphi_t(\mathbf{v}, \mathbf{v}_0, t) \in \mathbb{R}^M : \|\varphi_t - \mathbf{v}^*\| < \delta, \forall t \geq 0, \mathbf{v}_0 = \mathbf{v}(0)\}$. So we expect that $\delta_{\mathbf{y}^*} < \delta_{\tilde{\mathbf{y}}^*}$. Both $\mathbf{y}^*$ and $\tilde{\mathbf{y}}^*$ in *Env. 4* are empirically observed in the regime condition where the gradient $\dot{\mathbf{y}} = 0$ and $\dot{\tilde{\mathbf{y}}} = 0$. In particular, $\mathbf{y}^* \in \mathbb{R}^{4N}$ in *Env. 4* presents identical values y_i^*, for $i = 11, ..., 20$ and $i = 21, ..., 30$ as expected for the stable states shared by the controllers of the two central agents. Again, these equilibrium values are equal to the corresponding y_i^*, for $i = 11, ..., 20$ of the single central agent in *Env. 3* where $\mathbf{y}^* \in \mathbb{R}^{3N}$. All the considered equilibrium points $\mathbf{v}^*$ verify the condition $\mathbf{B}\mathbf{v}^* = \mathbf{A}\sigma(\mathbf{v}^*)$. Many results in neural networks analysis deal with the conditions for local (exponential) stability of the various $\mathbf{v}^*$ of an Hopfield network, some of which are based on the matrices measure [13] or on the Lyapunov direct method [14,15,16] in order to have an estimate of the domain of attraction. Here we follow the approach proposed by [17] for large scale dynamical systems. This approach splits the system of Equation 3 into M *free subsystems* corresponding to each neuron in the network, and an *interconnecting structure* that gives account of the relationships between the neurons. When analysing the stability properties of a given equilibrium point, we will be able to assume, without loss of generality, that this equilibrium is located at the origin of $\mathbb{R}^M$. To show this, assume that $\mathbf{y}^* \neq 0$ is an equilibrium point for Equation 3, and define

$$u_i = y_i - y_i^*, \quad S_i(u_i) = \sigma_i(u_i + y_i^*, \beta_i, g_i) - \sigma(y_i^*, \beta_i, g_i) \quad i = 1, ..., M \quad (4)$$

where $S_i(0) = 0$, S_i strictly monotonically increasing in u_i and $u_i S_i(u_i) > 0 \quad \forall u_i \neq 0$. With this notation and under the assumptions of $\mathbf{y}^*$ as an isolated equilibrium of the system 3, $\mathbf{u} = 0$ is an equilibrium point for the system $\dot{\mathbf{u}} = -\mathbf{B}\mathbf{u} + \mathbf{A}\mathbf{S}(\mathbf{u})$. Under this viewpoint, the latter system is described by M *free subsystems* of equation

$$\dot{u}_i = -B_i u_i + A_{ii} S_i(u_i) \quad (5)$$

and an *interconnecting structure* made up of the terms

$$s_i(u_1, ..., u_M) = \sum_{j=1, j \neq i}^{M} A_{ij} S_j(u_j), \quad i = 1, ..., M. \tag{6}$$

Here we make use of the method of analysis advanced in [10]. Specifically, the stability results for the entire neural network of Equation 3 make use of the stability results for the individual free neurons of Equation 5 and then for the system in Equation 6. The stability analysis of each of the M Equations 5 is based on the direct Lyapunov method for which we define a function

$$V_i(u_i) = \frac{1}{2} u_i^2, \quad i = 1, ..., M \tag{7}$$

ad the related Dini derivative (or rate of change)

$$DV_i(u_i) = u_i \dot{u}_i = u_i[-B_i u_i + A_{ii} S_i(u_i)]. \tag{8}$$

Hence, for being $u_i = 0$ the equilibrium point for all the M *free subsystems*, the Lyapunov function must be positive definite, i.e. $V_i(u_i) > 0$, and the Dini derivative negative definite, i.e. $DV_i(u_i) < 0$, for all $u_i \neq 0$. These conditions are satisfied if

$$\begin{cases} -B_i u_i + A_{ii} S_i(u_i) < 0 & u_i > 0 \\ -B_i u_i + A_{ii} S_i(u_i) = 0 & u_i = 0 \\ -B_i u_i + A_{ii} S_i(u_i) > 0 & u_i < 0 \end{cases} \tag{9}$$

for $u_i \in B_i(r_i) = \{u_i \in \mathbb{R} : -r_i < u_i < r_i\}$ for some $r_i > 0$. Note that the hypothesis in Equation 9 are nontrivial only for the neurons belonging to the hidden layer of each single controller. This is a further evidence of the role played by the hidden recurrently connected neurons in processing the information and determining the performances of the controller. Moreover, the input layer neurons satisfy the hypothesis in Equation 9 if the input **I** in Equation 1 are limited in $\mathbb{R}$ and constant for $u_i = 0$. Since the input neurons are not recurrently connected and the corresponding terms in the *interconnecting structure* are null, the convergence of input states to $u_i = 0$, for all $i \equiv \{inputs\}$, is obtained by a constant activation of the proximity sensors, i.e. keeping quasi-steady mutual positions among the agents. Also for the output neurons of each controller the hypothesis in Equation 9 is verified for all $\mathbb{R}$ and the convergence to the equilibrium point is influenced only by the *interconnecting structure*. Given the asymptotical stability of the M *free subsystems*, u_i are also exponentially stable if

$$\begin{cases} -B_i u_i + A_{ii} \rho_{i1} < 0 & Aii < 0 \\ -B_i u_i + A_{ii} \rho_{i2} < 0 & Aii > 0 \end{cases} \tag{10}$$

where ρ_i are defined as

$$\rho_{i1} < \frac{S_i(u_i)}{u_i} < \rho_{i2}, \quad -r_i < pi < ri, u_i \neq 0. \tag{11}$$

The stability analysis for the system 3 is completed with the stability results for the *interconnecting structure* of Equations 6. For the system 3, the interconnections satisfy the estimate

$$u_i A_{ij} S_j(u_j) \leq |u_i| k_{ij} |u_j| \tag{12}$$

for all $|u_i| < r_i$, $|u_j| < r_j$, $i, j = 1, ..., M$, where k_{ij} are real constants. There exists an M-vector $\alpha = [\alpha_1, ..., \alpha_M]^T$, $\alpha_i > 0 \ \forall i = 1, ..., M$ such that a test matrix $H = [h_{ij}]$ is defined as

$$h_{ij} = \begin{cases} \alpha_i(-B_i + k_{ii}) & i = j \\ (\alpha_i k_{ij} + \alpha_j k_{ji})/2 & i \neq j \end{cases} \tag{13}$$

where k_{ij} are given in Equation 12. If the hypothesis in Equations 12 is verified and the test matrix defined in Equation 13 is negative definite (i.e. all the eigenvalues of H are negative), the equilibrium $\mathbf{u} = 0$ of the entire network of Equation 3 is exponentially stable.

Once the stability of $\mathbf{u} = 0$ is verified for the M *free subsystems* and the *interconnecting structure*, we estimate the domain of attraction of $\mathbf{u} = 0$ as a subset of the domain that is not generally entirely determined. We make use of the Lyapunov direct method applied to system 3 adapting several similar results in neural networks analysis. We let

$$V(\mathbf{u}) = \sum_{i=1}^{M} \frac{1}{2} \alpha_i V_i(u_i) = \sum_{i=1}^{M} \frac{1}{2} \alpha_i u_i^2 \tag{14}$$

be a Lyapunov function where α_i are defined for Equation 13 and $V_i(u_i)$ are used also in Equation 7. The estimated domain for $\mathbf{u} = 0$ is defined as

$$G_\lambda = \{\mathbf{u} \in \mathbb{R}^M : V(\mathbf{u}) < \lambda\}, \qquad \lambda = \min_{1 \leq i \leq M} \left\{ \frac{1}{2} \alpha_i r_i^2 \right\} \tag{15}$$

where r_i are the extremes of the interval $|u_i| < r_i$ verifying the hypothesis 9. Note that $B_i(r_i) = \{u_i \in \mathbb{R} : |u_i| < r_i, r_i > 0\}$ is generally not symmetrical around $u_i = 0$, but hypothesis 9 may be verified in an interval $-r_{i1} < u_i < r_{i2}, r_{i1,2} > 0$, $r_{i1} \neq r_{i2}$. Recall that this condition is nontrivial only for the hidden layer neurons of the neural networks coded by *geno33*. So the values of the parameters $r_{i1,2}$ that maximize the range of stability for u_i depend on the parameters B_i, A_{ii} of each neurons in the hidden layers, the features of the firing-rate function of the neurons and the properties of the *interconnecting structure*. In this way, the extension of G_λ for each equilibrium point of the network 3 depend on the minimum r_i among those satisfying the hypotheses 9, 12 and 13 for all $i = 1, ..., M$. In the present experiments we consider the value of λ in Equation 15 as an estimated property of the domains of attraction for the two isolated equilibria that we want to compare. The larger is λ, the more chances has G_λ to attract the trajectory $\varphi(\mathbf{u}, \mathbf{u}_0, t)$ towards $\mathbf{u} = 0$. From an agent point of view, the stable configuration $\dot{\mathbf{y}} = 0$ in Equations 3 is more probable as G_λ of $\mathbf{u} = 0$ becomes larger. The agents, and consequently all the team, set their behaviour according to the more probable stable configuration. In *Env. 3* the corresponding $\mathbf{u} = 0$ for the successful solution is the only relevant equilibrium empirically observed. It verifies all the hypotheses 9, 12 and 13 for exponential asymptotical stability. The value of λ (2.99) is computed for $\alpha_i = 1 \ \forall i$, but there are no other domains of attraction than that of the unique equilibrium to compare. Now, in *Env. 4*, let the two equilibria observed in *Env. 4* be $\tilde{\mathbf{u}} = 0$ and $\mathbf{u} = 0$, as previously associated with the two independent couples of agents and the chain formation, respectively. We obtain, for $\alpha_i = 1 \ \forall i$, $\lambda = 2.19$ for the equilibrium related to the successful solution and $\tilde{\lambda} = 3.18$ for equilibrium related to the undesired behaviour. This result confirms our hypothesis about the reduction of the domain of attraction of the successful solution due to the emergence of a new relevant stable solution. Moreover, the decrease in the percentage of success of *geno33* in *Env. 4* is due to the fact that the undesired behaviour is achieved by the network 3 with higher probability than the desired one. We are now able to state that the addition of one agent in the team has a destabilising effect in the accomplishment of the task because of the emergence of a competitive undesired behaviour. To this end, the scalability property is conserved because the necessary condition of role assignment is verified and also the sufficient condition of local stability of the solution is verified, but the property presents a loss of robustness that prevents the team to totally assure the desired behaviour also in a scaled environment.

6   Conclusions

Generally speaking, the behavioural strategies of a multi-robot system can be defined as scalable if the performance of the system does not drop by increasing the cardinality of the group. In this paper we looked at the elements which are responsible for determining whether or not the behavioural strategies of robots controlled by dynamic neural networks are scalable. In particular, we focused on a navigation task, originally presented in [1], in which teams of three robots have to coordinate their actions in order to decide a common direction of motion. First, we designed, by artifcial evolution, dynamic neural network controllers for robots capable of solving the navigation task. Subsequently, we tested the scalability of the successful behavioural strategies by re-evaluating a controller designed to guide teams of three robots in teams of four robots. In synthesis, by analysing the dynamics of the robot controllers, we observed that in teams of three robots the controllers differentiate in those that guide the followers and in that one that guides the leader. We also observed that, teams of four robots do not require any further role. Therefore, a controller capable of online specialisation in between leader and follower is potentially capable of guiding teams of higher cardinality than those composed of three robots. This may be considered as the necessary condition to add an indefinite number of agents in the team without modifying the global strategy. In fact, the added agent in the experiment *Env. 4* shows an overlapped behaviour with a pre-existing role, as confirmed by the same equilibrium state in the dynamics of the controllers of the agents sharing the role. However, this necessary condition is not sufficient to support the scalability of the behavioural strategies, as confirmed by the different performances of the tested genotype in both the experiments. This is mainly due to the stability of the global dynamical system in the neighbourhood of the desired solution. Given the convergence to this solution, it does not have a domain of attraction large enough to attract the states of all the agents regardless the initial conditions and the states near the solution. These mechanisms undergo the unpredictability of the system resulting from the evolution and the complexity of the interaction among the agents.

References

1. Quinn, M., Smith, L., Mayley, G., Husbands, P.: Evolving controllers for a homogeneous system of physical robots: Structured cooperation with minimal sensors. Phil. Trans. of the Royal Soc. of London, Series A **361** (2003) 2321–2344
2. Nolfi, S., Floreano, D.: Evolutionary Robotics: The Biology, Intelligence, and Technology of Self-Organizing Machines. MIT Press, Cambridge, MA (2000)
3. Paolo, E.D.: Behavioral coordination, structural congruence and entrainment in a simulation of acoustically coupled agents. Adaptive Behavior **8** (2000) 27–48
4. Baldassarre, G., Nolfi, S., Parisi, D.: Evolving mobile robots able to display collective behaviour. Artificial Life **9** (2003) 255–267
5. Mondada, F., Pettinaro, G., Guignard, A., Kwee, I., Floreano, D., Deneubourg, J.L., Nolfi, S., Gambardella, L., Dorigo, M.: SWARM-BOT: A new distributed robotic concept. Autonomous Robots **17** (2004) 193–221
6. Dudek, G., Jenkin, M.: Computational Principles of Mobile Robotics. Cambridge University Press, Cambridge, UK (2000)
7. Vicentini, F., Tuci, E.: Swarmod: a 2d s-bot's simulator. Technical Report TR/IRIDIA/2006-005, IRIDIA, Université Libre de Bruxelles (2006) This paper is available at `http://iridia.ulb.ac.be/IridiaTrSeries`.
8. Hopfield, J.J., Tank, D.: Computing with neural circuits: a model. Science **233** (1986) 625–633
9. Goldberg, D.E.: Genetic Algorithms in Search, Optimization and Machine Learning. Addison-Wesley, Reading, MA (1989)
10. Michel, A.N., Farrell, J.A., Porod, W.: Qualitative analysis of neural networks. Circuits and Systems, IEEE Transactions on **36** (1989) 229–243
11. Jiang, H., Li, Z., Teng, Z.: Boundedness and stability for nonautonomous cellular neural networks with delays. Phys. Lett. A **306** (2003) 313–325
12. Liang, J., Cao, J.: Boundedness and stability for recurrent neural networks with variable coefficients and time-varying delays. Phys. Lett. A **318** (2003) 53–64
13. Qiao, H., Peng, J., Xu, Z.B.: Nonlinear measures: a new approach to exponential stabilityanalysis for hopfield-type neural networks. IEEE Tras. Neural Networks **12** (2001) 360–370
14. Cao, J., Tao, Q.: Estimation on domain of attraction and convergence rate of hopfield continuous feedback neural networks. J. Comput. Syst. Sci. **62** (2001) 528–534
15. Zhou, D., Shen, J., Ren, X.: Estimation of attraction domain and exponential convergence rate of dynamic feedback neural nets. In Kelemen, J., Sosik, P., eds.: Signal Processing Proceedings, 2000. WCCC-ICSP 2000. 5th International Conference on. Volume 3., Springer Verlag, Berlin, Germany (2000) 1598–1601
16. Yang, X., Liao, X., Li, C., Evans, D.J.: New estimate of the domains of attraction of equilibrium points in continuous hopfield neural networks. Phys. Lett. A **351** (2006) 161–166
17. Michel, A.N., Miller, R.K., eds.: Qualitative analysis of large scale dynamical systems. Academic Press [Harcourt Brace Jovanovich Publishers], New York (1977)

Author Index

Lecture Notes in Computer Science

For information about Vols. 1–4346

please contact your bookseller or Springer

Vol. 4398: S. Marchand-Maillet, E. Bruno, A. Nürnberger, M. Detyniecki (Eds.), Adaptive Multimedia Retrieval: User, Context, and Feedback. XI, 269 pages. 2007.

Vol. 4397: C. Stephanidis, M. Pieper (Eds.), Universal Access in Ambient Intelligence Environments. XV, 467 pages. 2007.

Vol. 4396: J. García-Vidal, L. Cerdà-Alabern (Eds.), Wireless Systems and Mobility in Next Generation Internet. IX, 271 pages. 2007.

Vol. 4395: M. Daydé, J.M.L.M. Palma, Á.L.G.A. Coutinho, E. Pacitti, J.C. Lopes (Eds.), High Performance Computing for Computational Science - VECPAR 2006. XXIV, 721 pages. 2007.

Vol. 4394: A. Gelbukh (Ed.), Computational Linguistics and Intelligent Text Processing. XVI, 648 pages. 2007.

Vol. 4393: W. Thomas, P. Weil (Eds.), STACS 2007. XVIII, 708 pages. 2007.

Vol. 4392: S.P. Vadhan (Ed.), Theory of Cryptography. XI, 595 pages. 2007.

Vol. 4391: Y. Stylianou, M. Faundez-Zanuy, A. Esposito (Eds.), Progress in Nonlinear Speech Processing. XII, 269 pages. 2007.

Vol. 4390: S.O. Kuznetsov, S. Schmidt (Eds.), Formal Concept Analysis. X, 329 pages. 2007. (Sublibrary LNAI).

Vol. 4389: D. Weyns, H.V.D. Parunak, F. Michel (Eds.), Environments for Multi-Agent Systems III. X, 273 pages. 2007. (Sublibrary LNAI).

Vol. 4385: K. Coninx, K. Luyten, K.A. Schneider (Eds.), Task Models and Diagrams for Users Interface Design. XI, 355 pages. 2007.

Vol. 4384: T. Washio, K. Satoh, H. Takeda, A. Inokuchi (Eds.), New Frontiers in Artificial Intelligence. IX, 401 pages. 2007. (Sublibrary LNAI).

Vol. 4383: E. Bin, A. Ziv, S. Ur (Eds.), Hardware and Software, Verification and Testing. XII, 235 pages. 2007.

Vol. 4381: J. Akiyama, W.Y.C. Chen, M. Kano, X. Li, Q. Yu (Eds.), Discrete Geometry, Combinatorics and Graph Theory. XI, 289 pages. 2007.

Vol. 4380: S. Spaccapietra, P. Atzeni, F. Fages, M.-S. Hacid, J. Mylopoulos, B. Pernici, P. Shvaiko, J. Trujillo, I. Zaihrayeu (Eds.), Journal on Data Semantics VIII. XV, 219 pages. 2007.

Vol. 4378: I. Virbitskaite, A. Voronkov (Eds.), Perspectives of Systems Informatics. XIV, 496 pages. 2007.

Vol. 4377: M. Abe (Ed.), Topics in Cryptology – CT-RSA 2007. XI, 403 pages. 2006.

Vol. 4376: E. Frachtenberg, U. Schwiegelshohn (Eds.), Job Scheduling Strategies for Parallel Processing. VII, 257 pages. 2007.

Vol. 4374: J.F. Peters, A. Skowron, I. Düntsch, J. Grzymała-Busse, E. Orłowska, L. Polkowski (Eds.), Transactions on Rough Sets VI, Part I. XII, 499 pages. 2007.

Vol. 4373: K. Langendoen, T. Voigt (Eds.), Wireless Sensor Networks. XIII, 358 pages. 2007.

Vol. 4372: M. Kaufmann, D. Wagner (Eds.), Graph Drawing. XIV, 454 pages. 2007.

Vol. 4371: K. Inoue, K. Satoh, F. Toni (Eds.), Computational Logic in Multi-Agent Systems. X, 315 pages. 2007. (Sublibrary LNAI).

Vol. 4370: P.P Lévy, B. Le Grand, F. Poulet, M. Soto, L. Darago, L. Toubiana, J.-F. Vibert (Eds.), Pixelization Paradigm. XV, 279 pages. 2007.

Vol. 4369: M. Umeda, A. Wolf, O. Bartenstein, U. Geske, D. Seipel, O. Takata (Eds.), Declarative Programming for Knowledge Management. X, 229 pages. 2006. (Sublibrary LNAI).

Vol. 4368: T. Erlebach, C. Kaklamanis (Eds.), Approximation and Online Algorithms. X, 345 pages. 2007.

Vol. 4367: K. De Bosschere, D. Kaeli, P. Stenström, D. Whalley, T. Ungerer (Eds.), High Performance Embedded Architectures and Compilers. XI, 307 pages. 2007.

Vol. 4366: K. Tuyls, R. Westra, Y. Saeys, A. Nowé (Eds.), Knowledge Discovery and Emergent Complexity in Bioinformatics. IX, 183 pages. 2007. (Sublibrary LNBI).

Vol. 4364: T. Kühne (Ed.), Models in Software Engineering. XI, 332 pages. 2007.

Vol. 4362: J. van Leeuwen, G.F. Italiano, W. van der Hoek, C. Meinel, H. Sack, F. Plášil (Eds.), SOFSEM 2007: Theory and Practice of Computer Science. XXI, 937 pages. 2007.

Vol. 4361: H.J. Hoogeboom, G. Păun, G. Rozenberg, A. Salomaa (Eds.), Membrane Computing. IX, 555 pages. 2006.

Vol. 4360: W. Dubitzky, A. Schuster, P.M.A. Sloot, M. Schroeder, M. Romberg (Eds.), Distributed, High-Performance and Grid Computing in Computational Biology. X, 192 pages. 2007. (Sublibrary LNBI).

Vol. 4358: R. Vidal, A. Heyden, Y. Ma (Eds.), Dynamical Vision. IX, 329 pages. 2007.

Vol. 4357: L. Buttyán, V. Gligor, D. Westhoff (Eds.), Security and Privacy in Ad-Hoc and Sensor Networks. X, 193 pages. 2006.

Vol. 4355: J. Julliand, O. Kouchnarenko (Eds.), B 2007: Formal Specification and Development in B. XIII, 293 pages. 2006.

Vol. 4354: M. Hanus (Ed.), Practical Aspects of Declarative Languages. X, 335 pages. 2006.

Vol. 4353: T. Schwentick, D. Suciu (Eds.), Database Theory – ICDT 2007. XI, 419 pages. 2006.

Vol. 4352: T.-J. Cham, J. Cai, C. Dorai, D. Rajan, T.-S. Chua, L.-T. Chia (Eds.), Advances in Multimedia Modeling, Part II. XVIII, 743 pages. 2006.

Vol. 4351: T.-J. Cham, J. Cai, C. Dorai, D. Rajan, T.-S. Chua, L.-T. Chia (Eds.), Advances in Multimedia Modeling, Part I. XIX, 797 pages. 2006.

Vol. 4349: B. Cook, A. Podelski (Eds.), Verification, Model Checking, and Abstract Interpretation. XI, 395 pages. 2007.

Vol. 4348: S.T. Taft, R.A. Duff, R.L. Brukardt, E. Ploedereder, P. Leroy (Eds.), Ada 2005 Reference Manual. XXII, 765 pages. 2006.

Vol. 4347: J. Lopez (Ed.), Critical Information Infrastructures Security. X, 286 pages. 2006.

Printing: Mercedes-Druck, Berlin
Binding: Stein+Lehmann, Berlin